THE MAKING OF
ECONOMIC SOCIETY

Colloquy on the Anatomy of Economic Man

Present at the colloquy (left to right): Adam Smith, Thomas Malthus, David Ricardo, Jeremy Bentham, John Stuart Mill, Francois Marie Charles Fourier, Claude Henri Saint-Simon, Auguste Comte, Karl Marx, and Pierre Joseph Proudhon.

Carrying on the Anatomical Studies

Left to right: Thorstein Veblen, Joseph Schumpeter, John Maynard Keynes, and Alfred Marshall.

Other books by Robert Heilbroner

The Worldly Philosophers
The Future as History
The Great Ascent
A Primer on Government Spending
    (with Peter L. Bernstein)
The Limits of American Capitalism
Between Capitalism and Socialism
An Inquiry into the Human Prospect
Business Civilization in Decline
Beyound Boom and Crash
The Economic Problem
    (with James K. Galbraith)
Marxism: For and Against
The Economic Transformation of America
    (with Aaron Singer)
The Nature and Logic of Capitalism
The Essential Adam Smith
Behind the Veil of Economics

9th
edition

THE MAKING OF ECONOMIC SOCIETY

Robert Heilbroner

Prentice Hall, Englewood Cliffs, New Jersey 07632

Library of Congress Cataloging-in Publication Data

Heilbroner, Robert L.
    The making of economic society / Robert L. Heilbroner. -- 9th ed.,
rev. and updated for the 1990s.
      p.   cm.
    Includes index.
    ISBN 0-13-555186-2
    1. Economic history.   I. Title.
HC51.H44 1993
330.9--dc20   92-9584
                                      CIP

Editorial/production supervision and
   interior design: Eleanor Perz
Cover design: Lundgren Graphics
Prepress buyer: Trudy Pisciotti
Manufacturing buyer: Robert Anderson

Chapter 13 uses material from Chapter 38 of *The Economic Problem*, 9th ed., by
Robert L. Heilbroner and James K. Galbraith (Englewood Cliffs, NJ: Prentice Hall, 1989).

Printed in the United States of America
10 9 8 7 6 5 4 3 2 1

ISBN 0-13-555186-2

Prentice-Hall International (UK) Limited, *London*
Prentice-Hall of Australia Pty. Limited, *Sydney*
Prentice-Hall Canada Inc., *Toronto*
Prentice-Hall Hispanoamericana, S.A., *Mexico*
Prentice-Hall of India Private Limited, *New Delhi*
Prentice-Hall of Japan, Inc., *Tokyo*
Simon & Schuster Asia Pte. Ltd., *Singapore*
Editora Prentice-Hall do Brasil, Ltda., *Rio de Janeiro*

To Peter Bernstein

CONTENTS

INTRODUCTION

No one has to tell students about to tackle their first economics course in these troubled times that the subject is of vital importance. Economics is no longer a mysterious aspect of the world, confined to the back sections of newspapers and newsmagazines—the sections we used to skip because they were so dull. It has become part of the headline fare of our day. Not since the Great Depression have economic problems been so insistent, so worrisome, so much a part of our everyday conversation. International competition, unemployment, and the fear of inflation have brought economics into the center of our lives. If there was ever a time when students actually *wanted* to learn about economic problems, it is today.

Nevertheless, as I write these words, caution plucks at my sleeve. Not so many years ago, when a preceding edition of this book was being written, the opening chapter began in a very different vein—"We Americans tend to think of ourselves as members of the richest society on earth"—after which the text went on to point out some of the seamier sides of American life, to which we paid too little attention. In those opening pages, there was no mention of inflation or recessions, or a collapse of the auto or steel industries before foreign competition.

This makes me wonder if the problems that will be in the headlines a few years from now will be those that seem most important as I write these pages. Perhaps three years hence we will be worrying about the economic plight of our cities more than we will be fretting about our place in the world economy. Perhaps we will be talking about automation rather than recession as the cause of unemployment. It is possible that we will be worried about America's competitive threat *to* other nations, not their threat to us. Maybe we will even be so lucky as to have economics as a whole once again relegated to the back pages of the papers, to the immense satisfaction of everyone but economics professors.

It is perhaps disconcerting for a student to be told right off that the ability of economists to forecast the emergence of new problems is very poor. Yet our experience tells us that the economic crystal ball is often clouded and that the wisest thing to expect in the economy is the unexpected. I bring up this somewhat embarassing state of affairs not to run down my profession, but to explain what our objectives should be in taking up the subject of economics. Of course we want to learn about the critical problems of the moment, and students should emerge from their first course with a clearer understanding of some of our present problems than before they started the course. But a moment's reflection on the unforeseen twists and turns of the past tells us that we want something more than information about a specific set of issues. *What we want is a general understanding of the economic system in which we live*—an understanding that will throw light across a large enough range of matters to illumine the unexpected problems we will encounter tomorrow, as well as those we face at the moment.

How can we obtain such a lantern? One way is through the study of *economic theory*—that is, by learning about the problems of the day from a very generalized and abstract point of view. Economic theory is a powerful intellectual tool, and its mastery is indispensable for anyone who aspires to become an economist. Yet I am inclined to think that theory is best reserved for—and best understood by—those who have already gained a grasp of economics that smells more of the real world than the diagrams and equations we find in a standard economics text.

Then why not plunge directly into a study of the real world, learning about the main elements of economic life—giant corporations, labor unions, government? There is much to be said for a study of economic institutions as the first step to a thorough mastery of economics, but here, too, I think something is missing without which the knowledge we gain will be less useful and flexible than we want.

The missing ingredient is a familiarity with the *history* of our economic society, a sense of how our dominant institutions came into being in the first place. Only from a standpoint of history can we see our institutions, and the problems they create, as part of the ongoing process of our economic life. Only from a point of view that places our present concerns as the outgrowth of the past can we hope to gain a perspective on the problems of the future that will emerge from those of today.

Hence we are off to a study of the present that necessarily begins in the past. For the first several chapters, we will be tracing the growth of our present-day society from its distant beginnings—not merely to rediscover our past, but also to see our present-day economic structure in a new, and I hope revealing, light.

Only after we have learned something about the "making" of our economic society will we turn to a consideration of the issues that trouble us so much. But by that time, I think, we will already see that the study of economics does not stop at the present, nor at our shores. Our perspective on the evolution of economic systems and the succession of problems to which economics gives rise will lead us first to place America's problems in the context of the world's economic problems, and thereafter to try to place them in the context of the sweep of history itself.

But I have said enough by way of introduction. The merit and the interest of a historical approach to our economic problems will have to prove themselves in the pages to come. I do not promise that you will be expert economists when you are done, but I hope you will want to be.

Concepts, Words, and Questions

All chapters end with summaries of key concepts, to help you focus on the important propositions in that chapter; key words, to add to your vocabulary; and a few questions, to make you think out for yourself some of the main points at issue.

ACKNOWLEDGMENTS

I wish to thank the many people who have reviewed this text and used it in their courses in earlier editions. Their criticisms, comments, and suggestions have helped shape the content of this book and have contributed to its success over the years. While I have not always been able to incorporate all of their suggestions, their advice is highly valued. In particular, I am grateful to Mathew Forstater for his superior research.

Robert L. Heilbroner

1 THE ECONOMIC PROBLEM

Now that we have decided on our course of exploration, it would be convenient if we could immediately begin to examine our economic past. But not quite yet. Before we can retrace economic history, we need to know what economic history *is*. And that, in turn, requires us to take a moment to clarify what we mean by economics and by the economic problem itself.

The answer is not a complicated one. Economics is essentially the study of a process we find in all human societies—"the" economic problem is simply *the process of providing for the material well-being of society*. In its simplest terms, economics is the study of how mankind earns its daily bread.

This hardly seems like a particularly exciting subject for historical scrutiny. Indeed, when we look back over the pageant of what is usually called "history," the humble matter of bread hardly strikes the eye at all. Power and glory, faith and fanaticism, ideas and ideologies are the aspects of the human chronicle that crowd the pages of history books. If the simple quest for bread is a moving force in human destiny, it is well concealed behind what one philosopher has called "that history of international crime and mass murder which has been advertised as the history of mankind."[1]

Yet, if mankind does not live by bread alone, it is obvious that it cannot live without bread. Like every other living thing, the human being must eat—the imperious first rule of continued existence. And this first prerequisite is less to be taken for granted than at first appears, for the human organism is not in itself a highly efficient mechanism for survival. From each 100 calories of food it consumes, it can deliver only about 20 calories of mechanical energy. On a decent diet, human beings can produce just about one horsepower-hour of work daily, and with that

---

[1] Karl Popper, *The Open Society and Its Enemies*, 3rd ed. (London: Routledge, 1957), II, 270.

they must replenish their exhausted bodies. With what is left over, they are free to build a civilization.

As a result, in many countries, the sheer continuity of human existence is far from assured. In the vast continents of Asia and Africa, in the Near East, even in some countries of South America, brute survival is the problem that stares humanity in the face. Millions of human beings have died of starvation or malnutrition in our present era, as countless hundreds of millions have died over the long past. Whole nations are acutely aware of what it means to face hunger as a condition of ordinary life; it has been said, for example, that a peasant in Bangladesh, from the day he or she is born to the day he or she dies, never knows what it is to have a full stomach. In many of the so-called underdeveloped nations, the life span of the average person is less than half of ours. Not so many years ago, an Indian demographer made the chilling calculation that of 100 Asian and 100 American infants, more Americans would be alive at age sixty-five than Indians at age *five*! The statistics, not of life but of premature death throughout most of the world, are overwhelming and crushing.

THE INDIVIDUAL AND SOCIETY

Thus we can see that economic history must focus on the central problem of survival and on how humankind has solved that problem. For most Americans, this may make economics seem very remote. Few of us are conscious of anything resembling a life-or-death struggle for existence. That it might be possible for us to experience severe want, that we might ever know in our own bodies the pangs of hunger experienced by an Indian villager or a Bolivian peon, is a thought nearly impossible for most of us to entertain seriously.*

Short of a catastrophic war, it is highly unlikely that most of us ever will know the full meaning of the struggle for existence. Nonetheless, even in our prosperous and secure society, there remains, however unnoticed, an aspect of life's precariousness, a reminder of the underlying problem of survival. *This is our helplessness as economic individuals.*

For it is a curious fact that as we leave the most primitive peoples of the world, we find the economic insecurity of the individual many times multiplied. The solitary Eskimo, Bushman, Indonesian, or Nigerian peasant, left to his own devices, will survive a considerable time. Living close to the soil or to his animal prey, such an individual can sustain his own life, at least for a while, singlehandedly. With a com-

---

* Although the sight of homeless people huddled on the sidewalks of our major cities tells us that even rich countries can harbor poverty.

munity numbering only a few hundred, he can live indefinitely. Indeed, a considerable percentage of the human race today lives in precisely such fashion—in small, virtually self-contained peasant communities that provide for their own survival with a minimum of contact with the outside world. This large portion of mankind may suffer great poverty, but it also knows a certain economic independence. If it did not, it would have been wiped out centuries ago.*

When we turn to the New Yorker or the Chicagoan, on the other hand, we are struck by exactly the opposite condition, by a prevailing ease of material life coupled with an extreme *dependence* on others. We can no longer envisage the solitary individual or the small community surviving unaided in the great metropolitan areas where most Americans live, unless they loot warehouses or stores for food and necessities. The overwhelming majority of Americans have never grown food, caught game, raised meat, ground grain into flour, or even fashioned flour into bread. Faced with the challenge of clothing themselves or building their own homes, they would be hopelessly untrained and unprepared. Even to make minor repairs in the machines that surround them, they must call on other members of the community whose business it is to fix cars or repair plumbing or whatever. Paradoxically, perhaps, the richer the nation, the more apparent is this inability of its average inhabitant to survive unaided and alone.

division of labor There is, of course, an answer to the paradox. We survive in rich nations because the tasks we cannot do ourselves are done for us by an army of others on whom we can all call for help. If we cannot grow food, we can buy it; if we cannot provide for our needs ourselves, we can hire the services of someone who can. This enormous *division of labor* enhances our capacity a thousandfold, for it enables us to benefit from other people's skills as well as our own. In our next chapter, it will play a central role.

Along with this invaluable gain, however, comes a certain risk. It is a sobering thought, for example, that we depend on the services of only about 200,000 people, out of a national labor force of over 120 million, to provide us with that basic commodity, coal. A much smaller number—roughly 50,000—makes up our total airline pilot crew. An even smaller number of workers are responsible for running the locomotives that haul all the nation's rail freight. Failure of any one of these groups to perform its functions would cripple us. As we know, when from time to time we face a bad strike, our entire economic machine may falter

---

* Recent anthropological investigation shows that primitive societies may also enjoy a kind of affluence, in that they voluntarily spend many hours at leisure rather than in hunting or gathering. See Marshall Sahlins, *Stone Age Economics* (New York: Aldine, 1972).

because a strategic few—even garbage collectors—cease to perform their accustomed tasks.

Thus, along with the abundance of material existence as we know it goes a hidden vulnerability: Our abundance is assured only insofar as the organized cooperation of huge armies of people is to be counted upon. Indeed, our continuing existence as a rich nation hinges on the tacit precondition that the mechanism of social organization will continue to function effectively. *We are rich, not as individuals, but as members of a rich society, and our easy assumption of material sufficiency is actually only as reliable as the bonds that forge us into a social whole.*

economics and scarcity

Strangely enough, then, we find that man, not nature, is the source of most of our economic problems, at least above the level of subsistence. To be sure, the economic problem itself—that is, the need to struggle for existence—derives ultimately from the *scarcity* of nature. If there were no scarcity, goods would be as free as air, and economics—at least in one sense of the word—would cease to exist as a social preoccupation.

And yet, if the scarcity of nature sets the stage for the economic problem, it does not impose the only strictures against which men must struggle. For scarcity, as a felt condition, is not solely the fault of nature. If Americans today, for instance, were content to live at the level of Mexican peasants, all our material wants could be fully satisfied with but an hour or two of daily labor. We would experience little or no scarcity, and our economic problems would virtually disappear. Instead, we find in America—and indeed, in all industrial societies—that as the ability to increase nature's yield has risen, so has the reach of human wants. In fact, in societies such as ours, where relative social status is importantly connected with the possession of material goods, we often find that "scarcity" as a psychological experience and good becomes *more* pronounced as we grow wealthier: Our desires to possess the fruits of nature race out ahead of our mounting ability to produce goods.

Thus the "wants" that nature must satisfy are by no means fixed. But, for that matter, nature's yield itself is not a constant. It varies over a wide range, depending on the social application of human energy and skill. Scarcity is therefore not attributable to nature alone but to "human nature" as well; and economics is ultimately concerned not merely with the stinginess of the physical environment, but equally with the appetite of the human being and the productive capability of the community.

the tasks of economic society

Hence we must begin a systematic analysis of economics by singling out the functions that social organization must perform to bring human nature into social harness. And when we turn our attention to this fundamental problem, we can quickly see that it involves the solution of two related and yet separate elemental tasks. A society must

1. organize a system to assure the production of enough goods and services for its own survival, and
2. arrange the distribution of the fruits of its production so that more production can take place.

These two tasks of economic continuity are, at first look, very simple. But it is a deceptive simplicity. Much of economic history is concerned with the manner in which various societies have sought to cope with these elementary problems; and what strikes us in surveying their attempts is that most of them were partial failures. (They could not have been *total* failures, or society would not have survived.) So we had better look more carefully into the two main economic tasks to see what hidden difficulties they may conceal.

PRODUCTION AND DISTRIBUTION

mobilizing effort

What obstacles does a society encounter in organizing a system to produce the goods and services it needs?

Since nature is usually stingy, it seems that the production problem must be essentially one of applying engineering or technical skills to the resources at hand, of avoiding waste and utilizing social effort as efficaciously as possible.

This is indeed an important task for any society, and a great deal of formal economic thought, as the word itself suggests, is devoted to economizing. Yet this it not the core of the production problem. Long before a society can concern itself about using its energies "economically," it must first marshal the energies to carry out the productive process itself. That is, *the basic problem of production is to devise social institutions that will mobilize human energy for productive purposes.*

This basic requirement is not always so easily accomplished. For example, in the United States in 1933, the energies of nearly one-quarter of our work force were somehow prevented from engaging in the production process. Although millions of unemployed men and women were eager to work, although empty factories were available for them to work in, despite the existence of pressing wants, a terrible and mystifying breakdown short-circuited the production process, with the result that an entire third of our previous annual output of goods and services simply disappeared.

We are by no means the only nation that has, on occasion, failed to find work for large numbers of willing workers. In the very poorest nations, where production is most desperately needed, we frequently find that mass unemployment is a chronic condition. The streets of many Asian cities are thronged with people who cannot find work. But this, too, is not a condition imposed by the scarcity of nature. There is, after all, an endless amount of work to be done, if only in cleaning the filthy streets or patching up the homes of the poor, building roads or digging ditches. What is lacking is a social mechanism to mobilize human energy for production purposes. And this is the case just as much when the unemployed are only a small fraction of the work force as when they constitute a veritable army.

These examples point out to us that the production problem is not solely a physical and technical struggle with nature. On these "scarcity" aspects of the problem will depend the ease with which a nation may forge ahead and the level of well-being it can reach with a given effort. But the original mobilization of productive effort itself is a challenge to its *social organization,* and on the success or failure of that social organization will depend the volume of the human effort that can be directed to nature.

allocating effort   But putting men and women to work is only the first step in the solution of the production problem. They must not only be put to work; they must be put to work *in the right places* to produce the goods and services that society needs. Thus, *in addition to assuring a large enough quantity of social effort, the economic institutions of society must also assure a viable allocation of that social effort.*

In a nation such as India or Bolivia, where the great majority of the population is born in peasant villages and grows up to be peasant cultivators, the solution to this problem offers little to tax our understanding. The basic needs of society—food and fiber—are precisely the goods that its peasant population "naturally" produces. But in an industrial society, the proper allocation of effort becomes an enormously complicated task. People in the United States demand much more than bread and cotton. They need such things as automobiles. Yet no one "naturally" produces an automobile. On the contrary, in order to produce one, an extraordinary spectrum of special tasks must be performed. Some people must make steel; others must make rubber. Still others must coordinate the assembly process itself. And this is but a tiny sampling of the far from "natural" tasks that must be performed if an automobile is to be produced.

As with the mobilization of its total production effort, society does not always succeed in the proper allocation of its effort. It may, for instance, turn out too many cars or too few. Of greater importance, it may devote its energies to the production of luxuries while large numbers of its people are starving. Or it may even court disaster by an inability to channel its productive effort into areas of critical importance.

Such allocative failures may affect the production problem quite as seriously as a failure to mobilize an adequate quantity of effort, for a viable society must produce not only goods, but the *right* goods. And the allocative question alerts us to a still broader conclusion. It shows us that the act of production, in and of itself, does not fully answer the requirements for survival. Having produced enough of the right goods, society must now *distribute* those goods so that the production process can go on.

distributing output   Once again, in the case of the peasant who feeds himself and his family from his own crop, this requirement of adequate distribution may seem simple enough. But when we go beyond the most primitive society, the problem is not always so readily solved. In many of the poorest nations of the East and South, urban workers have often been unable to deliver their daily horsepower-hour of work because they have not been given enough of society's output to run their human engines to capacity. Worse yet, they have often languished on the job while granaries bulged with grain and the well-to-do complained of the ineradicable laziness of the masses. At the other side of the picture, the distribution mechanism may fail because the rewards it hands out do not succeed in persuading people to perform their tasks. Shortly after the Russian Revolution in 1917, some factories were organized into communes in which managers and janitors pooled their pay, and from which all drew equal allotments. The result was a rash of absenteeism among the previously better-paid workers and a threatened breakdown in industrial production. Not until the old unequal wage payments were reinstituted did production resume its former course.

As was the case with failures in the production process, distributive failures need not entail a total economic collapse. Societies can exist—and most do exist—with badly distorted productive and distributive efforts. Only rarely, as in the instances noted above, does maldistribution interfere with the ultimate ability of a society to staff its production posts. More frequently, an inadequate solution to the distribution problem reveals itself in social and political unrest, or even in revolution.

Yet this, too, is an aspect of the total economic problem. For if society is to insure its steady material replenishment, it must parcel out its production in a fashion that will maintain not only the capacity but also the willingness to go on working. And thus again, we find the focus of economic inquiry directed to the study of human institutions. For a viable economic society, we can now see, must not only overcome the stringencies of nature, but also contain and control the intransigence of human nature.

THREE SOLUTIONS TO THE ECONOMIC PROBLEM

Thus, to the economist, society presents itself in what is to the rest of us an unaccustomed aspect. Underneath the problems of poverty or pollution or inflation, he or she sees a process at work that must be understood before we can turn our attention to the issues of the day, no matter how pressing. That process is society's basic mechanism for accomplishing the complicated tasks of production and distribution necessary for its own continuity.

But the economist sees something else as well, something that at first seems quite astonishing. Looking over the diversity of contemporary societies, and back over the sweep of all history, he sees that mankind has succeeded in solving the production and distribution problems in but three ways. That is, within the enormous diversity of the actual social institutions that guide and shape the economic process, the economist divines but three overarching *types* of systems that separately or in combination enable humankind to solve its economic challenge. These great systemic types can be called economies run by *Tradition*, economies run by *Command*, and economies run by the *Market*. Let us briefly see what is characteristic of each.

tradition   Perhaps the oldest and, until a very few years ago, by far the most generally prevalent way of solving the economic challenge has been that of tradition. Tradition is a mode of social organization in which both production and distribution are based on procedures devised in the distant past, ratified by a long process of historic trial and error, and maintained by the powerful forces of custom and belief.

Societies based on tradition solve the economic problems very manageably. First, they typically deal with the production problem—the problem of assuring that the needful tasks will be done—by assigning the jobs of fathers to their sons. Thus, a hereditary chain assures that skills will be passed along and jobs will be staffed from generation to generation. In ancient Egypt, wrote Adam Smith, the first great economist, "every man was bound by a principle of religion to follow the occupation of his father and was supposed to commit the most horrible sacrilege if he changed it for another."[2] And it was not merely in antiquity that tradition preserved a productive orderliness within society. In our own Western culture, until the fifteenth or sixteenth century, the hereditary allocation of tasks was also the main stabilizing force within society. Although there was some movement from country to town and

---

[2] *The Wealth of Nations* (New York: Modern Library, 1937), p. 62.

from occupation to occupation, birth usually determined one's role in life. One was born to the soil or to a trade; and on the soil or within the trade, one followed in the footsteps of one's forebears.

In this way tradition has been the stabilizing and impelling force behind a great repetitive cycle of society, assuring that society's work would be done each day very much as it had been done in the past. Even today, among the less industrialized nations of the world, tradition continues to play this immense organizing role. In India, for example, until very recently, one was born to a caste that had its own occupation. "Better thine own work is, though done with fault," preached the Bhagavad-Gita, the great philosophic moral poem of India, "than doing others' work, even excellently."

Tradition not only provides a solution to the production problem of society, but it also regulates the distribution problem. Take, for example, the Bushmen of the Kalahari Desert in South Africa, who depend for their livelihood on their hunting prowess. Elizabeth Marshall Thomas, a sensitive observer of these peoples, reports on the manner in which tradition solves the problem of distributing their kill.

The gemsbok has vanished. . . . Gai owned two hind legs and a front leg, Tsetchwe had meat from the back, Ukwane had the other front leg, his wife had one of the feet and the stomach, the young boys had lengths of intestine. Twikwe had received the head and Dasina the udder.

It seems very unequal when you watch Bushmen divide the kill, yet it is their system, and in the end no person eats more than the other. That day Ukwane gave Gai still another piece because Gai was his relation, Gai gave meat to Dasina because she was his wife's mother. . . . No one, of course, contested Gai's large share, because he had been the hunter and by their law that much belonged to him. No one doubted that he would share his large amount with others, and they were not wrong, of course; he did.[3]

The manner in which tradition can divide a social product may be, as the illustration shows, very subtle and ingenious. It may also be very crude and, by our standards, harsh. Tradition has regularly allocated to women in nonindustrial societies the most meager portion of the social product. But however much the end product of tradition may accord with, or depart from, our accustomed moral views, we must see that it is a workable *method* of dividing society's production.

the cost of tradition   Traditional solutions to the economic problems of production and distribution are most commonly encountered in primitive agrarian or nonindustrial societies where, in addition to serving an economic function, the unquestioning acceptance of the past provides the necessary per-

[3] *The Harmless People* (New York: Knopf, 1959), pp. 49–50.

severance and endurance to comfort harsh destinies. Yet even in our own society, tradition continues to play a part in solving the economic problem. It plays its smallest role in determining the distribution of our own social output, although the persistence of such traditional payments as tips to waiters, allowances to minors, or bonuses based on length of service are all vestiges of older ways of distributing goods, as are differentials between men's and women's pay for equal work.

More important is the continued reliance on tradition, even in America, as a means of solving the production problem—that is, in allocating the performance of tasks. Much of the actual process of selecting in employment in our society is heavily influenced by tradition. We are all familiar with families in which sons follow their fathers into a profession or a business. On a somewhat broader scale, tradition also dissuades us from certain employments. Children of American middle-class families, for example, do not usually seek factory work, although factory jobs may pay better than office jobs, because blue-collar employment is not in the middle-class tradition.

Even in our society, in other words, clearly not a "traditional" one, custom provides an important mechanism for solving the economic problem. But now we must note one very important consequence of the mechanism of tradition. *Its solution to the problems of production and distribution is a static one.* A society that follows the path of tradition in its regulation of economic affairs does so at the expense of large-scale, rapid social and economic change.

Thus, the economy of a Bedouin tribe or a Burmese village is in few essential respects changed today from what it was a hundred or even a thousand years ago. The bulk of the peoples living in tradition-bound societies repeat, in the daily patterns of their economic life, much of the routine that characterized them in the distant past. Such societies may rise and fall, wax and wane, but external events—war, climate, political adventures and misadventures—are mainly responsible for their changing fortunes. Internal, self-generated economic change is but a small factor in the history of most tradition-bound states. *Tradition solves the economic problem, but it does so at the cost of economic progress.*

command A second manner of solving the problem of economic continuity also displays an ancient lineage. This is the method of imposed authority, of economic command. It is a solution based not so much on the perpetuation of a viable system by the changeless reproduction of its ways as on the organization of a system according to the orders of an economic commander-in-chief.

Not infrequently we find this authoritarian method of economic control superimposed upon a traditional social base. Thus, the pharaohs of Egypt exerted their economic dictates above the timeless cycle of traditional agricultural practice on which the Egyptian economy was based. By their orders, the supreme rulers of Egypt brought into being the enormous economic effort that built the pyramids, the temples, the roads. Herodotus, the Greek historian, tells us how the pharaoh Cheops organized the task.

> [He] ordered all Egyptians to work for himself. Some, accordingly, were appointed to draw stones from the quarries in the Arabian mountains down to the Nile, others he ordered to receive the stones when transported in vessels across the river. . . . And they worked to the number of a hundred thousand men at a time, each party during three months. The time during which the people were thus harassed by toil lasted ten years on the road which they constructed, and along which they drew the stones; a work, in my opinion, not much less than the Pyramid.[4]

The mode of authoritarian economic organization was by no means confined to ancient Egypt. We encounter it in the despotisms of medieval and classical China that produced, among other things, the colossal Great Wall, or in the slave labor by which many of the great public works of ancient Rome were built, or, for that matter, in any slave economy, including that of the pre-Civil War United States. Only a few years ago we would have discovered it in the dictates of the Soviet economic authorities. In less drastic form, we find it also in our own society; for example, in the form of taxes—that is, in the preemption of part of our income by the public authorities for public purposes.

Economic command, like tradition, offers solutions to the twin problems of production and distribution. In times of crisis, such as war or famine, it may be the only way in which a society can organize its manpower or distribute its goods effectively. Even in America, we commonly declare martial law when an area has been devastated by a great natural disaster. On such occasions we may press people into service, requisition homes, impose curbs on the use of private property such as cars, or even limit the amount of goods a family may consume.

Quite aside from its obvious utility in meeting emergencies, command has a further usefulness in solving the economic problem. Unlike tradition, the exercise of command has no inherent effect of slowing down economic change. Indeed, the exercise of authority is the most powerful instrument society has for *enforcing economic change*. Authority in communist China or Russia, for example, effected radical alterations in their systems of production and distribution. Again, even in our own society, it is sometimes necessary for economic authority to intervene in the normal flow of economic life to speed up or bring about

---

[4] *Histories*, trans. Cary (London: 1901), Book II, p. 124.

change. The government may, for instance, utilize its tax receipts to lay down a network of roads that will bring a backwater community into the flux of active economic life. It may undertake an irrigation system that will dramatically change the economic life of a vast region. It may deliberately alter the distribution of income among social classes.

the impact of command

To be sure, economic command that is exercised within the framework of a democratic political process is very different from that exercised by a dictatorship: There is an immense social distance between a tax system controlled by Congress and outright expropriation or labor impressment by a supreme and unchallengeable ruler. Yet while the means may be much milder, the *mechanism* is the same. In both cases, command diverts economic effort toward goals chosen by a higher authority. In both cases, it interferes with the existing order of production and distribution to create a new order ordained from "above."

This does not in itself serve to commend or condemn the exercise of command. The new order imposed by the authorities may offend or please our sense of social justice, just as it may improve or lessen the economic efficiency of society. Clearly, command can be an instrument of a democratic as well as of a totalitarian will. There is no implicit moral judgment to be passed on this second of the great mechanisms of economic control. Rather, it is important to note that no society—certainly no modern society—is without its elements of command, just as none is devoid of the influence of tradition. *If tradition is the great brake on social and economic change, economic command can be the great spur to change.* As mechanisms for assuring the successful solution to the economic problem, both serve their purposes, both have their uses and their drawbacks. Between them, tradition and command have accounted for most of the long history of man's economic efforts to cope with his environment and with himself. The fact that human society has survived is testimony to their effectiveness.

the market

But there is a third solution to the economic problem, a third way of maintaining socially viable patterns of production and distribution. This is the *market organization of society*—an organization that, in truly remarkable fashion, allows society to insure its own provisioning with a minimum of recourse to either tradition or command.

Because we live in a market-run society, we are apt to take for granted the puzzling—indeed, almost paradoxical—nature of the market solution to the economic problem. But assume for a moment that we could act as economic advisers to a society that had not yet decided on its mode of economic organization. Suppose, for instance, that we were called on to act as consultants to one of the new nations emerging on the continent of Africa or Asia.

We could imagine the leaders of such a nation saying, "We have always experienced a highly tradition-bound way of life. Our men hunt and cultivate the fields and perform their tasks as they are brought up to do by the force of example and the instruction of their elders. We know, too, something of what can be done by economic command. We are prepared, if necessary, to sign an edict making it compulsory for many of our men to work on community projects for our national development. Tell us, is there any other way we can organize our society so that it will function successfully—or better yet, *more* successfully?"

Suppose we answered, "Well, there is another way. One can organize a society along the lines of a market economy."

"I see," say the leaders. "What would we then tell people to do? How would we assign them to their various tasks?"

"That's the very point," we answer. "In a market economy, no one is assigned to any task. In fact, the main idea of a market society is that each person is allowed to decide for himself what to do."

There is consternation among the leaders. "You mean there is no assignment of some men to farming and others to mining? No manner of designating some for transportation and others for weaving? You leave this to people to decide for themselves? But what happens if they do not decide correctly? What happens if no one volunteers to go into the mines, or if no one offers himself as a bus driver?"

"You must rest assured," we tell the leaders, "none of that will happen. In a market society, all the jobs will be filled because it will be to people's advantage to fill them."

Our respondents accept this with uncertain expressions. "Now look," one of them finally says, "let us suppose that we take your advice and allow our people to do as they please. Let's talk about something specific, like cloth production. Just how do we fix the right level of cloth output in this 'market society' of yours?"

"But you don't," we reply.

"We don't! Then how do we know there will be enough cloth produced?"

"There will be," we tell him. "The market will see to that."

"Then how do we know there won't be *too much* cloth produced?" he asks triumphantly.

"Ah, but the market will see to that too!"

"But what is this market that will do these wonderful things? Who runs it?"

"Oh, nobody runs the market," we answer. "It runs itself. In fact, there really isn't any such *thing* as 'the market.' It's just a word we use to describe the way people behave."

"But I thought people behaved the way they wanted to!"

"And so they do," we say. "But never fear. They will want to behave the way you want them to behave."

"I am afraid," says the chief of the delegation, "that we are wasting out time. We thought you had in mind a serious proposal. What you suggest is inconceivable. Good day."

Could we seriously suggest to such an emergent nation that it entrust itself to a market solution of the economic problem? That will be a problem to which we shall return at the very end of our book. But the perplexity that the market idea would rouse in the mind of someone unacquainted with it may serve to increase our own wonderment at this most sophisticated and interesting of all economic mechanisms. How does the market system assure us that our mines will find miners, our factories workers? How does it take care of cloth production? How does it happen that in a market-run nation each person can indeed do as he wishes and, withal, fulfill needs that society as a whole presents?

economics and the market system

Economics, as we commonly conceive it and as we shall study it in much of this book, is primarily concerned with these very problems. Societies that rely primarily on tradition to solve their economic problems are of less interest to the professional economist than to the cultural anthropologist or the sociologist. Societies that solve their economic problems primarily by the exercise of command present interesting economic questions, but here the study of economics is necessarily subservient to the study of politics and the exercise of power.

It is a society that solves its economic problems by the market process that presents an aspect especially interesting to the economist. Clearly, many (although not all) of the problems we encounter in America today have to do with the workings or misworkings of the market system. And precisely *because* our contemporary problems often arise from the operations of the market, we study economics itself. Unlike the case with tradition and command, where we quickly grasp the nature of the economic mechanism of society, when we turn to a market society we are lost without a knowledge of economics. For in a market society, it is not at all clear that even the simplest problems of production and distribution will be solved by the free interplay of individuals without guidance from tradition or command; nor is it clear how and to what extent the market mechanism is to be blamed for society's ills—after all, we can find poverty and misallocation and pollution in nonmarket economies too!

In subsequent parts of this book, we shall analyze these puzzling questions in more detail. But the task of our initial exploration must now be clear. As our imaginary interview with the leaders of an emergent nation has suggested, the market solution appears very strange to someone brought up in the ways of tradition or command. Hence the question arises: How did the market solution itself come into being? Was it imposed, full-blown, on our society at some earlier date? Or did it arise spontaneously and without forethought? This is the focusing question of economic history to which we now turn, as we retrace the evolution of our own market system out of the tradition- and authority-dominated societies of the past.

KEY CONCEPTS AND KEY WORDS

Provisioning wants
: 1. Economics is at bottom the study of how mankind assures its material sufficiency, of how societies arrange for their *material provisioning*.

Scarcity
: 2. Economic problems arise because the wants of most societies exceed the gifts of nature, giving rise to the general condition of *scarcity*.

3. Scarcity, in turn (whether it arises from nature's stinginess or man's appetites), imposes two severe tasks on society:

Production
: a) It must mobilize its energies for *production*—producing not only enough goods, but the right goods; and

Distribution
: b) It must resolve the problem of *distribution*, arranging a satisfactory solution to the problem of Who Gets What?

Division of labor
: 4. These problems exist in all societies, but they are especially difficult to solve in advanced societies in which there exists a far-reaching *division of labor*. People in wealthy societies are far more socially interdependent than people in simple societies.

5. Over the course of history, there have evolved three types of solutions to the two great economic problems. These are *Tradition, Command,* and the *Market System.*

Tradition
: 6. Tradition solves the problems of production and distribution by enforcing a continuity oftaand rewards through social institutions such as the caste system. *Typically, the economic solution imposed by tradition is a static one*, in which little change occurs over long periods of time.

Command
: 7. Command solves the economic problem by imposing allocations of effort or reward by *governing authority*. Command can be a means for achieving rapid and far-reaching economic *change*. It can take an extreme totalitarian or a mild democratic form.

Market
: 8. The market system is a complex mode of organizing society in which order and efficiency emerge "spontaneously" from a seemingly uncontrolled society. We shall investigate the market system in great detail in the chapters to come.

QUESTIONS

1. If we could produce all the food we needed in our own backyards, and if technology were so advanced that we could all make anything we wanted in our basements, would an "economic problem" exist?

2. Suppose that everyone were completely versatile—able to do everyone else's work just as well as his or her own. Would a division of labor still be useful in society? Why?

3. Modern economic society is sometimes described as depending on "bureaucrats" who allow their lives to be directed by the large corporations or government agencies for which they work. Assuming that this description has some glimmer of truth, would you think that modern society should be described as one of tradition, command, or the market?

4. In what way do your own plans for the future coincide with or depart from the occupations of your parents? Do you think that the so-called generational split is observable in all modern societies?

5. Economics is often called the science of scarcity. How can this label be applied to a society of considerable affluence such as our own?

6. What elements of tradition and command do you think are indispensable in a modern industrial society? Do you think that modern society could exist without any dependence on tradition or without any exercise of command?

7. Much of production and distribution involves the creation or the handling of *things*. Why are production and distribution *social* problems rather than engineering or physical problems?

8. Do you consider mankind's wants to be insatiable? Does this imply that scarcity must always exist?

9. Take some of the main problems that disturb us in America today: neglect, poverty, inflation, pollution, racial discrimination. To what extent do you find such problems in societies run by tradition? by command? What is your feeling about the responsibility the market system bears for these problems in America?

2 THE PREMARKET ECONOMY

"Nobody ever saw a dog make a fair and deliberate exchange of one bone for another with another dog," wrote Adam Smith in *The Wealth of Nations*. "Nobody ever saw one animal by its gestures and natural cries signify to another, this is mine, that yours; I am willing to give this for that."[1]

Smith was writing about "a certain propensity in human nature . . . ; the propensity to truck, barter, and exchange one thing for another." That such a propensity exists as a universal characteristic of humankind is perhaps less likely than Smith believed, but he was certainly not mistaken in putting the act of exchange at the very center of his scheme of economic life. For there can be no doubt that exchange—buying and selling—lies at the very heart of a market society such as he was describing. And so, as we now begin to study the rise of the market society, what could be more natural than to commence by tracing the pedigree of markets themselves?

It comes as something of a surprise, perhaps, to discover how very ancient is that pedigree. Communities have traded with one another at least as far back as the last Ice Age. We have evidence that the mammoth hunters of the Russian steppes obtained Mediterranean shells in trade, as did also the Cro-Magnon hunters of the central valleys of France. In fact, on the moors of Pomerania in northeastern Germany, archeologists have come across an oaken box, replete with the remains of its original leather shoulder strap, in which were a dagger, a sickle head, and a needle—all of Bronze Age manufacture. According to the conjectures of experts, this was very likely the sample kit of a prototype of the traveling salesman, an itinerant representative who collected orders for the specialized production of his community.[2]

---

[1] *The Wealth of Nations* (New York: Modern Library, 1937), p. 13.

[2] *Cambridge Economic History of Europe* (Cambridge, England: Cambridge University Press, 1952), II, 4.

And as we proceed from the dawn of civilization to its first organized societies, the evidences of trade and of markets increase rapidly. As Miriam Beard has written:

Millennia before Homer sang, or the wolf suckled Romulus and Remus, the bustling damkars (traders) of Uruk and Nippur . . . were buckling down to business. Atidum the merchant, in need of enlarged office facilities, was agreeing to rent a suitable location from Ribatum, Priestess of Shamash, for one and one-sixth shekels of silver per year—so much down and the rest in easy installments. Abu-wakar, the rich shipper, was delighted that his daughter had become Priestess of Shamash and could open a real estate office near the temple. Ilabras was writing to Ibi: "May Shamash and Marduk keep thee! As thou knowest, I had issued a note for a female slave. Now the time to pay is come."[3]

Thus, at first glance it seems we can discover evidences of market society deep in the past. But these disconcerting notes of modernity must be interpreted with caution. If markets, buying and selling, even highly organized trading bodies, were well-nigh ubiquitous features of ancient society, they must not be confused with the presence of a *market society*. Trade existed as an important adjunct to society from earliest times, but the fundamental impetus to production, or the basic allocation of resources among different uses, or the distribution of goods among social classes was largely divorced from the marketing process. That is, *the markets of antiquity were not the means by which those societies solved their basic economic problems*. They were subsidiary to the great processes of production and distribution rather than integral to them; they were "above" the critical economic machinery rather than within it. As we shall see, between the deceptively contemporary air of many markets of the distant past and the reality of our contemporary market economy lies an immense distance over which society would take centuries to travel.

THE ECONOMIC ORGANIZATION OF ANTIQUITY

We must ourselves traverse that distance if we are to understand how contemporary market society came into being and, indeed, if we are to understand what it is. Only by immersing ourselves in the societies of the past, only by seeing how they did, in fact, solve their economic problems, can we begin to understand clearly what is involved in the evolution of the market society that is our own environment.

Needless to say, it would make an enormous difference which of the many premarket societies of the past we visited as general observers.

[3] *A History of the Business Man* (New York: Macmillan, 1938), p. 12.

To trace economic history from the monolithic temple-states of Sumer and Akkad to the "modernity" of classical Greece or Rome is to undertake a cultural journey of immense distance. Yet, traveling only as economic historians, we will find that it makes much less difference in which of the societies of antiquity we light. For as we examine these societies, we can see that, underlying their profound dissimilarities of art or political rule or religious belief, there are equally profound similarities of economic structure, similarities we call to mind less frequently because they are in the "background" of history and rarely adorn its more exciting pages. But these identifying characteristics of economic organization are the ones that now interest us as we turn our gaze to the past. What is it that we see?

agricultural
foundation
of ancient
societies

The first and perhaps the most striking impression is the overwhelmingly agricultural aspect of all these economies.

In a sense, of course, all human communities, no matter how industrialized, live off the soil: All that differentiates an "industrial" society from an "agricultural" one is the number of the nonagricultural population that its food growers can support. Thus, an American farmer working a large acreage with abundant equipment, can feed more than eighty nonfarmers; while an Asian peasant, tilling his tiny plot with little more than a stick-plow, may be hard pressed to sustain his own family.

Over all of antiquity, the capacity of the agricultural population to sustain a nonfarming population was very limited. Exact statistics are unavailable, but we can project backwards to the situation that prevailed in all these ancient nations by looking at the underdeveloped regions of the world today, where the levels of technique and the productivity of agriculture bear a close—too close—resemblance to those of antiquity. Thus in India, in Egypt, in the Philippines, Indonesia, Brazil, Colombia, Mexico, we find that it takes two farm families to support one nonfarm family; while in tropical Africa, a survey made some years ago told us that "the productivity of African agriculture is so low that it takes anywhere from two to ten people—men, women, and children—to raise enough food to supply their own needs and those of *one* additional—non–food-growing—adult."[4] Those sad findings are still largely true.

Antiquity was not *that* badly off; indeed, at times it produced impressive agricultural outputs. But neither was it remotely comparable to American farm productivity, with its enormous capacity to support a nonagricultural population. All ancient societies were basically rural economies. This did not preclude, as we shall see, a very brilliant and wealthy urban society nor a far-flung network of international trade. Yet the typ-

[4] George H. T. Kimble, *Tropical Africa* (New York: Twentieth Century Fund, 1960), I, 572. (Italics added.)

ical economic personage of antiquity was neither trader nor urban dweller. He was a tiller of the soil, and it was in his rural communities that the economies of antiquity were ultimately anchored.

But this must not lead us to assume that economic life was therefore comparable to that of a modern agricultural community like Denmark or New Zealand. Contemporary farmers, like businessmen, are very much bound up in the web of transactions characteristic of a market society. They sell their output on one market; they buy their supplies on another. The accumulation of money, and not of wheat or corn, is the object of their efforts. Books of profit and loss regularly tell them if they are doing well or not. The latest news of agricultural technology is studied and is put into effect if it is profitable.

None of this properly describes the "farmer" of ancient Egypt, of antique Greece or Rome, or of the great Eastern civilizations. With few exceptions, the tiller of the soil was a peasant, and a peasant is a social creature very different from a farmer. He is not on the alert for new technologies, but, on the contrary, clings with stubborn persistence— and often with great skill—to his well-known ways. He must do so, since a small error might mean starvation. He does not buy the majority of his supplies, but fashions them himself; similarly, he does not produce for a "market," but principally for himself. Finally, he is often not even free to consume his own crop, but typically must hand over a portion—a tenth, a third, half, or even more—to the owner of his land.

For in the general case, the peasant of antiquity did not own his land. We hear of the independent citizen-farmers of classical Greece and republican Rome, but these were exceptions to the general rule in which peasants were but tenants of a great lord. And even in Greece and Rome, the independent peasantry tended to become swallowed up as the tenantry of huge commercial estates. Pliny mentions one such enormous estate or *latifundium* (literally, "broad farm") with a quarter of a million livestock and a population of 4,117 slaves.

Hence the peasant, who was the bone and muscle of the economies of antiquity, was himself a prime example of the nonmarket aspect of these economies. Although some cultivators freely sold a portion of their own crop in the city marketplaces, the great majority of agricultural producers scarcely entered the market at all. For many of these producers— especially those who were slaves—this was, accordingly, an almost cashless world, where a few coppers a year, carefully hoarded and spent only for emergencies, constituted the only link with a world of market transactions.*

* This is not, let us note, only an ancient condition. Traveling in Morocco, John Gunther reported of the local peasant-serfs, "formerly they got no wages—what would they need money for—but this is changing now." *Changing now—in 1953!* From *Inside Africa* (New York: Harper, 1955), p. 104.

Thus, whereas the peasant's legal and social status varied widely in different areas and eras of antiquity, in a broad view the tenor of his economic life was singularly constant. Of the web of transactions, the drive for profits of the modern farmer, he knew little or nothing. Generally poor, tax-ridden, and oppressed, prey to nature's caprices and to the exploitations of war and peace, bound to the soil by law and custom, the peasant of antiquity—like the peasant of today who continues to provide the agricultural underpinnings to some countries of the East and South—was dominated by the economic rule of tradition. His main stimulus for change was command—or, rather, obedience. Labor, patience, and the incredible endurance of the human being were his contributions to civilization.

economic life of the cities
The basic agricultural cast of ancient society and its typical exclusion of the peasant cultivator from an active market existence make all the more striking another common aspect of economic organization in antiquity. This is the diversity, vitality, and ebullience of the economic life of the cities.

Whether we turn to ancient Egypt, classical Greece, or Rome, we cannot help but be struck by this contrast between the relatively static countryside and the active city. In Greece, for example, a whole panoply of goods passed across the docks of the Piraeus: grain from Italy, metal from Crete and even Britain, books from Egypt, perfume from still more distant origins. Isocrates, in the *Panegyricus*, boasts: "The articles which it is difficult to get, one here, one there, from the rest of the world; all these it is easy to buy in Athens." So, too, Rome developed a thriving foreign and domestic commerce. By the time of Augustus, 6,000 loads of ox-towed barges were required to feed the city annually,[5] while in the city forum a crowd of speculators converged as on "an immense stock exchange."[6]

Thus, something that at least superficially approximated our own society was visible in many of the larger urban centers of antiquity. And yet we must not be beguiled into concluding that this was a market society similar to our own. In at least two respects, the differences were profound.

The first of these was the essentially restricted character and scope of the market function of the city. Unlike the modern city, which is not only a receiver of goods shipped in from the hinterlands but also an important exporter of goods and services back to the countryside, the cities of antiquity tended to assume an economically parasitic role vis-

[5] *Cambridge Economic History of Europe*, II, 47.
[6] W. C. Cunningham, *An Essay on Western Civilization* (New York: 1913), p. 164.

à-vis the rest of the economy. Much of the trade that entered the great urban centers of Egypt, Greece, and Rome (over and above the necessary provisioning of the city masses) was in the nature of luxury goods for its upper classes, rather than raw materials to be worked and then sent out to a goods-consuming economy. The cities were the vessels of civilization; but as centers of economic activity, they were separated by a wide gulf from the country, making them enclaves of economic life rather than nourishing components of integrated rural-urban economies.

slavery   Even more important was a second difference between the ancient city economies and a contemporary market society. This was their reliance on *slave labor.*

For slavery on a massive scale was a fundamental pillar of nearly every ancient economic society. In Greece, for instance, the deceptively modern air of the Piraeus masks the fact that much of the purchasing power of the Greek merchant was provided by the labor of 20,000 slaves who toiled under sickening conditions in the silver mines of Laurentium. At the height of "democratic" Athens, it is estimated that at least one-third of its population were slaves. In Rome of 30 B.C., some 1,500,000 slaves—on the latifundia, in the galleys, the mines, the "factories," the shops—provided a major impetus in keeping the economic machinery in motion.[7] Seneca even tells us that a proposal that they wear special dress was voted down lest, recognizing their own number, they might know their strength.

Slaves were not, of course, the only source of labor. Groups of free artisans and workmen, often banded together in *collegia* or fraternal bodies, also serviced the Roman city, as did similar free workmen in Greece and elsewhere. In many cities, especially latter-day Rome, a mass of unemployed (but not enslaved) laborers provided a source of casual work. Yet, without the motive power of the slave, it is doubtful if the brilliant city economies of the past could have been sustained. And this brings us to the central point. It is that the flourishing market economy of the city rested atop an economic structure run by tradition and command. Nothing like the free exercise and interplay of self-interest guided the basic economic effort of antiquity. If an astonishingly modern urban market structure greets our eye, we must not forget that its merchants are standing on the shoulders of innumerable peasants and slaves.

the social   The presence of great agglomerations of urban wealth amid a far poorer
surplus   rural setting alerts us to another characteristic of ancient economic soci-

---

[7] K. J. Beloch, *Die Bevölkerung der Griechisch-Römischen Welt* (Leipzig: 1886), p. 478.

ety. This is the special relationship between its wealth and its underlying economic organization.

In any society, wealth implies that a *surplus* has been wrung from nature, that society has not only solved its economic production problem but has achieved a margin of effort above whatever is required for its own existence. Perhaps what first astonishes us when we regard the civilizations of the ancient world is the size of surplus that could be got from a basically poor peasant population. The temples of the ancient Assyrian kings, the extraordinary treasures of the Aztecs, the pyramids and pleasure craft of the pharaohs of Egypt, the Acropolis of Athens, and the magnificent roads and architecture of Rome all testify to the ability of an essentially agricultural civilization to achieve a massive surplus, to pry considerable amounts of labor loose from the land, support it at whatever low level necessary, and put it to work building for posterity.

But the stupendous achievements of the past testify as well to something else. The surplus productive potential that society manages to achieve, whether by technology or by adroit social organization, can be applied in many directions. It can be directed to agricultural improvements, such as irrigation ditches or dams, where it is apt to increase the bounty of the harvest still further. It can be applied to the tools and equipment of the city workman, where it is apt to raise his ability to produce. Or the surplus may be used to support a nonworking religious order, or a class of courtiers and idle nobility. If it were not for its amazing capacity to produce a surplus, the United States could never support its armed forces—any more than the USSR could have, if *its* economy had not given rise to more output than it required for sheer self-perpetuation.

Thus, the social form taken by the accumulation of wealth reveals a great deal about any society. "To whom does the surplus accrue?" is a question that invariably sheds important light on the structure of power within that society.

wealth and power

To whom did the wealth of antiquity accrue? At first glimpse, it seems impossible to answer in a phrase. Emperors, nobles, religious orders, merchant traders—all enjoyed the wealth of antiquity at one time or another. But at second look, an interesting and significant generalization becomes possible: Most wealth did not go to those who played a strictly *economic* role. Although there are records of clever slaves in Egypt and Rome who became wealthy, and although rich merchants and bankers are visible throughout the annals of antiquity, theirs was not the primary route to wealth. Rather, *in ancient civilization, wealth was generally the reward for political, military, or religious power or status, and not for economic activity.*

There was a reason for this. Societies tend to reward most highly the activities they value most highly; and in the long and turbulent centuries of antiquity, political leadership, religious tutelage, and military prowess were unquestionably more necessary for social survival than trading expertise. In fact, in many of these societies, economic activity itself was disdained as essentially ignoble. As Aristotle wrote in his *Politics,* "in the best-governed polis . . . the citizens may not lead either the life of craftsmen or of traders, for such a life is devoid of nobility and hostile to perfection of character." It was a theme on which Cicero would later expand in his essay *De Officiis* (Book I):

> The toil of a hired worker, who is paid only for his toil and not for artistic skill, is unworthy of a free man and is sordid in character. For in his case, money is the price of slavery. Sordid too is the calling of those who buy wholesale in order to sell retail, since they would gain no profits without a great deal of lying. . . . Trade on a small retail scale is sordid, but if it is on a large wholesale scale including the import of many wares from everywhere and their distribution to many people without any misrepresentation, it is not to be too greatly censured. . . .

Especially, added the great lawyer, "if those who carry on such trade finally retire to country estates, after being surfeited or at least satisfied with their gains."

Over and above the lesser social function of the merchant compared with the general, the consul, or the priest, this disdain of wealth obtained from "ignoble" economic activity reflected an economic fact of great importance: Society had not yet integrated the production of wealth with the production of goods. Wealth was still a surplus to be seized by conquest or squeezed from the underlying agricultural population; it was not yet a natural adjunct of a system of continuously increasing production in which some part of an expanding total social output might accrue to many classes of society.

And so it would be for many centuries. Until the smallest as well as the largest activities of society received their price tag, until purchases and sales, bids and offers penetrated down to the lowest orders of society, the accumulation of wealth remained more a matter of political, military, or religious power than of economics. To sum it up: *In premarket societies, wealth tended to follow power; not until the market society would power tend to follow wealth.*

"economics" and social justice in antiquity

Before we move on to view the economic system of antiquity in transition and evolution, we must ask one more question: What did contemporary economists think of it?

The answer we find is an interesting one: There were no contemporary "economists." Historians, philosophers, political theorists, and writers on manners and morals abounded during the long span of history we here call "antiquity," but economists, as such, did not exist. The reason is not far to seek. The economics of society—that is, the mode by which society organized itself to meet the basic tasks of economic survival—was hardly such as to provoke the curiosity of a thoughtful man. There was little or no "veil" of money to pierce, little or no complexity of contractual relationship in the marketplace to unravel, little or no economic rhythm of society to interpret. As the harvest flourished, as the justice or injustice of the tax-gathering system varied, as the fortunes of war and politics changed, so went the lot of the peasant proprietor, the slave, the petty craftsman, and trader. As relative military strength rose or fell, as individual merchants fared luckily or otherwise, as the arts prospered or declined, so went the pulse of trade. As his prowess in war or politics permitted, as his chance at ransoms, local monopolies, or marriage dictated, so fared the individual acquisitor of wealth. In all of this, there was little to try the analytic powers of economic-minded observers.

If there was a problem of economics—aside from the eternal problems of poor harvests, fortunes of war, and so on—it was inextricably mingled with the problem of social justice. As far back as the early Assyrian tablets, we have records of reformers who sought to alleviate taxes on the peasantry, and throughout the Bible—indeed, down through the Middle Ages—a strain of primitive communism, of egalitarian sharing, runs through the background of religious thought. In the Book of Leviticus, for example, there is mentioned the interesting custom of the *jubilee*, a limit of fifty years on leases, after which each landowner was to "return to each man unto his possession."* But despite the fact that religion was concerned with riches and poverty, and thus with the distributive problem of economics, the span of antiquity saw little or no systematic inquiry into the *social system* that produced riches or poverty. If riches were an affront, this was due to the personal failings of greedy men; and if social justice were to be obtained, it must be achieved by personal redistribution, by alms and charity. The idea of an "economic" study of society, as contrasted with a political or moral one, was conspicuous largely by its absence.

There was, however, one exception we should note. Aristotle, the great pupil of Plato, turned his powerful scrutiny to economic affairs, and with him the systematic study of economics, as such, truly begins. Not that Aristotle, any more than the majority of the Church fathers, was a radical social reformer. Much is summed up in his famous sentence. "From the hour of their birth, some are marked out for subjection, others

---

* That is, lands that had been forfeited in debt, etc., were to be restored to their original owners. The wrath of the later prophets such as Amos indicates that the injunction must have been observed largely in the breach.

for rule."[8] But the student of the history of economic thought turns first to Aristotle for questions whose treatment he can subsequently trace down through the present time: questions such as, "What is value?" "What is the basis of exchange?" "What is interest?"

We will not linger here over Aristotle's formulations of these ideas. But one point we might note, for it accords with what we have already seen of the attitude of antiquity to economic activity itself. When Aristotle examined the economic process, he differentiated it into two branches—not production and distribution, as we have done, but *use* and *gain*. More specifically, he differentiated between *oeconomia*— whence "economics"—and *chrematistiké*, from which we have no precise derivative term. By *oeconomia*, the Greek philosopher meant the art of household management, the administration of one's patrimony, the careful husbanding of resources. *Chrematistiké*, on the other hand, implied the use of nature's resources or of human skill for acquisitive purposes; *chrematistiké* was trade for trade's sake, economic activity that had as its motive and end not use, but profit. Aristotle approved of *oeconomia* but not of *chrematistiké*, and within the scope of the essentially limited market structure of antiquity, where the city trader all too frequently exploited the country peasant, it is not hard to see why. The much more difficult problem of whether a market society, in which *everyone* strives for gain, might warrant approval or disapproval never appears in Aristotle's writings, as it never appeared in ancient history. The market society, with its genuinely perplexing questions of economic order and economic morality, had yet to come into being. Until it did, the philosophy needed to rationalize that order was understandably lacking.

ECONOMIC SOCIETY IN THE MIDDLE AGES

Our conspectus of economic organization has thus far scanned only the great civilizations of antiquity. Now we must turn in somewhat closer focus to the society far nearer in time and, what is more important, immediately precedent to ours in terms of social evolution. This is the vast expanse of history we call the Middle Ages, an expanse that stretches over and describes the Western world, from Sweden to the Mediterranean, "beginning" with the fall of Rome and "ending" with the Renaissance.

Modern scholarship emphasizes more and more the diversity that characterizes that enormous span of time and space, a diversity not alone of social appearance from century to century but also of contrast from

[8] *Politics*, Book I.

locality to locality within any given period. It is one thing to speak of "life" in the Middle Ages when one has in mind a tenth-century peasant community in Normandy where, it is estimated, the average inhabitant probably never saw more than two or three hundred persons in his lifetime or commanded a vocabulary of more than six hundred words;[9] it is another when we mean the worldly city of Florence in the fourteenth century, about which Boccaccio wrote so engagingly.

Even more relevant for our purposes is the need to think of the Middle Ages in terms of economic variety and change. The early years of feudal economic life are very different from the middle or later years, particularly insofar as general well-being is concerned. The commencement of feudalism coincided with a period of terrible retrenchment, deprivation, depopulation. During the fifth century, the population of Rome actually fell from 1,500,000 to 300,000. But by the twelfth century, towns had again expanded (after 600 years!) to the limits of their old Roman walls and even spilled out beyond; and by the beginning of the fourteenth century, a very considerable prosperity reigned in many parts of Europe.* Then came a series of catastrophes: a ghastly two-year famine in 1315; thereafter, in 1348, the Black Death, which carried off between one-third and two-thirds of the urban population; a century-long devastating struggle between England and France and among the petty principalities of Germany and Italy. All these misfortunes pulled down the level of economic existence to dreadful depths. Neither stasis nor smooth linear progress, but enormous and irregular secular tides mark the long history of feudalism, and they caution us against a simplistic conception of its development.

Our purpose, however, is not to trace these tides, but rather to form a generalized picture of the *economic structure* that, beneath the swings of fortune, marks the feudal era as a unique way station of Western economic history. And here we can begin by noting the all-important development that underlay the genesis of that economic structure. *This was the breakdown of large-scale political organization.*

the fall of Rome   For as Rome "fell" and as successive raids and invasions from north, east, and south tore apart the European countryside, the great administrative framework of law and order was replaced by a patchwork quilt of small-scale political entities. Even in the ninth century, when Charlemagne's Holy Roman Empire assumed such impressive dimensions

[9] George G. Coulton. *Medieval Village, Manor and Monastery* (New York: Harper, Torchbooks, 1960), p. 15.

* There is some evidence that in England around the year 1500 real wages for common laborers achieved a level that they would not surpass for at least three centuries. (*Economica*, November 1956, pp. 296–314.)

on the map, beneath the veneer of a unified "state" there was, in fact, political chaos: Neither a single language, nor a coordinated central government, nor a unified system of law, coinage, or currency, nor, most important, any consciousness of "national" allegiance bound the statelets of Charlemagne's day into more than temporary cohesion.

We note this striking difference between antiquity and the Middle Ages to stress the tremendous economic consequences that came with political dissolution. As safety and security gave way to local autarky and anarchy, long voyages of commodities became extremely hazardous, and the once-vigorous life of the great cities impossible. As a common coin and a common law disappeared, merchants in Gaul could no longer do business with merchants in Italy, and the accustomed network of economic connections was severed or fell into disuse. As disease and invasion depopulated the countryside, men turned of necessity to the most defensive forms of economic organization, to forms aimed at sheer survival through self-sufficiency. A new need arose, a need to compress the viable organization of society into the smallest possible compass. For centuries, this insularity of economic life, this extreme self-reliance, would be the economic hallmark of the Middle Ages.

manorial organization of society

The need for self-sufficiency brought with it a new basic unit of economic organization: the *manorial estate.*

What was such an estate like? Typically, it was a large tract of land, often including many thousands of acres, which was "owned" by a feudal lord, spiritual or temporal.* The word "owned" is properly in quotation marks, for the manor was not first and foremost a piece of economic property. Rather, it was a social and political entity in which the lord of the manor was not only landlord, but protector, judge, police chief, and administrator as well. Although himself bound into a great hierarchy in which each lord was some other lord's servant (even the pope was the servant of God), the feudal noble was, within the confines of his own manor, quite literally "lord of the land." He was also undisputed owner and master of many of the people who lived on the land, for the serfs (or villeins) of a manor, although not slaves, were in many respects as much the property of the lord as were his (or their) houses, flocks, or crops.

At the focal point of the estate was the lord's homestead, a great manor house, usually armed against attack from marauders, walled off from the surrounding countryside, and sometimes attaining the stature of a genuine castle. In the enclosed courtyard of the manor were work-

---

* That is, the lord might be the abbot or the bishop of the locality, or he might be a secular personage, a baron who came into his possessions by inheritance or by being made a knight and given lands for exceptional service in battle or for other reasons.

shops in which cloth might be spun or woven, grapes pressed, food stored, simple ironwork or blacksmithing work performed, coarse grain ground. Extending out around the manor was a patchwork of fields, typically subdivided into acre or half-acre "strips," each with its own cycle of crops and rest. Half or more of all these belonged directly to the lord; the remainder "belonged," in various senses of that legal term, to the hierarchy of free, half-free, and unfree families who made up an estate.

The exact meaning of the word "belonged" hinged on the obligations and rights accruing to a serf, a freeman, or whatever other category one might be born into. Note, however, that even a freeman who "owned" his land could not sell it to another feudal lord. At best, his ownership meant that he could not himself be displaced from his land short of extraordinary circumstances. A lesser personage than a freeman did not even have this security. A typical serf was literally tied to "his" plot of land. He could not, without specific permission, and, usually, without specific payment, leave his homestead for another, either within the domain of the manor or within that of another. With his status came, as well, a series of obligations that lay at the very core of the manorial economic organization. These consisted of the necessity to perform labor for the lord—to till his fields, to work in his shops, to provide him with a portion of one's own crop. From manor to manor, and from age to age, the labor dues varied: In some localities, they amounted to as much as four or even five days of labor a week, which meant that only by the labor of a serf's wife or children could his own fields be maintained. And finally, the serfs owed small money payments: head taxes, like the *chevage*; death duties, like the *heriot; merchet*, a marriage fee; or dues to use the lord's mill or his ovens.

providing security   There was, however, an extremely important quid pro quo for all this. If the serf gave the lord his labor and much of the fruits of his toil, in exchange the lord provided some things that the serf by himself could not have obtained.

The most important of these was a degree of physical security. It is difficult for us to reconstruct the violent tenor of much of feudal life, but one investigator has provided a statistic that may serve to make the point. Among the sons of English dukes, 46 percent of those born between 1330 and 1479 died violent deaths. Their life expectancy when violent death was excluded was thirty-one years; when violent death was included, it was but twenty-four years.[10] The peasant, although not a warrior and therefore not occupationally exposed to the dangers of continual combat, assassination, and so on, was preeminently fair prey

[10] T. H. Hollingsworth, "A Demographic Study of the British Ducal Families," *Population Studies*, XI (1957–58).

for the marauding lord, defenseless against capture, unable to protect his poor possessions against destruction. Hence we can begin to understand why even free men became serfs by "commending" themselves to a lord who, in exchange for their economic, social, and political subservience, offered them the invaluable cloak of his military protection.

In addition, the lord offered a certain element of *economic* security. In times of famine, it was the lord who fed his serfs from the reserves in his own manorial storehouses. And, although he had to pay for it, the serf was *entitled* to use the lord's beasts and equipment in cultivating his own strips as well as those of the lord. In an age when the average serf possessed almost no tools himself, this was an essential boon.[11]

These facts should not incline us to an idyllic picture of feudal life. The relation between lord and serf was often, even usually, exploitative in the extreme. Yet we must see that it was also mutually supportive. Each provided for the other services essential for existence in a world where overall political organization and stability had virtually disappeared.

economics of manorial life

Despite the extreme self-efficiency of manorial life, there is much here that resembles the economic organization of antiquity.

To begin with, like those earlier societies, this was clearly a form of economic society organized by tradition. Indeed, the hand of custom— the famous "ancient customs" of the medieval manor court, which served frequently as the counsel for the otherwise undefended serf—was never stronger. Lacking strong, unified central government, even the exercise of command was relatively weak. As a result, the pace of economic change, of economic development, although by no means lacking, was extremely slow during the early years of the medieval period.

Second, even more than with antiquity, this was a form of society that was characterized by a striking absence of money transactions. Unlike the latifundium of Rome, which sold its output to the city, the manor supplied only itself, and perhaps a local town. No manorial estate was

---

[11] For a picture of life among the various classes in medieval Europe, one might turn to Eileen Power's *Medieval People* (Garden City, N.Y.: Doubleday, Anchor Books, 1954), a scholarly but charming account of the reality of human existence that lies behind history. For a sense of the violent tenor of the times, see J. Huizinga, *The Waning of the Middle Ages* (Garden City, N.Y.: Doubleday, Anchor Books, 1954), Chap. 1. Let me call attention also to two other books that convey a vivid sense of feudal economic life. One is by H. S. Bennett, *Life on the English Manor* (Cambridge, England: Cambridge University Press, 1965); the other, by Marc Bloch, *French Rural History* (Berkeley: University of California Press, 1966). *French Rural History*, especially, is one of the real masterworks of economic history. Less concerned with economic life (one has to read between the lines to ferret it out), but marvelous as a microhistory of medieval life, is the account of a tiny, heresy-ridden town in fourteenth-century southern France, *Montaillou: The Land of Promised Error*, by Emmanuel Le Roy Ladurie (New York: George Braziller, 1978).

ever quite so self-sufficient that it could dispense with monetary links with the outside world; even serfs bought a few commodities and sold a few eggs; and the lord, on occasion, had to buy considerable supplies he could not produce for himself. But on the whole, very little money changed hands. As Henri Pirenne, an authority on medieval economic history, has put it:

> . . . the tenants paid their obligations to their lord in kind. Every serf . . . owed a fixed number of days of labour and a fixed quantity of natural products or of goods manufactured by himself, corn, eggs, geese, chickens, lambs, pigs, and hempen, linen or woollen cloth. It is true that a few pence had also to be paid, but they formed such a small proportion of the whole that they cannot prevent the conclusion that the economy of the domain was a natural economy . . . since it did not engage in commerce it had no need to make use of money. . . .[12]

town and
fair
It would, however, be a misrepresentation of medieval life to conclude that cash and cash transactions and the bargaining of a market society were wholly foreign to it. Rather, as was the case with antiquity, we must think of medieval economic society as consisting of a huge, static, largely moneyless foundation of agricultural production atop which flourished a considerable variety of more dynamic activities.

For one thing, in addition to manors, there also existed the shrunken descendants of Roman towns (and as we shall later see, the nuclei of new towns), and these small cities obviously required a network of markets to serve them. Every town had its stalls to which peasants brought some portion of their crop for sale. More important, towns were clearly a different social unit from manors, and the laws and customs of the manors did not apply to their problems. Even when towns fell under manorial protection, townspeople little by little won for themselves freedom from feudal obligations of labor and, more important, from feudal obligations of law.* In contrast to the "ancient customs" of the manor, a new, evolving "law of merchants" regulated much of the commercial activity within the town walls.

Another locus of active economic life was the fair. The fair was a kind of traveling market, established in fixed localities for fixed dates, in which merchants from all over Europe conducted a genuine inter-

---

[12] *Economic and Social History of Medieval Europe* (New York: Harcourt, Harvest Books, 1956), p. 105.

* Hence the saying, "City air makes men free"; for the serf who escaped to a city and remained there a year and a day was usually considered to have passed from the jurisdiction of his lord to that of the city burghers. Running away was one of the very few means open to serfs to protest against their condition. Runaway serfs, like runaway slaves, were ferociously punished. Yet serfs did continuously escape to the cities, in this tiny, desperate way exerting economic pressure against their masters. For a debate on the importance of this issue, see *The Transition from Feudalism to Capitalism*, ed. Rodney Hilton (London: NLB, 1978).

national exchange. Held usually but once a year, the great fairs were tremendous occasions, a mixture of social holiday, religious festival, and intense economic activity. At some fairs, like those at Champagne in France or Stourbridge in England, a wide variety of merchandise was brought for sale: silks from the Levant, books and parchments, horses, drugs, spices. Anyone who has ever been to the Flea Market, the famous open-air bazaar outside Paris, or to a country fair in New England or the Middle West has savored something of the atmosphere of such a market. One can imagine the excitement that fairs must have engendered in the still air of medieval life.

guilds   And finally, within the towns themselves, we find the tiny but highly important centers of medieval "industrial" production. For even at its grandest, the manor could not support every craft needed for its maintenance, much less its extension. The services or products of glaziers and masons, expert armorers and metalworkers, fine weavers and dyers had to be bought when they were needed, and typically they were to be found in the medieval institutions as characteristic of town life as the manors were of life in the country.

These institutions were the *guilds*—trade, professional, and craft organizations of Roman origin. Such organizations were the "business units" of the Middle Ages; in fact, one could not usually set oneself up in "business" unless one belonged to a guild. Thus, the guilds were a kind of exclusive union, but not a union of workers so much as of managers. The dominant figures in the guild were the guildmasters—independent manufacturers, working in their own houses and banding together to elect their own guild government, which then laid down the rules concerning the internal conduct of affairs. Under the master guildsmen were their few journeymen (from the French *journée*, or "day"), who were paid by the day, and their half-dozen or so apprentices, ten to twelve years old, who were bound to them for periods of three to twelve years as their legal wards. In time, an apprentice could become a journeyman and then, at least in medieval romance, graduate to the status of a full-fledged guildmaster on completion of his "masterpiece."

Any survey of medieval town life delights in the color of guild organizations: the broiders and glovers, the hatters and scriveners, the shipwrights and upholsterers, each with its guild hall, its distinctive livery, and its elaborate set of rules. But if life in the guilds and at the fairs provides a sharp contrast with the stodgy life on the manor, we must not be misled by surface resemblances into thinking that it represented a foretaste of modern life in medieval dress. It is a long distance from the guild to the modern business firm, and it is well to fix in mind some of the differences.

*functions of
the guild*
In the first place, the guild was much more than just an institution for organizing production. While most of its regulations concerned wages and conditions of work and specifications of output, they also dwelt at length on "noneconomic" matters: on the charitable contributions expected from each member, on his civic role, on his appropriate dress, and even on his daily deportment. Guilds were the regulators not only of production but also of social conduct: When one member of the mercer's guild in London "broke the hed" of another in an argument over some merchandise, both were fined £10 and bonded for £200 not to repeat the disgrace. In another guild, members who engaged in a brawl were fined a barrel of beer, to be drunk by the rest of the guild.

But between guild and modern business firm there is a much more profound gulf than this pervasive paternalism. *Unlike a modern firm, the purpose of a guild was not first and foremost to make money.* Rather, it was to preserve a certain orderly way of life—a way that envisaged a decent income for its master craftsmen but that was certainly not intended to allow any of them to become a "big" businessman or a monopolist. On the contrary, guilds were specifically designed to ward off any such outcome of an uninhibited struggle among their members. The terms of service, the wages, the route of advancement of apprentices and journeymen were all fixed by custom. So, too, were the terms of sale: A guild member who cornered the supply of an item was guilty of *forestalling*, for which rigorous penalties were invoked, and one who bought wholesale to sell at retail was similarly punished for the faults of *engrossing* or *regrating*. Thus, competition was strictly limited and profits were held to prescribed levels. Advertising was forbidden, and even technical progress in advance of one's fellow guildsmen was considered disloyal.

In the great cloth guilds of Florence in the fourteenth century, for instance, no merchant was permitted to tempt a buyer into his shop or to call out to a customer standing in another's doorway, nor even to process his cloth in a manner different from that of his brethren. Standards of cloth production and processing were subject to the minutest scrutiny. If a scarlet dye, for instance, was found to be adulterated, the perpetrator was condemned to a crushing fine and, failing payment, to loss of his right hand.[13]

Surely the guilds represent a more "modern" aspect of feudal life than the manor, but the whole temper of guild life was still far removed from the goals and ideals of modern business enterprise. There was no free play of price, no free competition, no restless probing for advantage. Existing on the margin of a relatively moneyless society, the guilds perforce sought to take the risks out of their slender enterprises. Their aim

---

[13] G. Renard, *Histoire du Travail à Florence* (Paris: 1913), pp. 190ff.

was not increase, but preservation, stability, orderliness. As such, they were as drenched in the medieval atmosphere as the manors.

medieval economics

Beyond even these differences, we must note a still deeper chasm between medieval economic society and that of a market economy. This is the gulf between a society in which economic activity is still inextricably mixed with social and religious activity, and one in which economic life has, so to speak, emerged into a special category of its own. In our next chapter, we shall be talking about the ways in which a market society creates a special sphere of economic existence. But as we complete our introduction to medieval economic society, the main point to which we should pay heed is that no such special sphere then existed. *In medieval society, economics was a subordinate and not a dominant aspect of life.*

And what was dominant? The answer is, of course, that in economic matters, as in so many other facets of medieval life, the guiding ideal was religious. It was the Church, the great pillar of stability in an age of disorder, that constituted the ultimate authority on economics, as on most other matters.

But the economics of medieval Catholicism was concerned not with the credits and debits of successful business operation so much as with the credits and debits of the souls of business operators. As R. H. Tawney, one of the great students of the problem, has written:

> . . . the specific contributions of medieval writers to the technique of economic theory were less significant than their premises. Their fundamental assumptions, both of which were to leave a deep imprint on social thought of the sixteenth and seventeenth centuries, were two: that economic interests are subordinate to the real business of life, which is salvation; and that economic conduct is one aspect of personal conduct, upon which, as on other parts of it, the rules of morality are binding. Material riches are necessary . . . since without them men cannot support themselves and help one another. . . . But economic motives are suspect. Because they are powerful appetites men fear them, but they are not mean enough to applaud them. Like other strong passions, what they need, it is thought, is not a clear field, but repression. . . .[14]

Thus, what we find throughout medieval religious thought is a pervasive uneasiness with the practices of economic society. Essentially, the Church's attitude toward trade was wary and nicely summed up in the saying, *"Homo mercator vix aut numquam Deo placere potest"*—The merchant can scarcely or never be pleasing to God.

the just price

We find such a suspicion of business motives in the Church's concern with the idea of a "just price." What was a just price? It was selling a

[14] *Religion and the Rise of Capitalism* (New York: Harcourt, 1947), p. 31.

thing for what it was worth, and no more. "It is wholly sinful," wrote Thomas Aquinas, "to practise fraud for the express purpose of selling a thing for more than its just price, inasmuch as a man deceives his neighbor to his loss."[15]

But what *was* a thing "worth"? Presumably, what it cost to acquire it or make it. Suppose, however, that a seller had himself paid too much for an article—then what was a "just price" at which he might resell it? Or suppose a man paid too little—was he then in danger of spiritual loss, offsetting his material gain?

These were the questions over which the medieval "economist-theologians" mulled, and they testify to the mixture of economics and ethics characteristic of the age. But they were not merely theoretical questions. We have records of the dismay that economic theology brought to actual participants in the economic process. One St. Gerald of Aurillac in the tenth century, having bought an ecclesiastical garment in Rome for an unusually low price, learned from some itinerant merchants that he had picked up a "bargain"; instead of rejoicing, he hastened to send to the seller an additional sum, lest he fall into the sin of avarice.[16]

St. Gerald's attitude was no doubt exceptional. Yet if the injunction to charge fair prices did not succeed in staying men's appetites for gain, it did bridle their enthusiasm. Men in ordinary business frequently stopped to assess the condition of their moral balance sheets. Whole towns would, on occasion, repent of usury and pay a heavy amend, or merchants like Gandoufle le Grand would, on their deathbeds, order restitution made to those from whom interest had been extracted. Men of affairs in the twelfth and thirteenth centuries occasionally inserted codicils in their wills urging their sons not to follow their footsteps into the snares of trade, or they would seek to make restitution for their commercial sins by charitable contributions. One medieval merchant of London founded a divinity scholarship with £14, "forasmoche as I fynde myn conscience aggrugged that I have deceived in this life divers persons to that amount."[17]

the disrepute of gain   Thus, the theological cast of suspicion injected a wholly new note into the moneymaking process. For the first time, it associated the making of money with *guilt*. Unlike the acquisitor of antiquity who unashamedly

---

[15] A. E. Monroe, ed., "Summa Theologica," in *Early Economic Thought* (Cambridge, Mass.: Harvard University Press, 1924), p. 54.

[16] Pirenne, *Economic and Social History of Medieval Europe*, p. 27.

[17] S. L. Thrupp, *The Merchant Class in Medieval London* (Chicago: University of Chicago Press, 1948), p. 177. Also Renard, *Histoire du Travail à Florence*, pp. 220 ff.

reveled in his treasures, the medieval profiteer counted his gains in the knowledge that he might be imperiling his soul.

Nowhere was this disapproval of moneymaking more evident than in the Church's horror of usury—lending money at interest. Money-lending had, since Aristotle's day, been regarded as an essentially parasitic activity, an attempt to make a "barren" commodity, money, yield a return. But what had always been a vaguely disreputable and unpopular activity became, under Church scrutiny, a deeply evil one. Usury was decreed to be a *mortal* sin. At the Councils of Lyons and Vienne in the thirteenth and fourteenth centuries, the usurer was declared a pariah of society, to whom no one, under pain of excommunication, might rent a house; whose confession might not be heard; whose body might not have Christian burial; whose very will was invalid. Anyone even defending usury was to be suspected of heresy.

These powerful churchly sentiments were not produced merely by theological scruples. On the contrary, many of the Church's injunctions against both usury and profiteering arose from the most secular of realities. Famine, the endemic scourge of the Middle Ages, brought with it the most heartless economic gouging; loans commanded 40 to 60 percent—for bread. Much of the dislike of profit seeking and interest taking rose from its identification with just such ruthless practices, with which medieval times abounded.

Finally, another, perhaps even more fundamental, reason underlay the disrepute of gain and profit. This was the essentially static organization of economic life itself. Let us not forget that that life was basically agricultural and that agriculture, with its infinite complexity of peasant strips, was far from efficient. To quote once more from Henri Pirenne:

> . . . the whole idea of profit, and indeed the possibility of profit, was incompatible with the position occupied by the great medieval landowner. Unable to produce for sale owing to the want of a market, he had no need to tax his ingenuity in order to wring from his men and his land a surplus which would merely be an encumbrance, and as he was forced to consume his own produce, he was content to limit it to his needs. His means of existence was assured by the traditional functioning of an organization which he did not try to improve.[18]

What was true of the country was also true of the city. The idea of an *expanding* economy, a *growing* scale of production, an *increasing* productivity, was as foreign to the guildmaster or fair merchant as to the serf and lord. Medieval economic organization was conceived of as a means of reproducing, but not enhancing, the material well-being of the past. Its motto was perpetuation, not progress. There is little wonder that

---

[18] *Economic and Social History of Medieval Europe*, p. 63.

in such a static organization profits and profit seeking were viewed as essentially disturbing rather than welcome economic phenomena.

PREREQUISITES OF CHANGE

We have traced the broad outlines of the economic organization of the West roughly up to the tenth or twelfth century. Once again, it is wise to emphasize the diversity of currents concealed within a landscape we have too often been forced to treat as undifferentiated. At best, our journey into antiquity and the Middle Ages can give us a few glimpses of the prevailing flavor of the times, a sense of the ruling economic climate, of the main institutions and ideas by which men organized their economic efforts.

But one thing is certain. We are very far from the temper and tempo of modern economic life. The few stirrings we have witnessed in the slow world of the manor and the town are but the harbingers of a tremendous change, which, over the course of the next centuries, would dramatically alter the basic form of economic organization itself, replacing the old ties of tradition and command with new ties of market transactions.

We shall have to wait until our next chapter to witness the actual process of change itself. But perhaps it will help us put into focus both what we have already seen and what we are about to witness if we anticipate our line of advance. We now have an idea of a premarket society, a society in which markets exist but that does not yet depend on a market mechanism to solve the economic problem. What changes will be required to transform such a society into a true market economy?

1. *A new attitude toward economic activity will be needed.*

For such a society to function, men must be free to seek gain. The suspiciousness and unease that surrounded the ideas of profit, of change, and of social mobility must give way to new ideas that would encourage those very attitudes and activities. In turn, this meant, in the famous words of the mid-nineteenth-century legal historian Sir Henry Maine, that the *society of status* must give way to the *society of contract*, that the society in which men were born to their stations in life must give way to a society in which they were free to define those stations for themselves.

Such an idea would have seemed to the medieval mind without any possible rationale. The idea that a general free-for-all should determine men's compensations, with neither a floor to prevent them from being ground down nor a ceiling to prevent them from rising beyond all

reason, would have appeared senseless—even blasphemous. If we may
listen again to R. H. Tawney:

> To found a science of society upon the assumption that the appetite for economic
> gain is . . . to be accepted, like other natural forces . . . would have appeared to
> the medieval thinker as hardly less irrational or less immoral than to make the
> premise of social philosophy the unrestrained operation of such necessary human
> attributes as pugnacity or the sexual instinct.[19]

Yet some such freeing of the quest for economic gain, some such
aggressive competition in the new contractual relationship of man to
man, would be essential for the birth of a market society.

2. *The monetization of economic life will have to proceed to its*
   ultimate conclusion.

One prerequisite of a market economy should by now be clear: Such an
economy must involve the process of exchange, of buying and selling,
at every level of society. But for this to take place, men must have the
wherewithal to enter a market; that is, they must have cash. And, in turn,
if society is to be permeated with cash, men must earn money for their
labors. In other words, *for a market society to exist, nearly every task*
must have a monetary reward.

Even in our highly monetized society, we do not pay for every
service: most conspicuously not for the housekeeping services of a wife.
But all through the premarket era, unpaid service—the amount of work
performed by law without monetary compensation—was vastly larger
than it is in our society. Slave labor was, of course, unpaid. So was most
serf labor. Even the labor of apprentices was remunerated more in kind,
in food and lodging, than in cash. Thus, probably 70 to 80 percent of the
actual working population of an ancient or medieval economy labored
without anything resembling regular payment in money.

Clearly, in such a society, the possibilities for a highly involved
exchange economy were limited. But a still more important consequence
must be noted. The absence of a widespread monetization of tasks meant
the absence of a widespread market for producers. Nothing like the flow
of "purchasing power" that dominates and directs our own productive
efforts could be forthcoming in a society in which money incomes were
the exception rather than the rule.

3. *The pressure of a free play of market "demand" will have to*
   take over the regulation of the economic tasks of society.

All through antiquity and the Middle Ages, as we have seen, tradition
or command solved the economic problem. These were the forces that

---

[19] *Religion and the Rise of Capitalism*, pp. 31–32.

regulated the distribution of social rewards. But in a market society, another means of control must rise to take their place. *An all-encompassing flow of money demand, itself stemming from the total monetization of all economic tasks, must become the great propulsive mechanism of society.* Men must go to their tasks not because they are ordered there, but because they will make money there; and producers must decide on the volume and the variety of their output not because the rules of the manor or the guild so determine, but because there is a market demand for particular things. From the top to the bottom of society, in other words, a new marketing orientation must take over the production and distribution tasks. The whole replenishment, the steady provisioning, the very progress of society must now be subject to the guiding hand of a universal demand for labor and goods.

What forces would ultimately drive the world of medieval economic organization into a world of money, of universal markets, of profit seeking? The stage is now set for us to attempt to answer this profoundly important and difficult question. Let us turn to a consideration of the causes capable of effecting so vast a change.

KEY CONCEPTS AND KEY WORDS

Markets

1. We must differentiate between markets, which have a very ancient pedigree, and market societies, which do not. *In a market society, the economic problem itself—both production and distribution—is solved by means of a vast exchange between buyers and sellers.* Many ancient societies had markets, but these markets did not organize the fundamental activities of those societies.

2. The economic societies of antiquity had several features in common, many of which contrast sharply with those of modern market economies:

Peasant farming
   - They rested on an agricultural base of *peasant farming*.
   - Their cities were—from an economic point of view—parasitic *centers of consumption, not active centers of production*.

Slavery
   - *Slavery* was a common and very important form of labor.

Surplus
   - In addition they produced very considerable *surpluses*, as do modern economic systems.

Wealth and power

3. As a result, in the economic societies of antiquity, we find the economic side of life subservient to the political side. Priest, warrior, and statesman were superior to merchant or trader; *wealth followed power*, not—as in the market societies to come—the other way around.

Feudalism

4. Medieval economic life emerged from the catastrophic disorganization that followed the decline of Roman law and order. It was characterized by a unique form of organization called the *manorial system* in which:

Lords
   - *Local lords were the centers of political, military, economic, and social power.*

Serfs
- *Most peasants were bound as serfs* to a particular lord, for whom they were required to work and to whom they owed both labor and taxes or dues.
- *Physical security* against brigands or other lords was provided by the lord, who also gave some economic security in times of distress.

Manorial system

5. *The manorial system*, particularly in its earlier days (sixth to tenth centuries), *was a static economic system*, in which monetary payments played only a minor role. Self-sufficiency was the main purpose and the most outstanding characteristic of the manor.

Fairs

6. Side by side with the manor existed the economic life of the *towns*. Here monetary exchange always played a more important role, as did the organization of a more active economic life in the institution of *fairs*.

Guilds

7. The *guild* was the main form of organizing production in the towns and cities. *Guilds were very different from modern-day businesses*, insofar as they discouraged competition or profit seeking and sought to impose general rules on the methods of production, rates of pay, practices of marketing, and so on.

Usury

8. All through medieval times, the Church—the main social organization of the age—was suspicious of buying and selling activity. In part, this reflected a dislike of the exploitative practices of the times; in part, it was a consequence of an ancient contempt for moneymaking (remember Aristotle's dislike of *chrematistiké*) and especially for moneylending (usury). The religious leaders of the day worried about "just prices," and did not admit that unregulated buying and selling could give rise to just prices.

Market society

9. Three profound and pervasive changes would be needed to convert medieval society into a market society:
- *A new attitude toward moneymaking* as a legitimate activity would have to replace the medieval suspicion of profit seeking.

Monetization

- *The web of monetization would have to expand* beyond its narrow confines—that is, buying and selling would have to control the output of all products and the performance of nearly all tasks.
- The flux of *"demand" and "supply" would have to be allowed to take over the direction of economic activity* from the dictates of lords and the usages of custom.

QUESTIONS

1. What differences, if any, characterize the economic attitudes and behavior of the American farmer and the American businessman? Can this comparison also describe the behavior and attitude of the Egyptian peasant and the Egyptian merchant? What accounts for the difference between the two societies?

2. Julius Caesar and J. P. Morgan were both wealthy and powerful men. What

is the difference in the origins of their wealth and their power? Does power still follow wealth in modern economic societies? Does wealth still follow power in nonmarket societies?

3. To what uses was the surplus of society put in ancient Rome? in feudal society? in modern America? in the USSR? What significance attaches to these different uses? What do they tell us about the structure of these societies?

4. What do you think of the validity of Aristotle's distinction between economic activity for *use* and for *gain*?

5. In what ways is a serf a different *economic* creature from a modern farm worker? How is a slave different from an industrial worker?

6. What changes would have to take place within a guild before it resembled a modern business?

7. The Bible has numerous hostile references to moneymaking—"It is easier for a camel to go through the eye of a needle than for a rich man to enter into the kingdom of God." How do you account for this ancient churchly antipathy toward wealth? Is religion today still suspicious of moneymaking? Why?

8. Is the idea of a "just" price (or a "just" wage) still encountered in our own society? What is usually meant by these terms? Do you think these ideas are compatible with a market system? *monopoly?*

9. The manorial system persisted for nearly 1,000 years. Why do you think change was so slow in coming?

10. Ancient Greece and Rome were a great deal more "modern" in their temper than feudal Europe. Yet neither was remotely a modern economic system. Why not?

3 THE EMERGENCE OF MARKET SOCIETY

Tradition, changelessness, order—these were the key concepts of economic society in the Middle Ages, and our preceding chapter introduced us to this unfamiliar and static way of economic life. But our purpose in this chapter is different. It is no longer to describe the factors that preserved the economic stability of medieval society, but to identify those forces that eventually burst it asunder.

Once again, we need to begin with a word of caution. Our chapter spans an immense variety of historical experience. We must beware of thinking that the forces of change that dominate this chapter were identical from region to region or from century to century, or that the transition they effected was uniform throughout the broad expanse of Europe. On the contrary, the great evolution that we will witness in these pages was not sharp and clear, but muddy and irregular. At the same time that the first evidences of a truly modern market society were beginning to manifest themselves in the medieval cities of Italy and Holland, archaic forms of feudal relationship still persisted in the agricultural sectors of these nations, and indeed in the city life of other nations. We must bear in mind that the historic processes of this chapter extended from the tenth to the seventeenth centuries (and even to the eighteenth and nineteenth centuries in some places), and manifested themselves in no two countries in precisely the same way.

With these cautions in mind, now let us turn to the great evolution itself. What agents were powerful enough to effect the major historic changes needed to bring about a market society?

FORCES OF CHANGE

the itinerant merchant

We meet the first of these forces of change in an unexpected guise. It is a small irregular procession of armed men, jogging along one of the rudimentary roads of medieval Europe: standard-bearer with colors in the lead, then a military chief, then a group of riders carrying bows and

42

swords, and finally a caravan of horses and mules laden with casks and bales, bags and packs.

Someone unacquainted with medieval life might easily take such a troop for part of the baggage train of a small army. But he would be mistaken. These were not soldiers but merchants, the traveling merchants whom the English of the twelfth century called "pie-powders," from *pieds poudreux*, dusty feet. No wonder they were dusty; many of them came immense distances along routes so bad that we know of one instance where only the intervention of a local ecclesiastical lord prevented the "road" from being ploughed up as arable land. In their bags and packs were goods that had somehow made a perilous journey across Europe, or even all the way from Arabia or India, to be sold from town to town, or from halt to halt, as these merchant adventurers wound their way across the medieval countryside.

And adventurers they were. For in the fixed hierarchies of the great manorial estates of Europe, there was no natural place for these unlanded peddlers of goods, with their unfeudal attributes of calculation and (often very crude) bookkeeping and their natural insistence on trade in money. The traveling merchants ranked very low in society. Some of them, without doubt, were the sons of serfs, or even runaway serfs themselves. Yet since no one could prove their bondage, they had, if only by default, the gift of "freedom." It is no wonder that in the eyes of the nobility, the merchants were upstarts and a disturbing element in the normal pattern of things.

Yet no one would have dispensed with their services. To their brightly canopied stalls at the fairs flocked the lords and ladies of the manors as well as the Bodos and Ermentrudes of the fields. After all, where else could one buy pepper or purple dye, or acquire a guaranteed splinter from the Cross? Where else could one buy the marvelous cloths woven in Tuscany or hear such esoteric words, derived from the Arabic, as "jar" or "syrup"? If the merchant was a disturbing leaven in the mix of medieval life, he was also a pinch of active ingredient without which the mixture would have been very dull indeed.

We first note the traveling merchant in Europe in the eighth and ninth centuries, and we can follow his progress until the fourteenth and fifteenth centuries. By this time, largely through the merchants' own efforts, commerce was sufficiently organized so that it no longer required these itinerant journeyers.* For what these travelers brought, together

---

* Records of an order for goods placed on the occasion of a funeral of a Swedish nobleman in 1328 include saffron from Spain or Italy, caraway seed from the Mediterranean, ginger from India, cinnamon from Ceylon, pepper from Malabar, anise from southern Europe, and Rhine and Bordeaux wines. The order was placed for immediate delivery from one local merchant, despite the fact that Sweden was then a laggard and even primitive land. Cf. Fritz Rorig, *Mittelaterliche Weltwirtschaft* (Jena: 1933), p. 17. (I am indebted to Goran Ohlin for this reference.)

with their wares, was the first breath of commerce and commercial intercourse to a Europe that had sunk to an almost tradeless and self-sufficient manorial stagnation. Even to towns as minuscule and isolated as Forcalquier in France—a dot on the map without so much as a road to connect its few hundred souls to the outer world—these hardy traders beat their path: We know from a primitive book of accounts that in May 1331 thirty-six itinerant merchants visited Forcalquier to transact business at the home and "shop" of one Ugo Teralh, a notary.[1] And so, in a thousand isolated communities, did they slowly weave a web of economic interdependence.

urbanization   An important byproduct of the rise of the itinerant merchant was the slow urbanization of medieval life, the creation of new towns and villages. When the traveling merchants stopped, they naturally chose the protected site of a local castle or burg, or of a church. And so we find growing up around the walls of advantageously situated castles—in the *foris burgis*, whence *faubourg*, the French word for "suburb"—more or less permanent trading places, which in turn became the inner core of small towns. Nestled close to the castle or cathedral wall for protection, the new burgs were still not "of" the manor. The inhabitants of the burg—the burgesses, burghers, bourgeois—had at best an anomalous and insecure relation to the manorial world within. As we have seen, there was no way of applying the time-hallowed rule of "ancient customs" in adjudicating their disputes, since there *were* no ancient customs in the commercial quarters. Neither were there clear-cut rules for their taxation or for the particular degrees of fealty they owed their local masters. Worse yet, some of the growing towns began to surround themselves with walls. By the twelfth century, the commercial burg of Bruges, for example, had already swallowed up the old fortress like a pearl around a grain of sand.

Curiously, it was this very struggle for existence in the interstices of feudal society that provided much of the impetus for the development of a new social and economic order within the city. In all previous civilizations, cities had been the outposts of central government. Now for the first time, they existed as independent entities outside the main framework of social power. As a result, they were able to define for themselves—they *had* to define for themselves—a code of law and social behavior and a set of governing institutions that were eventually to displace those of the feudal countryside.

The process was long drawn out, for the rate of growth of towns was often very slow. In the nearly two centuries between 1086 and 1279,

---

[1] *Cambridge Economic History of Europe* (Cambridge, England: Cambridge University Press, 1952), II, 325–26.

for example, the town of Cambridge, England, added an average of but one house *per year*.[2] One important reason for this almost imperceptible rate of expansion was the difficulty of moving men or materials over the terrible roads. Not the least consequence of the decline of Roman power had been the decay of its once magnificent system of highways, the very stones of which were pilfered for building materials during the years of worst social disorganization. Until the roads recovered, economic movement was perforce limited and limping. And it is worth remarking that in many ports of Europe a system of transportation as efficient as that of ancient Rome was not enjoyed until the eighteenth or even nineteenth century. It took Napoleon almost as long to invade Italy from France as it had taken Caesar to go the other way.

Yet if growth was slow, it was steady; and in some locales it was much faster than in Cambridge. During the 1,000 years of the Middle Ages, nearly 1,000 towns were fathered in Europe, a tremendous stimulus to the commercialization and monetization of life, for each town had its local marts, its local toll gates, often its local mint, its granaries and shops, its drinking places and inns, its air of "city life," which contrasted so sharply with that of the country. The slow, spontaneous growth of urban ways was a major factor in introducing a marketing flavor to European economic life.

the Crusades   The rise of the itinerant merchant and the town were two great factors in the slow evolution of a market society out of medieval economic life; a third factor was the Crusades.

It is an ironic turn to history that the Crusades, the supreme religious adventure of the Middle Ages, should have contributed so much toward the establishment of a society to which the Church was vigorously opposed. If we consider the Crusades, however, not from the point of view of their religious impulse, but simply as great expeditions of exploration and colonization, their economic impact becomes much more understandable.*

The Crusades served to bring into sudden and startling contact two very different worlds. One was the still slumbering society of European feudalism with all its rural inertia, its aversion to trade, and its naïve conceptions of business; the other was the brilliant society of Byzantium and Venice, with its urban vitality, its unabashed enjoyment of money-making, and its sophisticated business ways. The crusaders, coming from

[2] George Gordon Coulton, *Medieval Panorama* (New York: World Publishing, Medidian Books, 1955), p. 285.

* We might note here some of the complex interaction of the process we are watching. For the Crusades were not only a cause of European economic development, but also a *symptom* of the development that had previously taken place.

their draughty castles and boring manorial routines, thought they would find in the East only untutored heathen savages. They were astonished to be met by a people far more civilized, infinitely more luxurious, and much more money-oriented than they.

One result was that the simple-minded crusaders found themselves the pawns of commercial interests that they little understood. During the first three Crusades, the Venetians, who provided ships, gulled them as shamelessly as country bumpkins at a fair. The fact that they were fleeced, however, did not prevent the crusaders from reaching the Holy Land, albeit with inconclusive results. But in the notorious Fourth Crusade (1202–1204), Dandolo, the wiley ninety-four-year-old doge of Venice, managed to subvert the entire religious expedition into a gigantic plundering operation for Venetian profit.

First Dandolo held up the voyagers for an initial transportation price of 85,000 silver marks, an enormous sum for the unmoneyed nobility to scrape up. Then, when the funds had been found, he refused to carry out his bargain until the crusaders agreed first to attack the town of Zara, a rich commerical rival of Venice. Since Zara was a *Christian*, not an "infidel" community, Pope Innocent III was horrified and suggested that the attack be directed instead against heathen Egypt. But Egypt was one of Venice's best customers, and this horrified Dandolo even more. The crusaders, stranded and trapped, had no choice: Zara soon fell—after which, at Dandolo's urging, Christian Constantinople was also sacked. The "heathen" Orient was never reached at all, but Venice profited marvelously.

It was not only Venice that gained, however. The economic impact on the crusaders themselves was much more formidable than the religious. On many this impact was disastrous, as knights who had melted down their silver plate to join the Crusades came back penniless to their ruined manor houses. To others, however, the Crusades brought a new economic impetus. When in 1101, for example, the Genoese raided Caesarea, a Palestinian seaport, 8,000 soldiers and sailors reaped a reward of some 48 *solidi* each, plus 2 pounds of pepper—and thus were 8,000 petty capitalists born.[3] And in 1204 when Constantinople fell, not only did each knight receive 20 marks in silver as his share of the booty, but even the squires and archers were rewarded with a few marks each.

Thus, the Crusades provided an immense fertilizing experience for Europe. The old, landed basis of wealth came into contact with a new moneyed basis that proved much more powerful. Indeed, the old conception of life itself was forcibly revised before a glimpse of an existence not only wealthier, but gayer and more vital. As a means of shaking a

---

[3] *Cambridge Economic History of Europe*, II, 306.

sluggish society out of its rut, the Crusades played an immense role in speeding along the economic transformation of Europe.

growth of national power

Yet another factor in the slow commercialization of economic life was the gradual amalgamation of Europe's fragmented economic and political entities into larger wholes. As the disintegration of economic life following the breakup of the old Roman Empire had shown, a strong economic society requires a strong and broad political base. Hence, as political Europe began its slow process of reknitting, once again its economic tempo began to rise.

One of the most striking characteristics of the Middle Ages, and one of its most crippling obstacles to economic development, was the medieval crazy quilt of compartmented, isolated areas of government. Over a journey of 100 miles, a traveling merchant might fall under a dozen different sovereignties, each with different rules, regulations, laws, weights, measures, money. Worse yet, at each border there was apt to be a toll station. At the turn of the thirteenth and fourteenth centuries, there were said to be more than thirty toll stations along the Weser River and at least thirty-five along the Elbe; along the Rhine, a century later, there were more than sixty such toll stations, mostly belonging to local ecclesiastical princes. Thomas Wykes, an English chronicler, described the system as "the raving madness of the Teutons." But it was not only a German disease. There were so many toll stations along the Seine in France in the late fifteenth century that it cost half its final selling price to ship grain 200 miles down the river.[4] Indeed, among the European nations, England alone enjoyed an internally unified market during the middle and late Middle Ages. This was one powerful contributory factor to England's emergence as the first great European economic power.

[margin annotation: no consistency]

The amalgamation of Europe's fragmented markets was essentially a political as well as an economic process; it followed the gradual centralization of power that changed the map of Europe from the infinite complexity of the tenth century to the more or less "modern" map of the sixteenth. Here, once again, the burgeoning towns played a central and crucial role. It was the city burghers who became the allies of the nascent monarchies, thereby disassociating themselves still further from their local feudal lords while, in turn, supplying the shaky monarchs with an absolutely essential prerequisite for kingship: cash.

Thus, monarch and bourgeois combined to bring about the slow growth of centralized governments, and from centralized government, in turn, came not alone a unification of law and money but a direct

[4] *Cambridge Economic History of Europe*, II, pp. 134–35.

stimulus to the development of commerce and industry as well. In France, for example, manufacturing was promoted by royal patronage of the famous Gobelin tapestry and Sèvres porcelain works, and business was created for innumerable craftsmen and artisans by the demands of the royal palaces and banquet halls. In other fields, growing national power also imparted a new encouragement: Navies had to be built, armies had to be equipped, and these new "national" armed forces, many of whom were mercenaries, had to be paid. All this set into faster motion the pumps of monetary circulation.

exploration   Another economic impetus given by the gradual consolidation of political power was the official encouragement of exploration. All through the long years of the Middle Ages, a few intrepid adventurers, like Marco Polo, had beat their way to remote regions in search of a short route to the fabled riches of India; and as a matter of fact, by the early fourteenth century, the route to the Far East was well enough known so that silk from China cost but half the price of that from the Caspian area, only half the distance away.

Yet the network of all these hazardous and brave penetrations beyond Europe formed only the thinnest of spider webs. There still remained the systematic exploration of the unknown, and this awaited the kingly support of state adventurers. Columbus and Vasco da Gama, Cabral and Magellan did not venture on their epoch-making journeys as individual merchants (although they all hoped to make their fortunes thereby) but as adventurers in fleets bought with, and equipped by, royal money, bearing the royal mark of approval, and sent forth in hope of additions to the royal till.

The economic consequences of those amazing adventures were incalculably great. For one thing, they opened up an invigorating flow of precious metals into Europe. Gold and silver, coming from the great Spanish mines in Mexico and Peru, were slowly redistributed to other nations as Spain paid in gold specie for goods it bought abroad. As a result, prices rose throughout Europe—between 1520 and 1650 alone, it is estimated that they increased 200 to 400 percent, bringing about both stimulus and stress to industry, but setting in motion a great wave of speculation and commerce.

In addition, of course, the longer-run results of exploration brought an economic stimulus of still greater importance. The establishment of colonies in the sixteenth and seventeenth centuries and the subsequent enjoyment of trade with the New World provided a tremendous boost in propelling Europe into a bustling commercial society. The discovery of the New World was, from the beginning, a catalytic and revolutionizing influence on the Old.

change in
religious
climate

The forces of change that we have thus far summarized were actually visible. At any time during the long transition from a nonmarket into a market society, we could have witnessed with our own eyes the traveling merchants, the expanding towns, the Crusades, the evidences of a growing national power, the far-flung explorations. Yet these were not the only forces that undermined the feudal system and brought into being its commercial successor. There were, as well, powerful but invisible currents of change, currents that affected the intellectual atmosphere, the beliefs, and the attitudes of Europe. One of these, of special importance, was a change in the religious climate of the times.

In our last chapter, we saw how deeply the Catholic Church was imbued with theological aversions to the principle of gain—and especially to interest taking or usury. An amusing story of the times sums up the position of the Church very well. Humbertus de Romanis, a monk, tells of someone who found a devil in every nook and cranny of a Florentine cloister, although in the marketplace he found but one. The reason, Humbertus explains, was that it took only one to corrupt a marketplace, where every man harbored a devil in his own heart.[5] In such a disapproving climate, it was hard for the commercial side of life to thrive.

To be sure, for all its fulminations against gain and usury, the Church itself grew in time to a position of commanding economic importance. Through its tithes and benefices, it was the largest collector and distributor of money in all of Europe; and in an age in which banks and safe deposit boxes did not exist, it was the repository of much feudal wealth. Some of its suborders, such as the Knights Templar, became immensely wealthy and served as banking institutions, lending to needy monarchs on stiff terms. Nonetheless, all this faintly disreputable activity was undertaken despite, and not because of, the Church's deepest convictions. For behind the ecclesiastical disapproval of wealth seeking was a deep-seated theological conviction, a firm belief in the transient nature of this life on earth and the importance of preparing for the Eternal Morrow. The Church lifted its eyes, and sought to lift the eyes of others, above the daily struggle for existence. It strove to minimize the importance of life on earth and to denigrate the earthly activities to which an all-too-weak flesh succumbed.

Calvinism

What changed this dampening influence on the zest of wealth making? According to the theories of the German sociologist Max Weber and the English economic historian R. H. Tawney, the underlying cause lay in the rise of a new theological point of view contained in the teachings of the Protestant reformer John Calvin (1509–1564).

Calvinism was a harsh religious philosophy. Its core was a belief

[5] Miriam Beard, *A History of the Business Man* (New York: Macmillan, 1938), p. 160.

in *predestination*—the idea that from the beginning God had chosen the saved and the damned, and that nothing man could do on earth could alter that inviolable writ. Furthermore, according to Calvin, the number of the damned exceeded by a vast amount the number of the saved, so that for the average person the chances were great that this earthly prelude was but the momentary grace given before eternal Hell and Damnation commenced.

Perhaps only a man of Calvin's iron will could have borne life under such a sentence. For we soon find that in the hands of his followers in the Lowlands and England the inexorable and inscrutable quality of the original doctrine began to be softened. Although the idea of predestination was still preached, it was now allowed that in the tenor of one's worldly life there was a *hint* of what was to follow. Thus, the English and Dutch divines taught that whereas even the saintliest-seeming man might end in Hell, the frivolous or wanton one was certainly headed there. Only in a blameless life lay the slightest chance of demonstrating that Salvation was still a possibility.

And so the Calvinists urged a life of rectitude, severity, and, most important of all, diligence. In contrast to the Catholic theologians, who tended to look upon worldly activity as vanity, the Calvinists sanctified and approved of endeavor as a kind of index of spiritual worth. Indeed in Calvinist hands there grew up the idea of a man *dedicated* to his work: "called" to it, as it were. Hence the fervid pursuit of one's calling, far from evidencing a distraction from religious ends, came to be taken as evidence of a dedication to a religious life. The energetic merchant was, in Calvinist eyes, a *godly* man, not an ungodly one; and from this identification of work and worth, it was not long before the notion grew up that the more successful a man was, the more worthy he was. Calvinism thus provided a religious atmosphere that, in contrast to Catholicism, encouraged wealth seeking and the temper of a businesslike world.

Perhaps even more important than its encouragement of seeking wealth was the influence of Calvinism on the *use* of wealth. By and large, the prevailing attitude of the prosperous Catholic merchants had been that the aim of worldly success was the enjoyment of a life of ease and luxury, while Catholic nobility displayed on occasion a positively grotesque disdain for wealth. In an orgy of gambling that gripped Paris at the end of the seventeenth century, a prince who sent his mistress a diamond worth 5,000 *livres* had it pulverized and strewn over her reply when she rejected it as being too small. The same prince eventually gambled away an income of 600,000 *livres* a year. A *maréchal* whose grandson turned up his nose at a gift of a purse of gold threw it into the street: "Let the street cleaner have it then."[6]

---

[6] Werner Sombart, *Luxury and Capitalism* (New York: Columbia University Press, 1938), pp. 120ff. Also Thirion, *La Vie Privée des Financiers au XVIIIe Siècle* (Paris: 1895), p. 292.

The Calvinist manufacturer or trader had a very different attitude toward wealth. If his religion approved of diligence, it most emphatically did not approve of indulgence. Wealth was to be accumulated and put to good use, not frittered away.

the Protestant ethic

Calvinism promoted an aspect of economic life of which we have hitherto heard very little: *thrift.* It made saving, the conscious abstinence from the enjoyment of income, a virtue. It made investment, the use of saving for productive purposes, an instrument of piety as well as profit. It even condoned, with various *quids* and *quos*, the payment of interest. In fact, Calvinism fostered a new conception of economic life. In place of the old ideal of social and economic stability, of knowing and keeping one's "place," it brought respectability to an ideal of struggle, of material improvement, of economic growth.

Economic historians still debate the precise degree of influence that may properly be attributed to "the Protestant Ethic" in bringing about the rise of a new gain-centered worldly philosophy. After all, there was nothing much that a Dutch Calvinist would have been able to teach an Italian Catholic banker about the virtues of a businesslike approach to life. Yet, looking back on the subsequent course of economic progress, it is striking that without exception it was the Protestant countries with their "Puritan streak" of work and thrift that forged ahead in the economic race. As one of the powerful winds of change of the sixteenth and seventeenth centuries, the new religious outlook must be counted as a highly favorable stimulus for the evolution of the market society.

breakdown of the manorial system

The enumeration of all these currents does not exhaust the catalog of forces bearing against the old fixed economic order in Europe. The list could be expanded and greatly refined.* Yet, with all due caution, we can now begin to comprehend the immense coalition of events—some as specific as the Crusades, some as diffuse as a change in religious ideals—that jointly cooperated to destroy the medieval framework of economic life and to prepare the way for a new dynamic framework of market transactions.

One important aspect of this profound alteration was the gradual *monetization of feudal obligations.* In locality after locality, we can trace

---

* An extremely important influence (to which we will specifically turn in our next chapter was the rise of a new interest in technology, founded on scientific inquiry into natural events. Another important causative factor was the development of modern business concepts and techniques. The German economic historian Werner Sombart has even said that if he were forced to give a single date for the "beginning" of modern capitalism he would choose 1202, the year in which appeared the *Liber Abaci,* a primer of commercial arithmetic. Similarly, the historian Oswald Spengler has called the invention of double-entry book-keeping in 1494 an achievement worthy of being ranked with that of Columbus or Copernicus.

the conversation of the old feudal payments in *kind*—the days of labor or chickens or eggs a lord received from his tenants—into payments of *money* dues and money rents with which they now discharged their obligations to him.

A number of causes lay behind this commutation of feudal payments. One was the growing urban demand for food, as town and city populations began to swell. In concentric circles around the town, money filtered out into the countryside, simultaneously raising the capacity of the rural sector to buy urban goods and whetting its desire to do so. At the same time, in a search for larger cash incomes to buy a widening variety of goods, the nobility looked with increasing favor on receiving its rents and dues in money rather than in kind. In so doing, however, it unwittingly set into motion a cause for the further serious deterioration of the manorial system. Usually, the old feudal services were converted into *fixed* sums of money payments. This temporarily eased the cash position of the lord, but soon placed him in the squeeze that always hurts the creditor in times of inflation. And even when dues were not fixed, rents and money dues lagged sufficiently behind the growing monetary needs of the nobility so that still further feudal obligations were monetized to keep the lord in cash. But as prices rose and the monetized life-style expanded still further, these too failed to keep him solvent.

The result was that the rural nobility, which now depended increasingly on rents and dues for its income, steadily lost its economic power.* Indeed, beginning in the sixteenth century, we find a new class coming into being—the *impoverished* nobility. In the year 1530 in the Gevaudan district of France, we find that 121 lords had an aggregate income of 21,400 *livres*, but one of these seigneurs accounted for 5,000 *livres* of the sum, another for 2,000—and the rest averaged but a mean 121 *livres* apiece.[7] In fact, the shortage of cash afflicted not only the lesser nobility but even the monarchy itself. Maximilian I, Emperor of the Holy Roman Empire, on occasion lacked the cash to pay for even the overnight lodgings of his entourage on tour; and when two of his grandchildren married children of the King of Hungary, all the trappings of the weddings—2,000 caparisoned horses, jewels, and gold and silver plate—were borrowed from merchant bankers to whom Maximilian had written wheedling letters begging them not to forsake him in his moment of need.

rise of the cash economy   Clearly, the manorial system was incompatible with a cash economy; for while the nobility was pinched between rising prices and costs and static incomes, the merchant classes, to whom cash naturally gravitated, stead-

---

* This process of economic decline was considerably hastened by the ineptitude of the nobility as managers of their estates. The descendants of the crusaders were not much more businesslike than their ancestors.

[7] *Cambridge Economic History of Europe*, I, 557–58.

ily increased their power. In the Gevaudan district, for example, where the richest lord had his income of 5,000 *livres*, the richest town merchants had incomes up to 65,000 *livres*. In Germany, while Maximilian scratched for cash, the great banking families of Augsburg commanded incomes far larger than Maximilian's entire kingly revenue. In Italy, the Gianfigliazzi of Florence, who began as "nobodies" lending money to the Bishop of Fiesole, ended up stripping him of his possessions and leaving him a pauper; while in Tuscany, the descendants of lords who looked down their noses at usurers in the tenth century lost their estates to them in the twelfth and thirteenth. All over Europe men of mean social standing turned the monetary economy to good account. One Jean Amici of Toulouse made a fortune in English booty during the Hundred Years War; Guillaume de St.-Yon grew rich by selling meat at rapacious prices to Paris; and Jacques Coeur, the most extraordinary figure of all, rose from merchant to King's coiner, then to King's purchasing agent, then to financier not for, but *of*, the King, during the course of which he accumulated a huge fortune, estimated at 27 million *écus*.*

APPEARANCE OF THE ECONOMIC ASPECT OF LIFE

Behind all these profoundly disturbing events, we can discern an immense process of change that literally revolutionized the economic organization of Europe. Whereas in the tenth century, cash and money transactions were only peripheral to the solution of the economic problem, by the sixteenth and seventeenth centuries, cash and money transactions were already beginning to provide the very molecular force of economic cohesion.

But over and above this general monetization of life, another and perhaps even more profound change was taking place. This was the emergence of a separate *economic* sphere of activity visible within, and separable from, the surrounding matrix of social life. It was the creation of a whole aspect of society that had never previously existed, but was thenceforth to constitute a commanding facet of human existence.[8]

In antiquity and feudal times, as we have seen, one could not easily separate the economic motivations or even the economic actions of the great mass of men from the normal round of existence itself. The peasant following his immemorial ways was hardly conscious of acting according to "economic" motives; indeed, he did not—he heeded the orders of his lord or the dictates of custom. Nor was the lord himself economically

---

* Note, however, that Coeur eventually fell from power, was imprisoned, and died in exile. The countinghouse was not yet fully master of the castle.

[8] The following section owes much to the insights of Karl Polanyi's famous *The Great Transformation* (Boston: Beacon Press, 1957, paperback ed.), Part II.

oriented. His interests were military or political or religious, and not basically oriented toward the idea of gain or increase. Even in the towns, as we have seen, the conduct of ordinary business was inextricably mixed with noneconomic concerns. The undeniable fact that men were acquisitive, not to say avaricious, did not yet impart its flavor to life in general; the making of money, as we have been at some pains to indicate, was a tangential rather than a central concern of ancient or medieval existence.

labor, land, and capital come into being

With the ever-widening scope of monetization, however, a genuinely new element of life came slowly to the fore. Labor, for example, emerged as an activity quite different from what it was in the past. No longer was "labor" part of an explicit social relationship in which one man (serf or apprentice) worked for another (lord or guildmaster) in return for at least an assurance of subsistence. Labor was now a mere quantum of effort, a "commodity" to be disposed of in the marketplace for the best price it could bring, quite devoid of any reciprocal responsibilities on the part of the buyer, beyond the payment of wages. If those wages were not enough to provide subsistence—well, that was not the buyer's responsibility. He had bought his "labor," and that was that.

no relation

This emergence of "abstract" labor—labor as a quantity of effort detached from a man's life and bought on the market in fixed amounts—had a parallel in two other main elements of economic life. One of these was land. Formerly conceived of as the territory of a great lord, as inviolable as the territory of a modern nation-state, land was now also seen in its economic aspect as something to be bought or leased for the economic return it yielded. An estate that was once the core of political and administrative power became a "property" with a market price, available for any number of uses, even as a site for a factory. The dues, the payments in kind, the intangibles of prestige and power that once had flowed from the ownership of land gave way to the single return of *rent*; that is, to a money return derived from putting land to *profitable* use.

The same transformation became true of property. As it was conceived in antiquity and throughout most of the Middle Ages, property was a sum of tangible wealth, a hoard, a treasury of plate, bullion, or jewels. Very logically, it was realized in the form of luxurious homes, in castles and armaments, in costly robes and trappings. But with the monetization and commercialization of society, property, too, became expressible in a monetary equivalent: a man was now "worth" so many *livres*, or *écus*, or pounds, or whatever. Property became *capital*, manifesting itself no longer in specific goods, but as an abstract sum of infinitely flexible use whose "value" was its capacity to earn *interest* or *profits*.

None of these changes, it should be emphasized, was planned, clearly foreseen, or for that matter, welcomed. It was not with equanimity that the feudal hierarchies saw their prerogatives nibbled away by the mercantile classes. Neither did the tradition-preserving guildmaster desire his own enforced metamorphosis into a "capitalist," a man of affairs guided by market signals and beset by competition. But perhaps for no social class was the transition more painful than for the peasant, caught up in a process of history that dispossessed him from his livelihood and made him a landless laborer.

enclosures   This process, which was particularly important in England, was the *enclosure movement*, a byproduct of the monetization of feudal life. Starting as early as the thirteenth century, the landed aristocracy, increasingly squeezed for cash, began to view its estates not merely as ancestral fiefs but as potential sources of cash revenue. In order to raise larger cash crops, lords therefore began to "enclose" the pasture that had previously been deemed "common land." Communal grazing fields, which had in fact always belonged to the lord despite their communal use, were now claimed for the exclusive benefit of the lord and turned into sheepwalks. Why sheepwalks? Because a rising demand for woolen cloth was making sheep raising a highly profitable occupation. The medieval historian Eileen Power writes:

> The visitor to the House of Lords, looking respectfully upon that august assembly, cannot fail to be struck by a stout and ungainly object facing the throne—an ungainly object upon which in full session of Parliament, he will observe seated the Lord Chancellor of England. The object is a woolsack, and it is stuffed as full of pure history as the office of the Lord Chancellor itself. . . . The Lord Chancellor of England is seated upon a woolsack because it was upon a woolsack that this fair land rose to prosperity.[9]

The enclosure process in England proceeded at an irregular pace over the long centuries; not until the late eighteenth and early nineteenth centuries did it reach its engulfing climax.* By its end, some 10 million acres, nearly *half* the arable land of England, had been "enclosed"—in its early Tudor days by the more or less high-handed conversion of the "commons" to sheep raising; in the final period, by the forcible consolidation of strips and plots into tracts suitable for commercial farming, for which tenants presumably received "fair compensation."

---

[9] *Medieval People* (Garden City, N.Y.: Doubleday, Anchor Books, 1954), p. 125.

* In other European nations, an enclosure process also took place, but at a much slower pace. In France, Italy, and southern Germany, the small-holder peasant persisted long after he had virtually ceased to exist in England; in northeastern Germany, on the other hand, the small peasant was deprived of his holdings and turned into a landless proletarian.

From a strictly economic point of view, the enclosure movement was unquestionably salutary in that it brought into productive employment land that had hitherto yielded only a pittance. Indeed, particularly in the eighteenth and nineteenth centuries, enclosure was the means by which England "rationalized" its agriculture and finally escaped from the inefficiency of the traditional manorial strip system. But there was another, crueler side to enclosure. As the common fields were enclosed, it became ever more difficult for the tenant to support himself. In the fifteenth and sixteenth centuries, when the initial enclosure of the commons reached its peak, as many as three-fourths to nine-tenths of the tenants of some estates were simply turned off the farm. Whole hamlets were thus wiped out. Sir Thomas More described it savagely in Book I of his *Utopia*:

prole

> Your sheep that were wont to be so meek and tame, and so small eaters, now, as I hear say, be become so great devourers and so wild, that they eat up and swallow down the very men themselves. They consume, destroy and devour whole fields, houses and cities. For look in what parts of the realm doth grow the finest, and therefore dearest wool, there noblemen and gentlemen, yea and certain abbots, holy men God wot, not contenting themselves with the yearly revenues and profits that were wont to grow to their forefathers and predecessors of their land . . . leave no ground for tillage, they enclose all into pastures, they throw down houses, they pluck down towns and leave nothing standing, but only the church to make of it a sheep house. . . .

The enclosure process provided a powerful force for the dissolution of feudal ties and the formation of the new relationships of a market society. By dispossessing the peasant, it created a new kind of labor force—landless, without traditional sources of income, however meager, impelled to find work for wages wherever it might be available.

emergence of the proletariat

Together with this agricultural proletariat, we begin to see the emergence of an urban proletariat, partly brought about by a gradual transformation of guilds into more "businesslike" firms, partly by the immigration into the cities of some of the new landless peasantry. And then to exacerbate the whole situation, from the middle of the eighteenth century, a rising population (itself traceable in large measure to the increase in food output resulting from the enclosures) began to pour growing numbers into the labor market. As a result of this complicated interplay of causes and effects, we find England plagued with the problem of the "wandering poor." One not untypical proposal of the eighteenth century was that they be confined in what a reformer candidly termed "Houses of Terror."

Thus did the emergence of a market-oriented system grind into being a "labor force," and though the process of adjustment for other classes of society was not so brutal, it, too, exacted its social price. Tenaciously the guildmasters fought against the invasion of their protected trades by manufacturers who trespassed on traditional preserves or who upset established modes of production with new machinery. Doggedly, the landed nobility sought to protect its ancient privileges against the encroachment of the moneyed *nouveaux riches*.

Yet the process of economic enlargement, breaking down the established routines of the past, rearranging the power and prestige of all social classes, could not be stopped. Ruthlessly it pursued its historic course and impartially it distributed its historic rewards and sacrifices. Although stretched out over a long period, it was not an evolution but a slow revolution that overtook European economic society. Only when that society had run its long gauntlet, suffering one of the most wrenching dislocations of history, would the world of transactions appear "natural" and "normal" and the categories of "land," "labor," and "capital" become so matter-of-fact that it would be difficult to believe they had not always existed.

factors of production   Yet, as we have seen, it was not at all "natural" and "normal" to have free, wage-earning, contractual labor or rentable, profit-producing land or fluid, investment-seeking capital. They were *creations* of the great transformation of a premarket into a market society. Economics calls these creations the *factors of production*, and much of economics is concerned with analyzing the manner in which these three basic constituents of the productive process are combined in the market mechanism.

What we must realize at this stage of our inquiry, however, is that "land," "labor," and "capital" do not exist as eternal categories of *social* organization. Admittedly, they are categories of *nature*, but these eternal aspects of the productive process—the soil, human effort, and the artifacts that can be applied to production—do not take on, in every society, the specific separation that distinguishes them in a market society. In premarket economies, land, labor, and capital are inextricably mixed and mingled in the figure of slave and serf, lord and guildmaster—none of whom enters the production process as the incarnation of a specific economic function offered for a price. The slave is not a "worker," the guildmaster is not a "capitalist," nor is the lord a "landlord." *Only when a social system has evolved in which labor is sold, land is rented, and capital is freely invested do we find the categories of economics emerging from the flux of life.*

Nowhere do we see this astonishing social process more clearly illustrated than in the evolution of the concept of property in man himself. In ancient society, as we have seen, men owned men. That is, a slave was literally the chattel of his owner, to be used, abused, or even put to death under certain circumstances. In the Middle Ages, this idea of human property evolved into the conception of serfdom. A serf was also the property of his master and subject to the ties and bonds we have discussed, but the ownership was not so all-embracing and entailed reciprocal obligations on the part of the lord.

Finally, we reach modern commercial society, in which each person has property *in himself*. A worker who has become a "factor of production" owns his own labor, which he is free to sell as advantageously as possible, something that no slave or serf could do. At the same time, the free worker, who is no man's property, is also no man's obligation. The employer buys his employees' labor, not their lives. All responsibility for the laborer ends when he leaves his employer's office or factory, which is the owner's "property."

wage labor and capitalism   The employer also gains a unique economic advantage once labor becomes a commodity offered for sale. In exchange for buying labor power for a payment called a *wage*, the employer becomes entitled to all the output that "his" workers produce. To put it differently, men and women who enter into a waged relationship with their employers give up all claims to any output they will create while fulfilling their labor stint.

Waged (or salaried) labor is so normal a part of modern market society that it always comes as a surprise to reflect on the curious arrangement under which labor power is sold without any rights of ownership in its product. But consider for a moment who owns the cars coming off an assembly line. Is it the working force that has made them? The engineers who have designed them? The managers who have superintended the production process? The president of the company or its stockholders? The answer is that none of these individuals owns the cars. Even the president of General Motors, or the biggest stockholder in the company, cannot lay claim to a vehicle coming off the line, without paying for it.

Who, then, does own the cars? Any worker or manager can tell you: They are "company property." That means they are owned by the company, the fictive legal "person" who employs the president, the managers, and the engineers, as well as the workers. The stockholders in turn legally own and control the company, but it is the company itself that enters into the wage contract, and therefore it is the company that owns the cars. In a simpler establishment run by a single proprietor— say a bakery—we see the same thing when the boss takes home baked products without paying for them because—as he says, perfectly correctly—they *belong* to him.

Thus the wage contract becomes a critical landmark, identifying a new kind of economic society, organized along entirely different lines from the older lord-and-peasant or master-and-apprentice arrangements. In these older societies, surplus had taken the form of great monuments or edifices or luxuries that had gone directly into the hands of the ruling classes, where they remained, or were used, as objects of prestige. In the new capitalist form, the surplus generated by society—that is, all wealth over and above that needed to replenish the working force and the other factors of production—accrued to the employer-capitalist.

Two changes attended this shift in surplus allocation. First, the surplus now took the much humbler forms of commodities produced in workshops, farms, or nascent factories, rather than impressive monuments, courtly trappings, and the like. Second, the commodities, unlike those monuments and trappings, *had to be sold* before they counted as "wealth."

Thus the emergence of capitalism, with its central wage-labor relationship, signaled much more than a change in ruling classes, from aristocrats to capitalists. It signaled as well a new meaning for wealth: as commodities-for-sale, not as objects-for-display. Unlike the pyramids, cathedrals, and edifices of previous societies, the wealth of capitalism had no status until it was "realized" on the marketplace. This necessity for sale introduced a new note of urgency, a nervous intensity, into the economic life of capitalism. In a word, capitalism was more than just a change in social institutions. It was also a completely new *economic system.*

capitalism and the profit motive

Much of the rest of this book will be concerned with examining how this new system works—what problems inhere in its complicated process of commodity production and sale. This will take us to an examination of the changing institutional forms that capitalism has created, as well as into an inquiry into some of the economic mechanisms by which the system works.

But it is useful to focus immediately on one aspect of capitalism that would occupy a central and indispensable place in its scheme of things. This was a new form of behavior that capitalism generalized throughout society: a drive to *maximize income* (as the economists would describe it) by concluding the best possible bargain on the marketplace into which everyone ventured, either to sell his or her labor power or other resources, or to purchase goods. In the language of business, the same behavioral drive was described as the *profit motive.*

The market society had not, of course, invented this motive. Perhaps it did not even intensify it. But it did make it a *ubiquitous and necessitous* aspect of social behavior. Although men may have *felt* acquisitive during the Middle Ages or antiquity, they did not enter en masse into market transactions for the basic economic activities of their livelihoods. And even when, for instance, a peasant sold his few eggs at the town market, rarely was the transaction a matter of overriding importance for his continued existence. Market transactions in a fundamentally nonmarket society were thus a subsidiary activity, a means of supplementing a livelihood that, however sparse, was largely independent of buying or selling.

With the monetization of labor, land, and capital, however, transactions became *universal* and *critical* activities. Now everything was for sale, and terms of transactions were anything but subsidiary to existence itself. To a man who sold his labor on a market, in a society that assumed no responsibility for his upkeep, the price at which he concluded his bargain was all-important. So it was with the landlord and the budding capitalist. For each of these a good bargain could spell riches—and a bad one, ruin. Thus, the pattern of economic maximization was generalized throughout society and given an inherent urgency that made it a powerful force for shaping human behavior. In a word, the drive to maximize income became a new mode of *social coordination and control.*

THE INVENTION OF ECONOMICS

The new market society did more than merely bring about an environment in which men were not only free, but *forced*, to follow their self-interest. It also brought a puzzle of great importance and considerable difficulty. The puzzle was to understand the workings of a world in which profit-seeking individuals were no longer constrained to follow the ways of their forefathers or to shape their economic activities according to the dictates of a ruling lord or king.

the "philosophy" of trade

The new order needed a "philosophy"—a reasoned explanation of how such a society would hang together, would "work." And such a philosophy was by no means self-evident. In many ways, the new world of profit-seeking individuals appeared as perplexing and fraught with dangers to its contemporaries as it did to the imaginary leaders of a traditional society to whom we described it in our first chapter.

Hence it is not surprising that the philosophers of trade disagreed. In England, a group of pamphleteers and merchants, the so-called Mercantilists, put forward an explanation of economic society that stressed the importance of gold and extolled the role of the merchant whose activities were most likely to bring "treasure" into the state by selling goods to foreigners. In France, a school of thinkers we call the Physiocrats held quite different ideas. They exalted the virtues of the farmer, not the merchant. All wealth ultimately came from nature's bounty, the Physiocrats argued, dismissing merchants and even manufacturers as belonging to a "sterile" class that added nothing to the wealth produced by the farmer. Labor was assumed to be poor, although not necessarily "wretched."

With such diverse views, it is obvious that nothing like unanimity prevailed concerning proper economic policy. Should competition be regulated or left alone? Should the export of gold be prohibited, or should "treasure" be permitted to enter or leave the kingdom as the currents of trade dictated? Should the agricultural producer be taxed because he was the ultimate source of all wealth, or should taxes fall on the prosperous merchant class? The answers to these perplexing questions awaited the advent of Adam Smith (1723–1790), patron saint of our discipline and a figure of towering intellectual stature. His masterwork, *The Wealth of Nations*, published in 1776, the year of the American Revolution, gave to the Western world the first full account of something it dearly wanted to know—how its own economic mechanism worked.

division of labor The world that Smith described was very different from our own. It was a world of very small enterprises: Smith's famous description of a pin factory concerns a manufacturing establishment that employs ten people. It was still hampered by medieval guild restrictions: In Smith's time, no master hatter in England could employ more than two apprentices; in the famous Sheffield silver trade, no master cutler could employ more than one. Still more important, it was a world in which government-protected monopolies were accorded to certain fields of commerce, such as the trade with the East Indies. Yet, for all the differences from modern economic society, the basic vision that Smith gave to his time can still elucidate the tasks of economics in our own time.

Two main problems occupied Smith's attention. The first is implicit in the title of the book. This is Smith's theory of the most important tendency of a society of "perfect liberty"—its *tendency to grow*.*

Economic growth—that is, the steady increase in the output of goods and services enjoyed by a society—was hardly a concern for philosophers of tradition-bound societies, or even of societies ruled by imperial-minded emperors. But what Smith discerned amid the seeming turmoil of a market society was a hidden mechanism that would operate to enlarge the "wealth of nations"—at any rate, those nations that enjoyed a system of perfect liberty and did not tamper with it.

* By "perfect liberty" Smith emphasized that all agents in such a society were free to enter, or not to enter, into economic arrangements such as the wage contract, in sharp contrast to the *obligations* imposed on serfs and slaves. That "liberty" may not have appeared very precious to the "freely contracting" owner of labor power in a London slum. Nonetheless, there was a difference—a legal difference—that Smith correctly identified as crucial for the system of capitalism.

What was it that drove society to increase its riches? Basically, it was the tendency of such a society to encourage a steady rise in the *productivity* of its labor, so that, over time, the same number of working people could turn out a steadily larger output.

And what lay behind the rise in productivity? The answer, according to Smith, was the gain in productiveness that was to be had by achieving an ever-finer *division of labor*. Here Smith's famous pin factory serves as an example:

One man draws out the wire, another straits it, a third cuts it, a fourth points it, a fifth grinds it at the top for receiving the head; to make the head requires two or three distinct operations; to put it on is a peculiar business; to whiten it is another; it is even a trade by itself to put them into paper. . . . I have seen a small manufactory of this kind where ten men only were employed and where some of them consequently performed two or three distinct operations. But though they were poor, and therefore but indifferently accommodated with the necessary machinery, they could, when they exerted themselves, make among them about twelve pounds of pins in a day. There are in a pound upwards of four thousand pins of middling size. Those ten persons, therefore, could make among them upwards of forty-eight thousand pins in a day. . . . But if they had all wrought separately and independently . . . they could certainly not each of them make twenty, perhaps not one pin in a day.

Adam Smith's growth model

This begins to unravel the reasons why a society of free enterprise tends to grow. But it does not fully explain the phenomenon. For what is it that drives such a society to a division of labor? And how do we know that the tendency to growth will not peter out, for one reason or another?

This leads us to the larger picture that Smith had in mind. We would call it a growth model, although Smith used no such modern term himself. What we mean by this is that Smith shows us both a *propulsive force* that will put society on an upward growth path and a *self-correcting* mechanism that will keep it there.

First the driving force. One of the fundamental building blocks of Smith's conception of human nature was what he called the "desire for betterment"—what we have already described as the profit motive. And what does the desire for betterment have to do with growth? The answer is very important. *It impels every manufacturer to expand his business in order to increase his profits.*

And how does this business expansion result in a higher division of labor? The answer is very neat. The main road to profit consists in equipping workmen with the necessary machinery that Smith mentions in his description of the pin factory, for it is this machinery that will increase their productivity. Thus, the path to growth lies in what Smith called *accumulation*, or in more modern terminology, the process of *capital investment*. As capitalists seek money, they invest in machines and equipment. As a result of the machines and equipment, their men can produce more. Because they produce more, society's output grows.

the dynamics
of the system

This answers the first part of our query. But there is still the question of how we know that society will continue to grow, that its trajectory will not flatten out. Here we come to the cleverest part of Smith's model. For at first look, it might seem as if the drive to increase capital investments would be self-defeating. The reason is that the steady increase in the demand for workmen to run the new machines would drive up their wages; and as wages rose, they would cut into the manufacturer's profits. In turn, as profits were eaten away, the very source of new investment would dry up and the growth curve would soon level off.

Not so, according to Smith. To be sure, the rising demand for workmen *would* tend to drive up wages. But this was only half the picture. The same upward tendency of wages would also tend to increase the supply of workingmen. The reason is not implausible. In Smith's day, infant mortality was shockingly high: "It is not uncommon," Smith remarked, ". . . in the Highlands of Scotland for a mother who has borne twenty children not to have two alive." But as wages rose, infant and child mortality would tend to diminish, and therefore more of the population would survive to working age (ten or younger in Smith's day).

The outcome must already be clear. Along with an increase in the demand for workingmen (and working children) comes an increase in their supply. This increase in the number of available workers meant that the competition for jobs would increase. Therefore the price of labor would *not* rise, at least not enough to choke off further growth. Like a vast self-regulating machine, the mechanism of capital accumulation would provide the very thing it needed to continue unhampered: a force to prevent wages from eating up profits. And so the growth process could go on undisturbed.

We will not concern ourselves here with the full details of Smith's growth model. And of course, his "model" is not directly applicable to the modern world, where (at least in industrialized nations) most children do not die before they reach working age and where his "safety valve" therefore has no relevance. But nonetheless, in Smith's model we get a sense of the imaginative reach and capacity for enlightenment that economic analysis can bring.*

the market
mechanism

The wealth (we would say the output) of nations was not, however, the only major problem on which Smith's treatise threw a clarifying light.

---

* It seems necessary to add a word to the student who gets sufficiently interested in Smith's model to look into the *Wealth* itself. He will look in vain in this vast, discursive book for a clear-cut exposition of the interactions we have just described. The model is implicit in Smith's exposition, but it lies around the text like a disassembled machine, requiring us to put it together in our minds. Nonetheless it is there, if one fits together the pieces. For a full exposition, see A. Lowe, "Adam Smith's System of Equilibrium Growth," and W. A. Eltis, "Adam Smith's Theory of Economic Growth," both in *Essays on Adam Smith*, ed. Skinner and Wilson (Oxford: Clarendon Press, 1975), as well as my own essay in that volume.

There was also the question of how a market system held together, of how it provided an orderly solution to the problems of production and distribution.

This brings us to Smith's description and explanation of *the market mechanism.* Here Smith begins by elucidating a perplexing problem. The actors in Smith's drama, as we know, are driven by the desire for self-betterment and guided mainly by their self-interest. "It is not from the benevolence of the butcher, the brewer or the baker that we expect our dinner," writes Smith, "but from their regard to their self-interest. We address ourselves not to their humanity, but to their self-love, and never talk to them of our necessities, but of their advantages."[10]

The problem here is obvious. How does a market society prevent self-interested, profit-hungry men from holding up their fellow citizens for ransom? How does a socially workable arrangement emerge from such a socially dangerous set of motivations?

The answer introduces us to a central mechanism of a market society, the mechanism of *competition.* For each man, out to do the best for himself with no thought of others, is faced with a host of similarly motivated individuals who are in exactly the same position. Each is only too eager to take advantage of his competitor's greed if it urges him to raise his price above the level "set" by the market. If a pin manufacturer tried to charge more than his competitors, they would take away his trade; if a workman asked for more than the going wage, he would not be able to find work; if a landlord sought to exact a rent steeper than another with land of the same quality, he would get no tenants.

the market and allocation   But the market mechanism does more than impose a competitive safeguard on the price of products. It also arranges for the production of the right *quantities* of the goods that society desires. Suppose that consumers want more pins than are being turned out, and fewer shoes. The public will buy out the existing supply of pins, while business in the shoe stores will be dull. Pin prices will tend to rise as the public scrambles for shrinking supplies, and prices of shoes will tend to fall as merchants try to get rid of their burdensome stocks.

And now, once again, a restorative force comes into play. As pin prices rise, so will the profits of the pin business, and as shoe prices sag, so will profits in shoemaking. Again, self-interest and the desire for betterment go to work. Pin manufacturers will expand their output to take advantage of higher prices; shoe factories will curtail production to cut their losses. Employers in the pin business will seek to hire more factors of production—more workers, more space, more capital equipment; and employers in the shoe business will reduce their use of the factors of

[10] *Wealth of Nations*, (New York: Modern Library, 1937), p. 14.

production—letting workers go, giving up leases on land, cutting down on their capital investment.

Hence pin output will rise and shoe output will fall. *But this is exactly what the public wanted in the first place!* Through what Smith called, in a famous phrase, an "invisible hand," the selfish motives of men are transmuted by the market mechanism to yield the most unexpected of results: social well-being.

the self-regulating system

Thus Smith showed that a market system, far from being chaotic and disorderly, is in fact the means by which a solution of the strictest discipline and order is provided for the economic problem.

First, he explained how the motive of self-interest provides the necessary impetus to set the mechanism to work. Next, he showed how competition prevents any individual from exacting a price higher than that set by the marketplace. Third, he made clear how the changing desires of society lead producers to increase production of wanted goods and to diminish the production of goods that are no longer as highly desired.

Not least, he showed that the market system is a self-regulating process. For the beautiful consequence of a competitive market is that it is its own guardian. If prices or profits or wages stray away from their "natural" levels determined by cost, forces exist to drive them back into line. Thus a curious paradox emerges: The competitive market, which is the acme of individual economic freedom, is at the same time the strictest of economic taskmasters. One may appeal the ruling of a planning board or win the dispensation of a minister, but there is no appeal, no dispensation, from the anonymous pressures of the competitive marketplace. Economic freedom is thus more illusory than it appears. You may do as you please, but if you please to do that which the market disapproves of, the price of freedom is ruin.

the market system and the rise of capitalism

Does the market system really work as Smith's great treatise suggests? Much of the rest of this book will be devoted to that question—that is, to tracing the growth and the internal order of the system whose prospects Smith's model described so brilliantly. The fact that we have suffered business cycles and depressions, and that giant business firms and labor unions have taken the place of pin factories and child workers, is evidence enough that Smith's model alone will certainly not serve us as a dependable guide through economic history. But the fact that our economy has grown prodigiously and that it has hung together, despite all its problems, is also evidence that there is an important kernel of truth in Smith's conception.

Let us therefore return to our historical narrative, to see how much of what Smith foresaw came true, and how much did not, and for what reasons. For we must remember that *The Wealth of Nations* appeared before capitalism assumed anything like its present industrial guise. After all, serfdom was not formally abolished in France until 1789; and in Germany, not until a half century later. Even in Adam Smith's England, the market society had not yet reached the stage in which capitalism achieved full legal and political status. For example, the guild regulations that irked Smith did not vanish until the medieval Statute of Artificers was repealed in 1813. Likewise in France, an immense web of regulations bound the would-be capitalist. Rules and edicts, many of them seeking to standardize production, laid down the exact number of threads to be woven into the cloths of the French textile manufacturers, and to disregard these laws was to risk pillorying—first for the cloth, then for the manufacturer.

Thus, well into the eighteenth century, we find the great revolution of the market still incomplete; or rather, we find the nearly complete process of monetization and commercialization contained uncomfortably within a frame of legal and social organization not yet fully adapted to it. We will have to observe how capitalism burst through the restrictions of the precapitaliist, mercantilist era before we can see Adam Smith's marvelous market mechanism in full operation.

KEY CONCEPTS AND KEY WORDS

Feudalism

1. *Powerful forces of change* were operative within European feudalism, and served gradually to introduce the structure of a market society. Primary among these forces were:
   - The role of *the itinerant merchant* in introducing trade, money, and the acquisitive spirit into feudal life.
   - The *process of urbanization* as a source of economic activity, and as the locus of a new, trade-centered seat of power.
   - *The Crusades* as a force for the disruption of feudal life and the introduction of new ideas.
   - The rise of unifying, commerce-supporting *national states.*
   - The stimulus of the *Age of Exploration* and of the *gold* it brought into Europe.
   - The emergence of *new religious ideas* more sympathetic to business activity than Catholicism had been.
   - The *monetization of dues* within the manorial system.

Economic life

2. As a consequence of these forces, we begin to see the *separation of economic from social life.* The processes of production and distribution were no longer indistinguishably melded into the prevailing religious, social, and political customs and practices, but now began to form a sharply distinct area of life in themselves.

Enclosures   3. With the rise of the economic aspect of life, we see *deep-seated transformations* taking place. The peasant-serf is no longer bound to the land, but becomes a free, mobile laborer; the guildmaster is no longer hobbled by guild rules, but becomes an independent entrepreneur; the lord of the land becomes (in the modern sense of the word) a landlord. The transformation was a long and often violent one, especially in the complex case of the *enclosures*.

Factors of production   4. The advent of free laborers, capitalists, and landlords, each selling his services on the market for land and capital and labor, made it possible to speak of the *"factors of production."* By this was implied two things: the *physical categories* of land, labor, and capital as distinguishable agents in the production process; and the *social relationships* among laborers, landowners, and capitalists as distinct groups or classes entering the marketplace.

Wage labor   5. Central among these new relationships was that of *wage labor*. In the wage-labor relationship, a worker is paid a wage for his labor time, and the ownership of the entire product is vested in the hands of the employer-capitalist.

Wealth in capitalism   6. The emergence of capitalism changes the conception of wealth from objects for display or prestige into commodities that must be brought to market and sold. This necessity to sell introduces a hitherto unknown urgency into the economic system.

Profit motive   7. As part of this process of change, we find the emergence of the *profit motive* at all levels of society, not as an acquisitive drive (which may have existed for centuries), but as the pervasive necessity for all individuals in a *monetized society* to strive for higher incomes for economic survival.

Adam Smith's *Wealth of Nations*   8. Along with the new economic society came a new interest in the mechanism of a market society. The greatest of the early economists was *Adam Smith*, author of *The Wealth of Nations*. Essentially a philosopher, Smith turned his powerful and far-ranging inquiry to the understanding of a society of "perfect liberty" (a society of freely contracting agents).

Growth   9. In the *Wealth*, Smith described two attributes of such a society. The first was its *tendency to grow*. Smith showed how growth resulted from the increase in labor *productivity* that came from the ever-finer *division of labor*. This enhancement in productivity was brought about by capitalists' *investment* in *capital equipment* as a means to higher profit.

Self-regulation   10. Smith also described the *market mechanism*. In this mechanism, *competition* played a key role in preventing individuals from exacting whatever price they pleased from buyers. The *market mechanism* also revealed how changing demands for goods would change the production of goods, to match that demand. Thus the capstone of Smith's treatise was the demonstration of the *self-regulating* nature of a competitive market, in which an "invisible hand" brought socially useful ends from selfish and private means.

QUESTIONS

1. What was so disruptive to feudal life about the activities of the merchant? Are business activities today also the causes of social stress?

2. Why is waged labor completely incompatible with feudalism?

3. The underdeveloped nations today often resemble the economies of antiquity or of the Middle Ages, at least insofar as their poverty and stagnation are concerned. Discuss what relevance, if any, the forces of change mentioned in this chapter have on the modernization of these areas. Are there new forces of change?

4. The leading nations in the world, so far as per capita income is concerned, are the United States and the Scandinavian states. Among the less-affluent Western nations are Ireland, Spain, and Portugal. Do you think this proves the validity of the Weber-Tawney thesis as to the importance of the Protestant Ethic in economic growth? Does the addition of Latin America change the argument? Japan?

5. The process of monetization and commercialization was often a violent one in Europe. Do you think the Civil War, which ended slavery and displaced the southern semifeudal plantation system, could be considered part of the same transformation in America?

6. Is economic life distinctly separate from social and political life in America?

7. Do you think most people in the United States obey the profit motive? Are most people mobile in the United States? Do you know anyone who has changed his residence because of economic considerations? His profession?

8. Acquisitiveness is certainly as old as man. Do you think we can speak of the origins of capitalism as being equally old?

9. Describe what Smith meant by the "invisible hand." What is the mechanism by which selfish interests are made compatible with—indeed, made the agent for—successful social provisioning?

10. Can you see a relation between Smith's growth model and his market model? Would the growth model work if the forces of the market did not operate?

4 THE INDUSTRIAL REVOLUTION

Heretofore in our survey of economic history, we have concentrated almost entirely on two main currents of economic activity: agriculture and commerce. Yet there was, from earliest days, a third essential source of economic wealth—industry—which we have purposely let slip by unnoticed. For in contrast to agriculture and commerce, industrial manufacture did not leave a major imprint on economic society itself. As a peasant, a serf, a merchant, or a guildsman, the actor in the economic drama directly typified the basic activities of the times, but this would not have been true of someone in industry. Such a person as a "factory worker"—indeed, the very idea of an *industrial* "proletarian"—was singularly absent from the long years before the late seventeenth century. Only with the advent of Adam Smith's pin factory does he begin to enter the scene.

Let us note as well that the "industrial capitalist" was also lacking. Most of the moneymakers of the past gained their fortunes by trading, or transporting, or lending—not by making. It is amusing—more than amusing; instructive—to mark the best ways of getting rich enumerated by Leon Battista Alberti, a fifteenth-century architect, musician, and courtier. They are (1) wholesale trade; (2) seeking for treasure trove; (3) ingratiating oneself with a rich man to become his heir; (4) usury; and (5) the rental of pastures, horses, and the like. A seventeenth-century commentator adds to this: royal service, soldiering, and alchemy. Manufacturing is conspicuously absent from both lists.[1] It, too, enters the economic world only about the time of Smith.

Granted that in ancient Greece Demosthenes had an armor and a cabinet "factory"; and from long before his time, in ancient Egypt, we even have the attendance record of workers in "factories" for the production of cloth. Yet it is clear that this form of production was far less important than either agriculture or commerce in shaping the economic

---

[1] Werner Sombart, *The Quintessence of Capitalism* (New York: Dutton, 1915), pp. 34–35.

texture of the times. For one thing, the typical scale of manufacture was small. Note that the very word *manufacture* (from the Latin *manus*, "hand," and *facere*, "to make") implies a system of hand, rather than machine, technology. Demosthenes' enterprises, for example, employed no more than fifty men. It is true that from time to time we do come across quite large manufacturing operations; already in the second century A.D., a Roman brickworks employed forty-six foremen; and by the time we reach the seventeenth century, enterprises with several hundred workers are not unheard of. Yet such operations were the exception rather than the rule. In 1660, for instance, a steelsmith in France needed no more than three tons of pig iron a year for his output of swords or sickle blades or artistic cutlery. Similarly, most guild operations, as we have seen, were small. As late as 1843, a Prussian census showed only 67 working people for every 100 masters.[2] In the past—as today in the East and Near East—most "industry" was carried on in the backs of small shops or the dim cellars of houses, in sheds behind bazaars, or in the scattered homes of workers to whom materials would be supplied by an organizing "capitalist."

A GREAT TURNING POINT

pace of technical change

In addition to the smallness of the scale of industry, another aspect of the times delayed industrial manufacture from making known its social presence. This was the absence of any sustained interest in the development of an *industrial technology*. Throughout antiquity and the Middle Ages, little of society's creative energy was directed toward a systematic improvement of manufacturing techniques. It is indicative of the lack of interest attached to productive technology that so simple and important an invention as the horse collar had to await the Middle Ages for discovery; the Egyptians, Greeks, and Romans, who were capable of a magnificent technology of architecture, were simply not fundamentally concerned with the techniques of everyday production itself.[3] Even well into the Renaissance and Reformation, the idea of industrial technology hardly attracted serious thought. With the principal exception of Leonardo da Vinci, whose fecund mind played with inventions of the most varied kind, the serious thinkers of Europe, until well into the seven-

[2] *Cambridge Economic History of Europe* (Cambridge, England: Cambridge University Press, 1952), II, 34; John U. Nef, *Cultural Foundations of Industrial Civilization* (New York: Harper, Torchbooks, 1960), p. 131; R. H. Tawney, *Equality*, 4th ed. (London: Macmillan, 1952), p. 59.

[3] E. M. Jope, in *History of Technology*, ed. Charles J. Singer et al. (New York: Oxford University Press, 1956), II, 553. There was, however, considerable improvement in mining techniques, especially for silver and copper.

teenth century, were both ignorant of and uninterested in the technology of basic production.

There was good reason for this prevailing indifference: In the societies of the premarket world, the necessary economic base for any large-scale industrial manufacture was totally lacking. In economies sustained by the labor of peasants, slaves, and serfs, economies in which the stream of money was small and the current of economic life—accidents of war and nature aside—relatively changeless from year to year, who could dream of a process in which avalanches of goods would be turned out? The very idea of industrial production on the large scale was inconceivable in such an unmonetized, static setting.

For all these reasons, the pace of industrialization was slow. It is a question whether Europe in the year 1200 was significantly more technologically advanced than it had been in the year 200 B.C. The widespread use of waterpower in industry, for instance, did not appear until the fifteenth century, and it would be still another century before windmills provided a common means for tapping the energy of nature. The mechanical clock dates from the thirteenth century, but not for 200 years would significant improvements be made in instruments for navigation, surveying, or measuring. Movable type, that indispensable forerunner of mass communication, did not appear until 1450.

In short, despite important pockets of highly organized production, notably in the thirteenth-century Flanders cloth industry and in Northern Italian towns, not until the late sixteenth century can we discern the first signs of a general ground swell of industrial technology, and even in that time it would have been impossible to foresee that one day industry would be the dominant form of productive organization. As a matter of fact, as late as the eighteenth century, when manufacturing had already begun to reach respectable proportions as a form of social endeavor, it was not generally thought of as inherently possessing any but secondary importance. Agriculture, of course, was the visible foundation of the nation itself. Trading was regarded as useful insofar as it brought a nation gold. But at best, industry was seen as a handmaiden of the others, providing the trader with the goods to export, or serving the farmer as a secondary market for the products of the earth.*

What finally conspired to bring manufacturing into a position of overwhelming prominence?

It was a complex concatenation of events that finally brought about the eruption we call the Industrial Revolution. As with the Commercial

---

* Remember that in the mid-eighteenth century, when the French doctor François Quesnay propounded one of the first systematic explanations of economic production and distribution (called *Physiocracy*), only the farmer was regarded as a producer of net worth; and the manufacturer, while his utility was not ignored, was nonetheless relegated to the "sterile" (i.e., non–wealth-producing) classes.

Revolution and the Mercantile era, which preceded it and formed its indispensable preparation, it is impossible in a few pages to do justice to the many currents that contributed to that final outburst of industrial technology. But if we cannot trace the process in detail, we can at least gain an idea of its impetus and of the main forces behind it if we turn now to England around 1750. Here, for the first time, industrial manufacture as a major form of economic activity began to work its immense social transformations. Let us observe the process as it took place.

England in
1750   Why did the Industrial Revolution originally take place in England and not on the Continent? Why did the pin factory attract Smith's attention? To answer these questions we must look at the background factors that distinguished England from most other European nations in the eighteenth century.

The first of these factors was simply that England was relatively wealthy. In fact, a century of successful exploration, slave trading, piracy, war, and commerce had made her the richest nation in the world. Even more important, her riches had accrued not solely to a few nobles, but also to a large upper-middle stratum of commercial *bourgeoisie*. England was thus one of the first nations to develop, albeit on a tiny scale, a prime requisite of an industrial economy: a "mass" consumer market. As a result, a rising pressure of demand inspired a search for new techniques. Very typically, the Society for the Encouragement of Arts and Manufacturers (itself a significant child of the age) offered a prize for a machine that would spin six threads of cotton at one time, thus enabling the spinner to keep up with the technologically more advanced weaver. It was this that led, at least in part, to Arkwright's spinning jenny, of which we shall hear more shortly.

Second, England was the scene of the most successful and thoroughgoing transformation of feudal society into commercial society. The process of enclosures was a significant clue to a historic change that sharply marked off England from the Continent. It was that in England the aristocracy had early on made its peace with (and more than that, found its profits in) commerce. Although sharp conflicts of interest remained between the "old" landed power and the "new" monied power, by 1700, the ruling orders in England had decisively opted for adaptation rather than resistance to the demands of the market economy.[4]

Third, England was the locus of a unique enthusiasm for science and engineering. The famous Royal Society, of which Newton was an early president, was founded in 1660 and was the immediate source of much intellectual excitement. Indeed, a popular interest in gadgets, ma-

[4] See Barrington Moore, *Social Origins of Dictatorship and Democracy* (Boston: Beacon Press, 1966), Chap. 1.

chines, and devices of all sorts soon became a mild national obsession: *Gentlemen's Magazine*, a fashionable periodical of the time, announced in 1729 that it would henceforth keep its readers "abreast of every invention"—a task that the mounting flow of inventions soon rendered quite impossible. No less important was the enthusiasm of the British landed aristocracy for scientific farming: English landlords displayed an interest in matters of crop rotation and fertilizer that their French counterparts would have found quite beneath their dignity.

Then there were a host of other background causes, some as fortuitous as the immense resources of coal and iron ore on which the British sat; others as purposeful as the development of a national patent system that deliberately sought to stimulate and protect the act of invention itself.* And then, as the revolution came into being, it fed upon itself. The new techniques (especially in textiles) simply destroyed their handicraft competition around the world and thus enormously increased their own markets. But what finally brought all these factors into operation was the energy of a group of New Men who made of the latent opportunities of history a vehicle for their own rise to fame and fortune.

rise of the new men　　One such, for instance, was John Wilkinson. The son of an old-fashioned, small-scale iron producer, Wilkinson was a man possessed by the technological possibilities of his business. He invented a dozen things: a rolling mill and a steam lathe, a process for the manufacture of iron pipes, and a design for machining accurate cylinders. Typically, he decided that the old-fashioned leather bellows used in the making of iron itself were not efficient, and so he determined to make iron ones. "Everybody laughed at me," he later wrote. "I did it and applied the steam engine to blow them and they all cried: 'Who could have thought of it?' "

He followed his success in production with a passion for application; everything must be made of iron: pipes, bridges, even ships. After a ship made of iron plates had been successfully launched, he wrote a friend: "It answers all my expectations, and has convinced the unbelievers, who were nine hundred and ninety-nine in a thousand. It will be a nine-days wonder, and afterwards, a Columbus' egg."[5]

* Phyllis Deane, in *The First Industrial Revolution* (paperback ed., Cambridge, England: Cambridge University Press, 1965), ascribes the onset of industrialism in England to a somewhat different set of causes: a rise in population, better food-producing techniques, a boom in foreign trade, and a vast improvement in transportation. There is no doubt that these were also indispensable elements in the process. I mention Deane's book so that a student will not think that there is only one "right" way of accounting for very complex historical transformations. For another excellent account of the process, one might turn to the fascinating book by David Landes, *Prometheus Unbound* (Cambridge: Cambridge University Press, 1969); and for still another highly suggestive account, see Joel Mokyr, *The Lever of Riches: Technological Creativity and Economic Progress* (New York: Oxford University Press, 1990).

[5] Paul Mantoux, *The Industrial Revolution in the Eighteenth Century*, 2nd ed. (New York: Harcourt, 1928), pp. 313*n*, 315.

But Wilkinson was only one of many. The most famous was, of course, James Watt—well known to Adam Smith—who, together with Matthew Boulton, formed the first company for the manufacture of steam engines. Watt was the son of an architect, shipbuilder, and maker of nautical instruments. At thirteen he was already making models of machines, and by young manhood he was an accomplished artisan. He planned to settle in Glasgow, but the guild of hammermen objected to his making mathematical instruments—the last remnants of feudalism thus coming into an ironic personal conflict with the man who, more than any other, would create *the* invention that would destroy guild organization. At any rate, Watt found a haven at the university and there, in 1764, had his attention turned to an early and very unsatisfactory steam engine invented by Newcomen. In his careful and systematic way, Watt experimented with steam pressures, cylinder designs, and valves, until by 1796 he had developed a truly radical and (by the standards of those days) extraordinarily powerful and efficient engine. Interestingly, Watt could never have done so well with his engines had not Wilkinson perfected a manner of making good piston-cylinder fits. Previously, cylinders and pistons were made of wood and rapidly wore out. Typically, too, it was Wilkinson who bought the first steam engine to be used for purposes other than pumping: It worked the famous iron bellows.

There was needed, however, more than Watt's skill. The new engines had to be produced and sold, and the factory that made them had to be financed and organized. Watt at first formed a partnership with John Roebuck, another iron magnate, but it shortly failed. Thereafter, luck came his way. Matthew Boulton, already a wealthy and highly successful manufacturer of buttons and buckles, took up Roebuck's contract with Watt, and the greatest combination of technical skill and business acumen of the day was born.

Even then the firm did not prosper immediately. Expenses of development were high, and the new firm was not out of debt for twelve years. Yet from the beginning, interest was high. By 1781, Boulton was able to claim that the people of London, Birmingham, and Manchester were all "steam mill mad"; and by 1786, when two steam engines were harnessed to fifty pairs of millstones in the largest flour mill in the world, all London came to see the marvel.

The steam engine was the greatest single invention, but by no means the sole mainstay, of the Industrial Revolution. Hardly less important were a group of textile inventions, of which the most famous was Arkwright's jenny, or water frame, as it was called to distinguish it from other hand-operated spinning jennies.*

---

* Essentially, what the water frame did was enable cotton thread of much greater strength to be produced. As a result, for the first time it was possible to use cotton thread instead

Arkwright's career is, in itself, interesting. A barber, he plied his trade near the weaving districts of Manchester and so heard the crying need for a machine that would enable the cottage spinners to keep up with the technically more advanced weavers. Good fortune threw him into contact with a clockmaker named John Kay, whom he hired to perfect a machine that Kay had already begun with another employer-inventor. What happened thereafter is obscure: Kay left the business accused of theft and embezzlement, and Arkwright appeared as the "sole inventor" of a spinning jenny in 1769.

He now found two rich hosiers, Samuel Need and Jedediah Strutt, who agreed to set up business with him to produce water frames, and in 1771, the firm built its own spinning mill. It was an overnight success; by 1779, it had several thousand spindles and more than 300 workmen, and ran night and day. Within not many years, Arkwright had built an immense fortune for himself and founded an even more immense textile industry for England. "O reader," wrote Carlyle, looking back on his career, "what a historical phenomenon is that bag-cheeked, pot-bellied, much enduring, much inventing barber! . . . It was this man that had to give England the power of cotton."[6]

the industrial entrepreneur

It is interesting, as we watch the careers of these New Men, to draw a few generalizations concerning them. For this was an entirely new class of economically important persons. Peter Onions, who was one of the inventors of the puddling process, was an obscure foreman; Arkwright was a barber; Benjamin Huntsman, the steel pioneer, was originally a maker of clocks; Maudslay, who invented the automatic screw machine, was a bright young mechanic at the Woolwich Arsenal. None of the great industrial pioneers came of noble lineage; and with few exceptions, such as Matthew Boulton, none even possessed money capital. In agriculture, the new revolutionary methods of scientific farming enjoyed aristocratic patronage and leadership, especially from the famous Sir Jethro Tull and Lord Townshend; but in industry, the lead went to men of humble origin and descent.

Let us note, therefore, that this required a social system flexible enough to permit the rise of such obscure "adventurers." It is not until we see the catalytic effect of unleashing and harnessing the energies of talented men in the lower and middle ranks of the social order that we begin to appreciate the immense liberating effect of the preceding eco-

---

of linen thread for the warp (the vertical threads that take most of the strain in weaving) as well as for the weft. Not until Arkwright's invention was "cotton cloth" made wholly of cotton. The new cloth was incomparably superior to the old and instantly enjoyed a huge demand.

[6] Mantoux, *The Industrial Revolution in the Eighteenth Century,* p. 225.

nomic and political revolutions. In the medieval hierarchy, the meteoric careers of such New Men would have been unthinkable. In addition, the New Men were the product of the unique economic preparation of England itself. They were, of course, the beneficiaries of the rising demand and the technical inquisitiveness of the times. Beyond that, many of the small manufacturers were themselves former small proprietors who had been bought out during the late period of the enclosure movement and who determined to use their tiny capital in the promising area of manufacture.

the new rich   Many of these New Men made great sums of money. A few, like Boulton and Watt, were modest in their wants. Despite an iron-clad patent, they charged for their engines only the basic cost of the machine and installation plus one-third the saving in fuel the customer got. Some, like Josiah Wedgwood, founder of the great china works, actually refused on principle to take out patents. But most of them did not display such fine sensibilities. Arkwright retired a multimillionaire, living in ostentatious splendor; Huntsman, Wilkinson, and Samuel Walker (who began life as a nailsmith and stole the secret of cast steel) all went on to roll up huge fortunes.* Indeed, Wilkinson's iron business became a minor industrial state with credit stronger than many German and Italian principalities. It even coined its own money, and its copper and silver tokens (with a profile and legend of John Wilkinson, Ironmaster) were much in use between 1787 and 1808.

Besides being avaricious, the manufacturers have been described by the economic historian Paul Mantoux as

tyrannical, hard, sometimes cruel: their passions and greeds were those of up-starts. They had the reputation of being heavy drinkers and of having little regard for the honour of their female employees. They were proud of their newly acquired wealth and lived in great style with footmen, carriages and gorgeous town and country houses.[7]

It is not surprising, then, that Adam Smith, while recognizing their usefulness, looked with distrust on the "mean rapacity, the monopolizing spirit" of merchants and manufacturers, warning that "they neither are, nor ought to be, the rulers of mankind."[8]

Pleasant or unpleasant, these men's personal characteristics fade beside one overriding quality. These were all interested in expansion,

---

* In contrast to the manufacturers, the inventors did not usually fare successfully. Many of them, who did not have Watt's good fortune in finding a Boulton, died poor and neglected, fruitlessly suing for stolen inventions, unpaid royalties, ignored claims.

[7] Mantoux, *The Industrial Revolution in the Eighteenth Century*, p. 397.

[8] *The Wealth of Nations* (New York: Modern Library, 1937), p. 460.

in growth, in <u>investment for investment's s</u>ake. All of them were identified with technological progress, and none of them disdained contact
with the physical process of production. An employee of Maudslay once
remarked, "It was a pleasure to see him handle a tool of any kind, but
he was *quite splendid* with an 18-inch file."[9] Watt was tireless in ex-
perimenting with his machines; Wedgwood stomped about his factory
on his wooden leg, scrawling, "This won't do for Jos. Wedgwood," wherever he saw evidence of careless work. Richard Arkwright was a bundle
of ceaseless energy in promoting his interests, jouncing about England
over execrable roads in a post chaise driven by four horses, pursuing his
correspondence as he traveled.

"With us," wrote a French visitor to a calico works in 1788, "a man
rich enough to set up and run a factory like this would not care to remain
in a position which he would deem unworthy of his wealth."[10] This was
an attitude entirely foreign to the rising English industrial capitalist. His
work was its own dignity and reward; the wealth it brought was quite
aside. Boswell, on being shown Watt and Boulton's great engine works
at Soho, declared that he never forgot Boulton's expression, as the latter
declared, "I sell here, sir, what all the world desires to have—Power."[11]

The New Men were first and last *entrepreneurs*—organizers. They
brought with them a new energy, as restless as it proved to be inex-
haustible. In an economic, if not a political, sense, they deserve the
epithet "revolutionaries," for the change they ushered in was nothing
short of total, sweeping, and irreversible.

industrial
and social
repercussions

The first and most striking element of that change was a sharp rise in
the output of the newly industrialized industries. The import of raw
cotton for spinning weighed 1 million pounds in 1701; 3 million pounds
in 1750; 5 million in 1781. That was a respectable rate of increase. But
then came the sudden burst in textile technology. By 1784, the figure
was over 11 million pounds; by 1789, it was three times greater yet, and
still it grew: to 43 million pounds in 1799; 56 million in 1800; 60 million
in 1802.[12] So was it with much else where the new technology penetrated. The output of coal increased tenfold in forty years; that of pig
iron leaped from 68,000 tons in 1788 to 1,347,000 tons in 1839.[13]

Thus, the first impact of the <u>Industrial Revolution was an immense</u>
<u>quickening of the pace of production in the new industrial sector of the</u>

---

[9] Lewis Mumford, *Technics and Civilization* (New York: Harcourt, 1934), p. 210.

[10] Mantoux, *The Industrial Revolution in the Eighteenth Century*, p. 404.

[11] H. R. Fox Bourne, *English Merchants* (London: 1866), p. 119.

[12] Mantoux, *The Industrial Revolution in the Eighteenth Century*, p. 258.

[13] J. L. and B. Hammond, *The Rise of Modern Industry* (New York: Harcourt, 1937), p.
160.

economy, an effect we find repeated in every nation that goes through an "industrial revolution." In France, for example, the impact of industrial techniques did not make its influence felt until about 1815; between that date and 1845, the French output of pig iron grew fivefold; her coal production, sevenfold; her rate of importation, tenfold.[14]

The Industrial Revolution itself did not immediately exert a comparable leverage on the *overall* increase of output. The industrial sector, to begin with, was small; and the phenomenal rates of increase in those industries where its leverage was first and most fruitfully applied were by no means mirrored in every industry. What is of crucial importance, however, is that the Industrial Revolution ushered in the technology by which large-scale, sustained growth was eventually to take place. This is a process into which we must look more carefully at the end of this chapter.

rise of the factory   But first we must pay heed to another immediate and visible result of the Industrial Revolution in England. We can describe it as the transformation of an essentially commercial and agricultural society into one in which industrial manufacture became the dominant mode of organizing economic life. To put it more concretely, the Industrial Revolution was characterized by *the rise of the factory to the center of social as well as economic life.* After 1850, the factory was not only the key economic institution of England, it was also the economic institution that shaped its politics, its social problems, the character of its daily life, just as decisively as the manor or the guild had done a few centuries earlier.

It is difficult for us today to realize the pace or the quality of change that this rise of factory work brought about. Until the mid-eighteenth century, Glasgow, Newcastle, and the Rhondda Valley were mostly waste or farm land, and Manchester in 1727 was described by Daniel Defoe as "a mere village." Forty years later, there were 100 integrated mills and a whole cluster of machine plants, forges, leather and chemical works in the area. A modern industrial city had been created.

By the 1780s, the shape of the new environment was visible. A French mineralogist visiting England in 1784 wrote:

[The] creaking, the piercing noise of the pulleys, the continuous sound of hammering, the ceaseless energy of the men keeping all this machinery in motion, presented a sight as interesting as it was new. . . . The night is so filled with fire and light that when from a distance we see, here a glowing mass of coal, there darting flames leaping from the blast furnaces, when we hear the heavy hammers striking the echoing anvils and the shrill whistling of the air pumps, we do not

[14] A. Dunham, *The Industrial Revolution in France, 1815–48* (New York: Exposition Press, 1955), p. 432.

know whether we are looking at a volcano in eruption or have been miraculously transported to Vulcan's cave. . . .[15]

The factory provided not merely a new landscape but a new and uncongenial social habitat. In our day, we have become so used to urban industrial life that we forget what a wrench is the transition from farm to city. For the peasant, this transfer requires a drastic adjustment. No longer does he work at his own pace, but at the pace of a machine. No longer are slack seasons determined by the weather, but by the state of the market. No longer is the land, however miserable its crop, an eternal source of sustenance close at hand, but only the packed and sterile earth of the industrial site.

It is little wonder that the English laborer, still more used to rural than urban ways, feared and hated the advent of the machine. Throughout the early years of the Industrial Revolution, workmen literally attacked the invading army of machinery, burning and wrecking factories. During the late eighteenth century, for instance, when the first textile mills were built, whole hamlets rose in revolt rather than work in the mills. Headed by a mythical General Ludd, the Luddites constituted a fierce but fruitless opposition to industrialism. In 1813, in a mass trial that ended in many hangings and transportations, the movement came to an end.*

conditions of labor   Distasteful as was the advent of the factory itself, even more distasteful were the conditions within it. Child labor, for instance, was commonplace and sometimes began at age four; hours of work were generally dawn to dusk; abuses of every kind were all too frequent. A Committee of Parliament, appointed in 1832 to look into conditions, gives this testimony from a factory overseer.

> **Q.** At what time in the morning, in the brisk time, did these girls go to the mills?
>
> **A.** In the brisk time, for about six weeks, they have gone at three o'clock in the morning and ended at ten or nearly half past at night.
>
> **Q.** What intervals were allowed for rest and refreshment during those nineteen hours of labour?
>
> **A.** Breakfast a quarter of an hour, and dinner half an hour, and drinking a quarter of an hour.
>
> **Q.** Was any of that time taken up in cleaning the machinery?
>
> **A.** They generally had to do what they call dry down; sometimes this took the whole time at breakfast or drinking.

[15] Mantoux, *The Industrial Revolution in the Eighteenth Century*, p. 313.

* Even in our day, however, we use the word *Luddite* to describe an attempt to "fight back" at the threat of machinery.

Q. Had you not great difficulty in awakening your children to the excessive labour?

A. Yes, in the early time we had to take them up asleep and shake them.

Q. Had any of them any accident in consequences of this labour?

A. Yes, my eldest daughter . . . the cog caught her forefinger nail and screwed it off below the knuckle.

Q. Has she lost that finger?

A. It is cut off at the second joint.

Q. Were her wages paid during that time?

A. As soon as the accident happened the wages were totally stopped.[16]

It was a grim age. The long hours of work, the general dirt and clangor of the factories, the lack of even the most elementary safety precautions, all combined to give early industrial capitalism a reputation from which, in the minds of many people of the world, it has never recovered. Worse yet were the slums to which the majority of workers returned after their travail. Life expectancy at birth in Manchester was seventeen years—a figure that reflected a child mortality rate of over 50 percent. This is not so surprising when we read this government commissioner's report of 1839 on one such workers' quarter in Glasgow called "the wynds."

The wynds . . . house a fluctuating population of between 15,000 and 30,000 persons. This district is composed of many narrow streets and square courts and in the middle of each court there is a dunghill. Although the outward appearance of these places was revolting, I was nevertheless quite unprepared for the filth and misery that were to be found inside. In some bedrooms we visited at night we found a whole mass of humanity stretched on the floor. There were often 15 to 20 men and women huddled together, some being clothed and others naked. There was hardly any furniture there and the only thing which gave these holes the appearance of a dwelling was fire burning on the hearth. Thieving and prostitution are the main sources of income of these people.[17]

early capitalism and social justice

Without question, the times were marked by tremendous social suffering. But it is well, in looking back on the birth years of industrial capitalism, to bear several facts in mind:

1. *It is doubtful if the poverty represented a deterioration in life for the masses in general.*

In at least some sections of England, industrialism brought immediate benefits. Wedgwood (an exceptionally good employer, it is true) used to

[16] Tawney, Bland, and Brown, *English Economic History, Selected Documents* (London: Bell, 1914), p. 510.

[17] Quoted in F. Engels, *The Condition of the Working Class in England* (New York: Macmillan, 1958), p. 46.

tell his employees to ask their parents for a description of the country as *they* first knew it and to compare their present state. So, too, the twelve-hour day in Arkwright's mills was a two-hour *improvement* over previous Manchester standards. Furthermore, the existing poverty was not by any means new. As we know from Hogarth's etchings, long before the Industrial Revolution, "Gin Lane" already sported its pitiful types. As one reformer of the mid-nineteenth century wrote, those whose sensibilities were revolted by the sight of suffering factory children thought "how much more delightful would have been the gambol of free limbs on the hillside; the sight of the green mead with its spangles of buttercups and daisies; the song of the bird and the humming of the bee . . . [but] we have seen children perishing from sheer hunger in the mud hovel or in the ditch by the wayside."[18]

> **2.** *Much of the harsh criticism to which early industrial capitalism was subjected was derived not so much from its economic as from its political accompaniments.*

For, coincident with the rise of capitalism, and indeed contributory to it, was a deep-seated change in the vantage point of political criticism. New ideas of democracy, of social justice, of the "rights" of the individual charged the times with a critical temper of mind before which *any* economic system would have suffered censure.

To be sure, the political movements by which capitalism was carried to its heights were not working-class movements, but middle-class, bourgeois movements; the rising manufacturers in England and France had little "social conscience" beyond a concern for their own rights and privileges. But the movement of political liberalism that they set in motion had a momentum beyond the narrow limits for which it was intended. By the first quarter of the nineteenth century, the condition of the working classes, now so exposed to public view in the new factory-slum environment, had begun to curry public sympathy.

Thus, one of the unexpected consequences of the Industrial Revolution was a sharp reorientation of political ideas. In the creation of an industrial working class and an industrial environment, the revolution bequeathed a new economic framework to politics.* Karl Marx and Friedrich Engels were to write in 1848 that "all history" was the history of class struggle, but never did that struggle emerge so nakedly into the open as after the industrial environment had been brought into being.

Equally important was that the rise of political liberalism not only

---

[18] Friedrich Hayek, ed., *Capitalism and the Historians* (Chicago: University of Chicago Press, 1954), p. 180.

* For a stirring account of the birth of a self-conscious working-class movement, see E. P. Thompson, *The Making of the English Working Class* (New York: Pantheon, 1964).

roused feelings of hostility toward the prevailing order, but initiated the slow process of amelioration. *From the outset, a reform movement coincided with capitalism.* In 1802, pauper apprentices were legally limited to a twelve-hour day and barred from night work. In 1819, the employment of children under nine was prohibited in cotton mills; in 1833, a forty-eight– to sixty-nine–hour week was decreed for workers under eighteen (who comprised about 75 percent of all cotton-mill workers), and a system of government inspection of factories was inaugurated; in 1842, children under ten were barred from the coal mines; in 1847, a ten-hour daily limit (later raised to ten and a half) was set for children and women.

The nature of the reforms is itself eloquent testimony to the conditions of the times, and the fact that the reforms were bitterly opposed and often observed in the breach is testimony to the prevailing spirit. Yet capitalism, unlike feudalism, was from the beginning subject to the corrective force of democracy. Karl Marx, using the material of the 1830s, drew a mordant picture of the capitalist process in all its economic squalor, but he overlooked (or shrugged off) this countervailing force whose power was steadily to grow.

> **3.** *The most important effect of the Industrial Revolution we have left for last: its long-term leverage on economic well-being.*

The ultimate impact of the Industrial Revolution was to usher in a rise of living standards on a mass scale unlike anything that the world had ever known before.

This did not happen overnight. In 1840, according to the calculations of Arnold Toynbee, Sr., the wage of an ordinary laborer came to 8 shillings a week, which was 6 shillings less than he needed to buy the bare necessities of life.[19] He made up the deficit by sending his children or his wife, or both, to work in the mills. If, as we have noted, some sections of the working class gained from the early impact of industrialization, others suffered a *decline* from the standard of living enjoyed in 1795 or thereabouts. A Committee of Parliament in the 1830s, for example, discovered that a hand weaver at that earlier date could have bought more than three times as many provisions with his wages as at the later date. Although not every trade suffered equally, the first flush of the Industrial Revolution brought its hardships to bear full force, while its benefits were not as immediately noticeable.

By 1870, however, the long-run effects of the Industrial Revolution were beginning to make themselves felt. The price of necessities had by then risen to 15 shillings, but weekly earnings had crept up to meet

---

[19] *The Industrial Revolution* (Boston: Beacon Press, 1956), p. 113.

and even exceed that sum. Hours were shorter, too. At the Jarrow Shipyards and the New Castle Chemical Works, the workweek had fallen from sixty-one to fifty-four hours; and even in the notoriously long-working textile mills, the stint was down to "only" fifty-seven hours. It was still a far cry from an abundant society, much less an "affluent" one, but the corner had been turned.

THE INDUSTRIAL REVOLUTION IN THE PERSPECTIVE OF THEORY

We have reviewed very briefly the salient historic features of the rise of industrial capitalism. Now we must reflect on the great economic and social changes we have witnessed and ask a pertinent economic question: *How did the process of industrialization raise material well-being?* To answer the question, we must turn to economic theory to elucidate systematically the insights we have already gained from Smith's *Wealth of Nations.*

Let us begin by asking what is necessary for a rise in the economic well-being of a society. The answer is not difficult. If we are to enjoy a greater material well-being, generally speaking, we must produce more. This is particularly true when we begin at the stage of scarcely-better-than-subsistence that characterized so much of Europe before the Industrial Revolution. For such a society to raise the standard of living of its masses, the first necessity is unquestionably higher production. Despite all the inequities of distribution that attended the society of serf and lord, capitalist and child-employee, underlying the meanness of the times was one overriding reality: the sheer inadequacy of output. There was simply not enough to go around, and if somewhat less lopsided distributive arrangements might have lessened the moral indignity of the times, they would not have contributed much to a massive improvement in basic economic well-being. Even assuming that the wage of the city laborer and the income of the peasant could have been doubled had the rich been deprived of their share—and this is a wildly extravagant assumption—still, the prime characteristic of rural and urban life would have been its poverty.

We must add only one important qualification to this emphasis on increased output as the prerequisite of economic improvement. Overall living standards will not improve if a country's population is growing even faster than its increased output. The production of goods and services must rise *faster* than population if individual well-being is to improve.

How does a society raise its *per capita* output?

We cannot fully analyze this problem here. But our glimpse into the pin factory and our study of the Industrial Revolution in England enable us to understand a great deal about the problem. For clearly, *the key to higher output lies in enhancing the human energies of the community with the leverage of industrial capital.* Our analytic understanding of the growth must begin by looking further into this extraordinary power that capital possesses.

capital and productivity   We have already frequently used the word *capital*, but we have not yet defined it. We can see that, in a fundamental sense, capital consists of anything that can enhance man's power to perform economically useful work. An unshaped stone is capital to the caveman who can use it as a hunting implement. A hoe is capital to a peasant; a road system is capital to the inhabitants of a modern industrial society. Knowledge is capital, too—indeed, perhaps the most precious part of society's stock of capital.

When economists talk of capital, however, they usually confine their meaning to *capital goods*—the stock of tools, equipment, machines, and buildings that society produces in order to expedite the production process.* All these capital goods have one effect in common on the productive process: They all operate to make human labor more productive. They make it possible for a worker to produce more goods in an hour (or a week, or a year) than he could produce without the aid of that capital. Capital is therefore a method of raising per capita *productivity*, which is an individual's output in a given span of time; it is the lesson of the pin factory extended to all branches of output. For example, in a forty-hour week, a typical modern worker using power-driven mechanical equipment can physically outproduce three men working seventy hours a week with the simpler tools available at the beginning of this century. To put it differently, in one day, a modern worker will turn out more output than his counterpart of 1900 did in a full week—not because the modern worker works harder, but because he has at his command thousands of dollars' worth of capital equipment rather than the few hundred dollars' worth available to a worker in 1900.

Why does capital make labor so much more productive?

The most important reason is that capital goods enable people to use principles and devices such as the lever and the wheel, heat and

---

* A personal footnote: there is also another meaning to the word *capital*. This is the social relationship that binds the wage-worker and the capitalist, the owner of the capital goods (the factory) where the worker seeks employment. Capital as a social relationship establishes the prerogatives of both capitalist and worker in their mutual dealings. It is perhaps the most important meaning of the word if we seek to define *capitalism* as a distinct period of social history. A student who wishes to pursue this meaning of the word, first proposed by Marx, might look into my book *The Nature and Logic of Capitalism* (New York: Norton, 1985). In this book, we will stay with the conventional economic usage, and speak of capital in terms of capital goods.

cold, combustion and expansion in ways that the unaided body cannot. *Capital goods give people mechanical and physicochemical powers of literally transhuman dimensions.* They enormously magnify muscular strength; they refine powers of control; they embody intelligence; they endow men and women with endurance and resilience far beyond those of flesh and bone. In using capital, human beings utilize the natural world as a supplement to their own feeble capacities.

capital and specialization
Another reason for the augmentation of production lies in the fact that capital facilitates the *specialization of human labor.* Once again, Smith's example serves us well. A team of people working together, each one tending to one job alone in which he or she is expert, can usually far outproduce the same number of people, each of whom does a variety of jobs. The prime example is, of course, the auto production line, in which a thousand workers cooperate to produce an immensely larger output of cars than could be achieved if each one built a car alone. Auto assembly lines, of course, use prodigious quantities of capital in the overhead conveyor belts, the inventories of parts on hand, the huge factory with its power system, and so on. And while not all specialization of labor depends on capital, capital is usually necessary for the large-scale industrial operations in which specialization becomes most effective.

In our next chapter, we will return to these important matters in the context of the development of modern industry. But while we are still discussing the basic question of the rise of industry itself, there is a fundamental problem to be disposed of. This is the question of how capital is made in the first place, of how a society generates the capital equipment it needs in order to grow.

capital and saving
The question brings us for the first time to a relationship that we will encounter many more times in our study of economics, both in a perspective of history and from a later vantage point of theory. The relationship is between the creation of those physical artifacts that we call capital and the inescapable prior act that we call *saving.*

When we think of saving, we ordinarily picture it in financial terms; that is, as a decision not to spend part of our money income. Behind this financial act, however, lies a "real" act that we must now clearly understand. *When we save money, we also abstain from using a certain quantity of goods and services we might have bought.* To be sure, our money savings represent a claim on goods and services, a claim that we may later exercise. Until we do, however, we have freed resources that would otherwise have been used to satisfy our immediate wants. When Smith's pin manufacturer "accumulated," he deliberately denied himself the higher standard of living that he could have enjoyed by spending his profits on riotous living. From these freed resources—the unused labor and capital that might have produced silks and coaches—society builds its capital, or, in more technical language, carries out the act of *investment.**

saving and investment

Thus, the acts of saving and investment are inextricably linked: Saving is the releasing of resources from consumption; investment is the employment of these resources in making capital. Indeed, from society's point of view, saving and investment are only two sides of the same coin. Why do we then separate them in economic discourse? The reason is that different people may perform the saving and investing functions, especially in modern societies. Those who release the resources of society are often not the same individuals as those who gather up those resources for investment purposes. Nonetheless, we can see that every act of capital building, no matter who performs it, requires that resources be devoted to that purpose.

This does not mean that investment necessarily entails a *diminution* of consumption. A rich society does not feel its normal, recurrent saving as a "pinch" on its spending, and Smith's manufacturers were not known for their modest ways. A society with unemployed factors can put its idle resources to work building capital without diminishing its expenditure on consumption. (It is still saving, of course, insofar as it is not using those newly employed resources to make consumption goods.) But—and this is a crucial point—when a *fully employed* society builds more capital, it *must* curtail its consumption. In this case, there is nowhere the needed capital-building resources can come from but their erstwhile consumption employments.

Let us go on still further. We can now see that the *rate* at which an economy can invest—that is, the size of the yearly addition it can make to its stock of capital goods—depends on its capacity to save. If its living standards are already close to the margin of existence, it will not be able to transfer much labor from consumption effort to capital-building effort. However badly it may wish for more tools, however productive those tools would prove to be, it cannot invest beyond the point at which its remaining consumption activity would no longer be adequate to maintain subsistence. At the other extreme, if a society is well-to-do, it may be able to abstain from a great deal of current consumption effort to provide for the future. Accordingly, its growth will be fast. *Whether*

---

* Note that *investment* in economics means devoting labor and other inputs to the creation of capital goods. It does not mean putting money into stocks and bonds, although that may lead to, or assist, the capital-building process. Economists call the process of making money investments *financial* investment, to distinguish it from *real* investment in capital goods.

growth is fast or slow, it is a hard economic reality that the amount of construction for the future can never exceed the amount of resources and effort that are unused, or that can be released from consumption in the present.

growth in early capitalism

This seems to imply that the process of economic growth must perforce be very slow in a poor economy. And so it is. In England, as we have already seen, nearly three-quarters of a century elapsed before the new process of industrialization brought about an increase in productivity sufficiently large to be felt as a general improvement in the lot of the worker. In the underdeveloped nations, as we shall see in Chapter 10, the prospect is equally or even more sluggish. At its best, growth is a gradual and cumulative rather than an "instant" phenomenon; and where the initial level of savings is low because of poverty, the rate of advance is correspondingly slower.

Perhaps we can better appreciate this overall determinant of the pace of growth if we now examine the actual social circumstances under which saving arose in early-nineteenth-century England.

For who did the saving? Who abstained from consumption? Well-to-do agriculturalists and manufacturers (for all their ostentatious ways) were certainly important savers who plowed substantial sums into more new capital investments. Yet the savers were not just the manufacturers or the gentry but also another class—the industrial workers. Here, in the low level of industrial wages, a great sacrifice was made—not voluntarily, by any manner of means, but made just the same. From the resources the workers could have consumed was built the industrial foundation for the future.

We can also see something that is perhaps even more significant. This is the fact that England *had* to hold down the level of its working-class consumption in order to free productive effort for the accumulation of capital goods. In point of historic actuality, the "holding down" was accomplished largely by the forces of the marketplace—with a liberal assist, to be sure, from the capitalists and from a government quick to oppose the demands of labor in the interests of its upper classes. But social inequities aside, the hard fact remains that had industrial wages risen very much, a vast demand for consumer goods would have turned the direction of the English economy away from capital building, toward the satisfaction of current wants. This would certainly have redounded to the immediate welfare of the English worker (although the increase in per capita consumption would have been small). At the same time, however, it would have *postponed* the day when society's overall productive powers were capable of generating an aggregate output of very large size.

This bitter choice must be confronted by every industrializing society, capitalist or socialist, democratic or totalitarian. To assuage the needs of today or to build for tomorrow is *the* decision a developing society must make.

incentives
for growth

There remains but one last question. We have gained some insight into the mechanics of growth, but we have not yet answered the question: How are these mechanics brought about? How does society arrange the reallocation of its factors of production to bring about the creation of the capital it needs?

This query brings us again to a consideration of our original division of economic societies into three types: Traditional, Command, and Market. It also leads to some very important conclusions.

The first of these is obvious: It is that tradition-bound societies are not apt to grow. In such societies, there is *no* direct social means of inducing the needed reallocation of factors. Worse yet, there are often strong social and religious barriers that create obstacles to the needed shifts in employment.

The situation is very different, however, when we turn to command societies. We have seen a striking use of command as the industrializing agency in modern times. In at least one country, the Soviet Union, command was the principal mechanism for a dramatic transition from peasanthood to industrialization, and in many other collectivist economies, command has been used, with varying results, to bring into effect such a transition.

In Chapter 13, we shall return to the Russian experience. Meanwhile, let us not forget that command was also one of the principal ways by which Europe began its industrialization. In the state-directed establishment of shipyards and armories, the construction of royal palaces and estates, tapestry works and chinaware factories, a very important organizing impetus was given to the creation of an industrial sector in the Mercantile era. True, in those days, command was never so ruthlessly applied nor so widely directed as with the communist states. But however much milder the dosage, the medicine was in essence the same: The *initial* transfer of labor from the traditional pursuits of the land to the new tasks of the factory depended on a commanding authority that ordered the new pattern into being.*

* As Barbara Ward has written in *India and the West*: "A developing society must at some point begin to save, even though it is still poor. This is the tough early stage of growth which Marx encountered in Victorian England and unfortunately took to be permanent. It is a difficult phase in any economy—so difficult that most societies got through it by *force majeure*. . . . No one asked the British laborers moving into the Manchester slums whether they wanted to save. . . . The Soviet workers who came to Sverdlovsk and Magnitogorsk from the primitive steppes had no say in the scale or the condition of their work. Nor have the Chinese in their communes today."

the market as a capital-building mechanism

But command was by no means the main agency for the final industrialization of the West. Rather, the organizing force that put men to work in making capital equipment was the market.

How did the market bring about this remarkable transformation? It achieved its purposes by the lure of monetary rewards. It was the hope of *profits* that lured manufacturers into turning out more capital goods. It was the attraction of better *wages* (or sometimes of *any* wages) that directed workers into the new plants. It was the signal of rising prices that encouraged, and falling prices that discouraged, the production of this or that particular capital good. Here is Smith's market mechanism, joined to his growth model.

And what, we may next ask, opened the prospect of profits large enough to induce entrepreneurs to risk their savings in new capital goods? The answer brings us full circle to the focal point of this chapter. For the answer is to be found primarily in the body of technological advance constituting the core of the Industrial Revolution. It was the pin-making *machinery* that opened the possibility of a profitable and expanding pin industry.

Not that every new invention brought with it a fortune for its pioneering promoters, or that every new product found a market waiting for it. The path of technical advance is littered with inventions born "too soon" and with enterprises founded with great hopes and closed down six months later. But looking back over the vast process of capital accumulation that, beginning in the late eighteenth century, lifted first England and then America into the long flight of industrial development, there is little doubt that the impelling force was the succession of inventions and innovations that successfully opened new aspects of nature to human control. Steam power, the cheap and efficient spinning and weaving of cloth, the first mass production of iron and, later, steel—these were the great breakthroughs of industrial science that opened the way for the massive accumulation of capital. And once the great inventions had marked out the channel of advance, secondary improvements and subsidiary inventions took on an important supporting role. To the entrepreneur with a cost-cutting innovation went the prize of a market advantage in costs and correspondingly higher profit. More than that, once one pioneer in a field had gained a technical advantage, competition quickly forced everyone else in the field to catch up as quickly as they could. Most of the cost-cutting innovations involved adding machinery to the production process—and this in turn boosted the formation of capital.

Capitalism as a whole proved an unparalled machine for the accumulation of capital. In its development we find the first economic system in history in which economic growth became an *integral* part of daily life. As Marx and Engels were to write in the *Communist Mani-*

festo: "The bourgeoisie, during its scarce one hundred years, has created more massive and more colossal productive forces than have all preceding generations together." And the compliment, all the more meaningful coming from the two archenemies of its social order, was true.

KEY CONCEPTS AND KEY WORDS

Industrial Revolution

1. The Industrial Revolution *was a great turning period* in history, during which manufacturing and industrial activity became primary forms of social production.

2. The Industrial Revolution began in England in the mid- to late-eighteenth century (although its roots are far deeper). There are numerous reasons why it occurred there and then:
   - England was *a wealthy trading nation* with a well-developed middle class.
   - England's *aristocracy was much more commerce-minded* than the artistocracies of the Continent.
   - England was the home of a widespread vogue of *scientific investigation* and of "gentlemen farmers" interested in *agricultural innovation*.
   - England's relatively *open social structure* permitted the rise of New Men, such as Watt and Wilkinson, who brought to manufacturing a burst of new social energies.
   - Many other causes could be cited as well. The Industrial Revolution was a *many-sided, complex chain of events*.

Output

3. The Industrial Revolution brought with it changes of the greatest importance in society.
   - It ushered in a slow but cumulative *rise in output* that was eventually to lift the industrial world out of an age-old poverty.
   - It brought the *factory* (and the *industrial slum*) as a new environment for work and life.
   - It gave rise to new kinds of *social abuses*, but also greatly sharpened the general *awareness of economic conditions*.

Capital building

4. The Industrial Revolution was essentially a *capital-building process* (machines, buildings, canals, railways), as a result of which the productivity of labor was greatly increased.

Productivity

5. *Capital generally enhances productivity* because it gives people far greater physical and technical capabilities than they enjoy with unaided labor alone. It also enables people to combine and *specialize* their labor, as in modern factory production lines.

Saving

6. *Capital building requires saving*. Capital can be built only if society has the use of resources normally used for filling its consumption needs. Saving releases these resources; investing puts them to use.

Investment 7. Society cannot devote more resources or energies to capital building than those it releases from other uses (or those it has available as unemployed resources). Hence, by and large, *saving regulates the pace at which investment can proceed.* Poor societies, in which it is difficult to give up consumption, accordingly have great problems in amassing enough resources for investment.

Consumption 8. The saving necessary for investment can come from agriculture, manufacturing enterprises, and many other sources. In poor nations, it must also often be wrung from workers or peasants, by denying them the use of all the nation's economic potential to fill their consumption needs.

9. Hence, *saving in poor nations is usually an involuntary process.* Capital building in many developing nations today, particularly those under authoritarian regimes, is attempted by the agency of command, not very successfully, on the whole. In the Industrial Revolution, it was accomplished in part by command, but mainly by the market system. The remarkable inventions of the Industrial Revolution served as sources of profits that resulted in great accumulations of capital.

QUESTIONS

1. It is interesting to note that technical improvements in agriculture or manufacturing have generally been slow to arise in countries that have relied on slave labor. Can you think of a reason why this might be so?

2. What forces do you think would be necessary to bring a new "industrial revolution" to the underdeveloped world today? Is an industrial revolution there apt to resemble the one that took place in England in the eighteenth century?

3. Industrialization in England was marked by a sharp growth of bitter political feeling on the part of the new factory proletariat. Do you think this must be an accompaniment of industrialization everywhere, or was it a particular product of early capitalism?

4. How does capital help human productivity? Discuss this in relation to the following kinds of labor: farm labor, office help, teaching, government administration.

5. When General Motors devotes a billion dollars to new investment (building new factories, warehouses, offices, etc.), who does the saving that is required? Stockholders? Workers? The public? Buyers of cars?

6. It is estimated that the value of the private capital structures and equipment in the United States in 1989 was some $15 trillion. Assume that half of it were wiped out in some catastrophe. What would happen to U.S. productivity? To average U.S. well-being? How could the damage be repaired?

7. Does all investment require saving? Why?

8. Is capital building in the United States today directed by the market alone? Does the government accumulate capital? Does public capital improve productivity as well as private capital?

9. Is building a school an "investment"? Is building a hospital? a sports stadium? a housing project? a research lab? What do you think distinguishes investment, in general, from consumption?

5 THE IMPACT OF INDUSTRIAL TECHNOLOGY

With this chapter, we enter a new major period of economic history. Formerly we dealt largely with the past, giving only an occasional glance to later echoes of the problems we encountered. Commencing with this chapter, our focus turns toward and into the actual present. We have reached the stage of economic history whose nearest boundary is our own time. Simultaneously, our point of geographic focus shifts. As economic history enters the mid-nineteenth century, the dynamic center of events comes increasingly to be located in the United States. Not only do we now begin to enter the modern world, but the economic trends in which we will be interested take us directly into our own society.

What will be the theme of this chapter? Essentially it will continue a motif we began with the Industrial Revolution—the impact of technology on economic society. Looking back, we can see that the burst of inventions that marked the revolution was not in any sense the completion of a historic event. Rather, it was merely the inception of a process of technological change that would continually accelerate down to the present time.

We can distinguish three or even four stages of this continuous process. The "first" industrial revolution was largely concentrated in new textile machinery, improved methods of coal production and iron manufacture, revolutionary agricultural techniques, and steam power. It was succeeded in the middle years of the nineteenth century by a "second" industrial revolution: a clustering of industrial inventions centering on steel, railroad and steamship transportation, agricultural machinery, and chemicals. By the early years of the twentieth century, there was a third wave of inventions: electrical power, automobiles, the gasoline engine. In our own time, there is a fourth: the revolution of electronics, air travel, automation, and, of course, nuclear energy. Some people speak of today's computerization of the world as constituting a fifth such revolution.

It is difficult, perhaps impossible, to exaggerate the impact of this continuing industrial advance. Now moving rapidly, now slowly; now on a broad front, now on a narrow salient; now in the most practical of inventions, again in the purest of theoretical discoveries, the cumulative application of science and technology to the productive process was *the* great change of the nineteenth and twentieth centuries. The initial Industrial Revolution was thus in retrospect a kind of discontinuous leap in human history; a leap as important as that which had lifted the first pastoral settlements above the earlier hunting communities. We have already noted that in the factory the new technology brought a new working place for man, but its impact was vastly greater than that alone. The enormously heightened powers of transportation and communication, the far more effective means of wresting a crop from the soil, the hugely enhanced ability to apply power for lifting, hauling, shaping, binding, cutting—all this conspired to bring about a literal remaking of the human environment, and by no means an entirely benign one.

IMPACT OF ONE INVENTION

In this book, we cannot do more than inquire into some of the economic consequences of the incursion of industrial technology into modern society, but it may help us gain some insight into the dimensions of that penetrative process if we follow for a short distance the repercussions of a single invention.

Let us therefore look in on the Paris Exposition of 1867, where curious visitors are gathered around an interesting exhibit: a small engine in which illuminating gas and air are introduced into a combustion chamber and ignited by a spark. The resulting explosion pushes a piston; the piston turns a wheel. There is but one working stroke in every four, and the machine requires a large flywheel to regularize its movement, but, as the historian Allan Nevins writes, the effect of the machine "was comparable to the sudden snapping on of an electric globe in a room men had been trying to light with smoky candles."[1] It was the world's first internal combustion engine.

It was not long before the engine, invented by Dr. N. A. Otto of Germany, was a regular feature of the American landscape. Adapted to run on gasoline, a hitherto uninteresting byproduct of kerosene manufacture, it was an ideal stationary power plant. Writes Nevins, "Soon every progressive farm, shop, and feed-mill had its one-cylinder engine chugging away, pumping water, sawing wood, grinding meal, and doing other small jobs."[2] By 1900, there were more than 18,500 internal com-

[1] *Ford, the Times, the Man, the Company* (New York: Scribner's, 1954), I, 96.
[2] *Study in Power, John D. Rockefeller* (New York: Scribner's, 1953), II, 109.

bustion engines in the United States; and whereas the most powerful model in the Chicago World's Fair in 1893 was 35 horsepower, at the Paris Exposition seven years later, it was 1,000 horsepower.

The internal combustion engine was an extraordinary means of increasing, diffusing, and giving mobility to a basic requirement of material progress: power. And soon the new engine opened the way for a yet more startling advance. In 1886, Charles E. Duryea of Chicopee, Massachusetts, had already decided that the gasoline engine was a far more promising power source than steam for a self-propelling road vehicle. By 1892, he and his brother had produced the first gas-powered "automobile," a weak and fragile toy. The next model in 1893 was a better one, and by 1896, the Duryea brothers actually sold thirteen cars. In that same year, a thirty-two-year-old mechanic named Henry Ford sold his first "quadricycle." The history of the automobile industry had begun.

the auto-mobilization of America

Its growth was phenomenal. By 1905, there were 121 establishments making automobiles, and 10,000 wage earners were employed in the industry. By 1923, the number of plants had risen to 2,471, making the industry the largest in the country. In 1960, its annual payroll was as large as the national income of the United States in 1890. Not only that, but the automobile industry had become the single greatest customer for sheet steel, zinc, lead, rubber, leather. It was the buyer of one out of every three radios produced in the nation. It absorbed 25 billion pounds of chemicals a year. It was the second largest user of engineering talent in the country, bowing only to national defense. It was the source of one-sixth of all the patents issued in the nation and the object of one-tenth of all consumer spending in the country. In the 1980s, it was estimated that roughly one job out of every seven owed its existence directly or indirectly to the car, as did one business out of every six—not just factories, of course, but repair shops, garages, gas stations, and traffic police departments.

Even this impressive array of figures by no means exhausts the impact of the internal combustion engine and its vehicular mounting. Out of 91 million U.S. households, 81 million own 147 million passenger cars; over one in two own two or more cars. As a result, some 50,000 towns manage to flourish without rail or water connections, an erstwhile impossibility; and seven out of ten workers no longer live within walking distance of their places of employment but drive to work. In fact, 1,300,000 of them drive fifty miles or more to work. To an extraordinary extent our entire economy has become "mobilized"—which is to say, dependent for its very functioning on the existence of wheeled, self-propelled transportation. If by some strange occurrence our automotive fleet were put out of commission—say by a spontaneous change in the nature of the gasoline molecule, rendering it incombustible—the effect would be as grave and socially disastrous as a catastrophic famine in the Middle Ages.* No wonder that the Arab oil embargos of 1974 and 1979 shook the industrialized world!

THE GENERAL IMPACT OF TECHNOLOGY

We dwell on the impact of the car to stress the *economic* consequences of technology. These may not be its most ultimately important consequences. We live in a world that is threatened in many ways by the extraordinary disruptive power of man's inventive capacity. Technology has progressed to the point at which whole species (including man himself) are endangered by the poisons we manufacture and carelessly spew into the air and water, by the vast quantities of heat we throw into the atmosphere, and of course by the capacity for explosive disintegration that has come with the mastery of the atomic nucleus.

Later we will look into some of these problems when we turn to the immediate issues confronting the United States. But at this point, while we are studying the general effects of man's gradually increasing technological powers, we leave aside these very large problems to focus on the ways in which technology has silently affected our economic system. Let us look into some of these effects.

urbanization The first has been a *vast increase in the degree of urbanization of society*. To an extraordinary extent (as we shall see in our next chapters), technology has enhanced the ability of the farmer to support the nonfarmer. As a result, society has more and more taken on the aspects and problems of the city rather than the country. In 1790, only 24 towns and cities in all of the United States had a population of more than 2,500, and together they accounted for only 6 percent of the total population. By 1860, the 392 biggest cities held 20 percent of the population; thirty years later, over three-quarters of the nation's people lived in 323 great "standard or consolidated metropolitan areas," and the belt from Boston to Washington was in fact, if not in government, one vast sprawling "city." Industrial technology has literally refashioned the human environment, bringing with it all the gains—and all the terrible problems—of city life on a mass scale.

---

* I believe it was the economist Kenneth Boulding who suggested that if the United States were to be visited by intelligent beings from another part of the universe, their initial impression would probably be that the dominant form of life here consists of creatures with hard shells and soft pulpy insides, who are propelled by wheels, although the creatures are capable of sluggish motion on their own when not encased in their natural exoskeletons.

inter-
dependence   Second, *the steady growth of industrial technology has radically less-ened the degree of economic independence of the average citizen.* In our opening chapter, we noted the extreme vulnerability of the "unsupported" inhabitants of a modern society, dependent on the work of a thousand others to sustain their own existence. This, too, we can now trace to the effect of the continuing industrial revolution. Technology has not only moved people off the soil and into the city, but has vastly increased the specialized nature of work. Unlike the man of all trades of the early nineteenth century—the farmers who could perform so many of their necessary tasks themselves—the typical factory worker or office worker is trained and employed to do only one small part of a social operation that now achieves staggering complexity. Technology has vastly increased the degree of economic interdependence of the modern community and has made the solution of the economic problem hinge on the smooth coordination of an ever-widening network of delicately connected activities.

work
and its
discontents   Third, *the expansion of industrial technology has radically altered the character of work.* For the greater part of human history, work was a strenuous physical activity, largely carried on alone or in small groups in the open air, requiring considerable dexterity to match human strength to the infinite variations of the natural environment, and culminating in an end product as unambiguously identifiable as the grain in the field or the cloth on a loom.

   The Industrial Revolution profoundly altered these attributes of work. Work now consisted more and more of repetitive movements that, however exhausting after a full day, rarely involved more than a fraction of a person's full muscular ability. In place of the judgments and aptitudes required to meet the variations of nature, it demanded only the ability to repeat a single task adapted to a changeless work surface. No longer alone in nature, workers performed their jobs in vast sheds with regiments like themselves. And most wrenching of all, in place of "their" product, what they saw emerging from the factory was an object in which they could no longer locate, much less appreciate, their own contribution.

I work on a small conveyor which goes around in a circle. We call it a "merry-go-round." I make up zigzag springs for front seats. Every couple of feet on the conveyor there is a form for the pieces that make up the seat springs. As the form goes by me, I clip several pieces together, using a clip gun. I then put the pieces on the form, and it goes around to where other men clip more pieces together. . . . The only operation I do is work the clip gun. It takes just a couple of seconds to shoot six or eight clips into the spring and I do it as I walk a few steps. Then I start right over again. . . .[3]

[3] Charles R. Walker and Robert H. Guest, *The Man on the Assembly Line* (Cambridge: Harvard University Press, 1952), p. 46.

A worker in an automobile plant in the early 1950s described his job in these terms. Since then, there have been efforts to lessen the routine on auto assembly lines, but the description would not be much different today in many mass-production factories.

alienation   What has been the effect on workers of this basic alteration in the pace and pattern of labor? Looking around us at factories (and offices), we find that industrial technology often subjects people to stultifying and enervating discipline—that it makes work a singularly joyless and meaningless process to which they must subordinate their individual personalities. This is an aspect of technology that has disturbed observers since Adam Smith commented, 200 years ago, that a person who endlessly performed the same task "generally becomes as stupid and ignorant as it is possible for a human creature to become."[4] Later, Karl Marx wrote with passion and perception about the terrible effects of industrial capitalism in divorcing the worker from the fruits of his own toil; and since Marx, writers in capitalist as well as in socialist nations have articulated the feelings of impotence and estrangement experienced in a vast, mechanized environment.

TABLE 5-1 Occupational Distribution of the Employed Labor Force
1900–1991

	Percentage of labor force	
	1900	1991
Managerial and professional		
Professional and technical workers	4.1	16.6
Managers and administrators	5.9	12.5
White-collar		
Clerical workers	3.1	15.6
Sales workers	4.8	11.8
Blue-collar		
Skilled workers and foremen	10.3	11.3
Semiskilled workers	12.8	10.7
Unskilled workers	12.4	4.2
Household and other service workers	8.9	13.9
Farm		
Farmers and farm managers	20.0	3.4
Farm laborers	17.6	

SOURCE: 1900 figures calculated from *Historical Statistics of the United States*, Series D 72-122, p. 74; 1991 figures from *Employment and Earnings*, Bureau of Labor Statistics, September 1991 (data regrouped).

[4] *The Wealth of Nations* (New York: Modern Library, 1937), p. 734.

Is industrial technology, in fact, the cause of a pervasive "alienation" of human beings? The question is not easy to answer. People today are certainly as much the servants as the masters of their industrial apparatus. Yet we must guard against too easy an indictment of technology as the great dehumanizer. Let us not forget the terrible toll on the human personality of preindustrial labor, with its exhausted peasants and brutalized common laborers. Further, let us bear in mind that if the repressive and disciplinary aspects of technology predominate in our time, it may be because we are still only in the inception of the advanced technological history of humankind, and because technology is pressed into the service of profit, not human enrichment. In a longer perspective, this same mechanization of work holds forth the promise of an eventual emancipation of humanity, as machinery gradually takes over the onerous, monotonous tasks of society.

distribution of the labor force

We will return again to some of these problems of technology, as well as to its larger environmental impact. But meanwhile we must pay heed to another important aspect of the technological invasion. This is the striking alteration it has brought about in the tasks of social provisioning. It is obvious that the inventory of work skills that we possessed in 1800 would never suffice to operate the social machine of almost 200 years later. But even in the much shorter span since 1900, the required distribution of skills has significantly changed, as can be seen in Table 5-1.

Note how different is our profile of occupations today from those of the not-so-distant past. We have already commented on the sharp drop in the number of people needed to feed the nation, but we can also see a shift within the blue-collar group from unskilled to skilled and semiskilled jobs as more people labor with capital equipment than with their hands. In addition, as the sharp increase in the number of managers and clerical workers indicates, a swifter and more complex production process requires ever more people to coordinate and oversee the actual making of goods. In 1899, there was one nonproduction worker for every thirteen production workers in manufacturing; by the late 1980s, there was about one for every two.

THE RISE OF UNIONISM

Before we leave this discussion of the general impact of technology on economic society, we must look briefly into one last attribute of industrialism—the rise of labor unions within the market system during the late nineteenth and early twentieth centuries.

Actually, we can trace the origins of trade unionism back to early Roman times, when some workers organized semifraternal orders. But unionism as an important social institution obviously had to await the creation of a free labor force, and that, as we know, did not occur until relatively recent times. Even after labor had been pried loose from its feudal status and thrown upon the market for survival, unionism still awaited as a final stimulus the advent of an industrial technology that brought masses of people together in the insecure and impersonal environment of the factory.

Thus, all through the nineteenth century, as industrial technology entered nation after nation, we also find a strong impetus toward union organization. In nearly every nation, it should also be noted, these movements were met at first with determined and often ferocious resistance: Under the so-called Conspiracy Doctrine and the Combination Laws (1800) of Great Britain, for example, thousands of workers were punished for combining to raise wages—although in no case were employers punished for combining to lower them. Indeed, for a quarter of a century, British unionists were treated as rebels or common criminals, as they also were, for that matter, in France and Germany.

In America, trade union progress was also slow. The strong American belief in "rugged individualism"—a belief shared by many workers as well as by their bosses—a reliance on docile immigrant labor in the heavy industries, and the use of every legal and many illegal weapons on the part of employers kept American unionism largely limited to the skilled crafts long after the union movement had finally gained acceptance and some measure of power in Europe.

During the 1920s, for example, union membership *dropped* some 30 percent, partly as a result of an all-out attack by the National Association of Manufacturers, partly as a consequence of labor's own indifference to unionism. By 1929, less than one nonagricultural worker in five belonged to a union, and not a single industrial union of consequence had yet organized a mass-production industry.*

industrial unionism   The coming of industrial unionism in America was compressed into a few dramatic years in the mid-1930s. Then, under the combined impetus of the New Deal and the newly formed Congress of Industrial Organizations (CIO), the long-pent-up pressures of labor frustration finally broke the barriers of corporate resistance. In a series of dramatic strikes,

---

* Craft unions seek to organize the workers of a particular skill (regardless of where they work) into one union; examples are the Newspaper Guild and the carpenters' or the plumbers' unions. Industrial unions, on the other hand, join all the members of a given industry (regardless of their craft or level of skill); examples are the Steelworkers and the United Auto Workers.

the CIO won contracts from Ford and General Motors, United States Steel and Bethlehem Steel, all bastions of antilabor resistance. It was not the terms of the contracts that mattered so much as the fact that in signing any contract at all, the companies *for the first time* recognized the unions as bargaining agents for their workers regarding wages, hours, and working conditions.

As a result, unionism boomed. By 1940, the number of the unionized had jumped from less than 4 million to over 8 million, and big-business resistance to unions was effectively finished.

It is difficult today to reconstruct that era, not so very long past, when Walter Reuther, the great organizer of the United Auto Workers, was thrown down a flight of concrete stairs and kicked by the hired strongmen of the Ford Motor Company, when coal miners carried rifles to fight the local police, or when strikers actually seized and occupied General Motors and Chrysler plants. The tumultuous history of this turning point in labor history has today given way to a much calmer era, in which tensions and conflicts continue to mark the relations of business and labor (as they always will in a market society), but the extreme attitudes and actions of the antilabor past already seem to be ancient history.

We cannot trace here the full story of American unionism (including the very important and checkered history of its efforts at self-government), but one point seems worth making before we return to our main narrative. It is that a high point in union membership seems to have been reached in the mid-1950s, when over a third of all nonagricultural workers in the private sector were members of unions—either AFL-CIO or independent. This percentage plummeted to less than 14 percent by 1990. Although this fall was offset by a considerable rise in local, state, and federal (public-sector) unions, the overall decline has been marked. Over the thirty years in question, the percentage of all American workers belonging to unions dropped from roughly a third to about a fifth, far below the percentages in other industrial nations.*

MASS PRODUCTION

Despite the recent American experience, there is no doubt that in general industrialization has been a powerful force for unionization. This interests us as another example of the indirect, often unexpected, ways in

---

* Examples: 98 percent of nonagricultural workers are unionized in Denmark; 52 percent in England; 42 percent in Germany; 35 percent in Switzerland; 29 percent in Japan. None of these countries shows the rapid decline in unionism we have observed in the United States. The reason seems to have been the aggressive (although not violent) antiunion campaign mounted by business during the Reagan administration. For a fascinating analysis of these trends, see the articles by Richard Freeman and Melvin Reder in the *Journal of Economic Perspectives*, Spring 1988.

which changes in the mode of production filter into other aspects of our social life. At this still early point in our studies, however, we must pursue further a more direct and immediate effect of technology. This is the development of a new method of industrial production first visible after the 1860s, although not fully realized until the turn of the twentieth century—*mass production*.

Allan Nevins described what mass-production techniques looked like in the early Ford assembly lines.

Just how were the main assembly lines and lines of component production and supply kept in harmony? For the chassis alone, from 1,000 to 4,000 pieces of each component had to be furnished each day at just the right point and right minute; a single failure, and the whole mechanism would come to a jarring standstill. . . . Superintendents had to know every hour just how many components were being produced and how many were in stock. Whenever danger of shortage appeared, the shortage chaser—a familiar figure in all automobile factories—flung himself into the breach. Counters and checkers reported to him. Verifying in person any ominous news, he mobilized the foreman concerned to repair deficiencies. Three times a day he made typed reports in manifold to the factory clearing-house, at the same time chalking on blackboards in the clearing-house office a statement of results in each factory-production department and each assembling department.[5]

Such systematizing in itself resulted in astonishing increases in productivity. With each operation analyzed and subdivided into its simplest components, with a steady stream of work passing before stationary men, with a relentless but manageable pace of work, the total time required to assemble a car dropped astonishingly. Within a single year, the time required to assemble a motor fell from 600 minutes to 226 minutes; to build a chassis, from 12 hours and 28 minutes to 1 hour and 33 minutes. A stopwatch man was told to observe a 3-minute assembly in which men assembled rods and piston, a simple operation. The job was divided into three jobs, and half the men turned out the same output as before.[6]

economies of large-scale production

But what interests us in the context of our study is not the technical achievements of mass production as much as its economic results: *Increases in productivity bring reductions in cost*. Even though the machinery needed for mass production is extremely expensive, output increases so fast that costs *per unit* of output drop dramatically.

Imagine, for instance, a small plant turning out 1,000 items a day with the labor of ten workers and a small amount of equipment. Suppose

[5] *Ford, the Times, the Man, the Company*, I, 507.
[6] *Ford*, pp. 504, 506.

each worker is paid $50, each item of material before manufacture costs 50¢, and the daily amount of "overhead"—that is, the daily share of costs such as rent, plant maintenance, office salaries, and wear and tear on equipment—comes to $500. Then our total daily cost of production is $1,500 ($500 of payroll, $500 of material costs, and $500 of overhead). Divided among 1,000 items of output, our cost per item is $1.50.

Now imagine that our product lends itself to mass-production techniques. Our payroll may then jump to $1,000 and, with our much larger plant and equipment, our daily overhead to $5,000. Nevertheless, mass production may have boosted output as much as 100 times. Then our total daily cost of production is $56,000 ($1,000 of payroll, $5,000 of overhead, and $50,000 of material costs). Divided among our 100,000 items of output, our cost per item has fallen to 56¢. Despite more than a thirty-fold rise in overall expense, our cost per unit has been almost cut to one-third.

This is not a far-fetched example of what economists call *the economies of large-scale production.* A glance at Table 5-2 shows how mass-production techniques did, in fact, boost output of Ford cars by more than 100 times while reducing their cost by seven-eighths.

Nor do the dynamics of the industrial process come to a halt with these formidable economies of large-scale production. For this technological achievement brings into the market system itself a new element of primary importance. That element is *size.*

It is not difficult to see why. Once a firm—by virtue of adroit management, improved product, advantages of location, or whatever other reason—steps out decisively in front of its competitors in size, *economies of large-scale production operate to push it out still further in front.* Bigger size usually means lower cost, at least for a young, expanding

TABLE 5-2

Year	Unit sales, Ford cars	Price of typical model (*touring*)
1907–1908	6,398	$2,800 (Model K)
1908–1909	10,607	850 ⎫
1909–1910	18,664	950 ⎪
1910–1911	34,528	780 ⎪
1911–1912	78,440	690 ⎪
1912–1913	168,304	600 ⎬ Model T
1913–1914	248,307	550 ⎪
1914–1915	221,805 (10 mos.)	490 ⎪
1915–1916	472,350	440 ⎪
1916–1917	730,041	360 ⎭

SOURCE: Compiled from Nevins, *Ford, the Times, the Man, the Company,* pp. 644, 646–47.

industry. Lower cost means bigger profits. Bigger profits mean the ability to grow to still larger size. Thus, the techniques of large-scale manufacturing bring about a situation threatening to alter the whole meaning of competition. From a mechanism that prevents any single firm from dominating the market, competition now becomes a force that may drive an ever-larger share of the market into the hands of the largest and most efficient producer.*

AGENTS OF INDUSTRIAL CHANGE

the great entrepreneurs We shall have much more to say about the economics of the drive to bigness when we study the evolution of the market system in Chapter 6. Yet it may be helpful if we look once again at the actual historic scene in which this internal growth took place. For the processes of economic change described in this chapter did not occur in a vacuum. They were brought about by a social "type" and a business milieu that powerfully accelerated and abetted the process of industrial enlargement, much as the New Men had speeded along the initial industrializing process in England in the late eighteenth century.

The agents of change during the late nineteenth century in America were very much the descendants of their industrial forebears a century earlier. Like Arkwright and Watt, many of the greatest American entrepreneurs were men of humble origin, endowed with an indomitable drive for business success. There was Carnegie in steel, Harriman in railroads, Rockefeller in oil, Frick in coke, Armour and Swift in meat packing, McCormick in agricultural machinery—to mention but a few. To be sure, the *typical* businessman was very different from these Horatio Alger stereotypes of the business hero. Economic historians, such as F. W. Taussig, looking back over the careers of the business leaders of the late nineteenth century, have discovered that the average entrepreneur was not a poor, industrious immigrant lad, but the son of well-circumstanced people often in business affairs themselves. Nor was the average businessman nearly so successful as a Carnegie or a Rockefeller.

captains of industry Yet in nearly every line of business, at least one "captain of industry" appeared who dominated the field by his personality and ability. Though few achieved their supreme degree of pecuniary success, the number who climbed into the "millionaire class" was impressive. In 1880, it was

* In an important book, *The Visible Hand: The Managerial Revolution in American Business* (Cambridge: Harvard University Press, 1977), Alfred D. Chandler looks into why some industries displayed a tendency toward the emergence of big business (such as steel), and others did not (such as furniture). The crucial elements, he shows, were a cost-cutting, mass-producing technology, which did not develop in all industries, and an equally important technology of mass distribution, also not available to every industry.

estimated that there were 100 millionaires in the country. By 1916, the number had grown to 40,000.

Interesting and significant differences distinguish these nineteenth-century business leaders from those of a century earlier. The American captains of industry were not typically men whose leadership rested on inventive or engineering skills. With the growth of large-scale production, the engineering functions became the province of salaried production experts, of second-echelon plant managers. What was required now was the master touch in guiding industrial strategy, in making or breaking alliances, choosing salients for advance, or overseeing the logistics of the whole operation. More and more, the great entrepreneurs were concerned with the strategy of finance, of competition, of sales, rather than with the cold techniques of production itself.

Then, too, we must make note of the entrepreneurial tactics and tone of the period. In a phrase that has stuck, Matthew Josephson once called the great men of business in this era "the robber barons." In many ways, they did indeed resemble the predatory lords of the medieval era. For example, in the 1860s, a small group of California entrepreneurs under the guiding hand of Collis Huntington performed the astonishing feat of building a railroad across the hitherto impassable Rockies and Sierras. Aware that Huntington and his associates would thereby have a monopolistic control of all rail traffic to California, Congress authorized the construction of three competing lines. But the legislators had not taken the measure of the wily pioneers. Before their own line was completed, they secretly bought the charter of one competitive line; and when the second proved somewhat harder to buy out, they simply built it out, recklessly flinging their lines into its territory until it, too, was forced to surrender. Thereafter it was no great trick to buy out the third, having first blocked it at a critical mountain pass. Only one competitive source of transportation remained: the Pacific Mail Steamship Company. Fortunately, this was owned by the obliging Jay Gould, a famous robber baron in his own right; and for the payment of a proper tribute, he agreed to eliminate San Francisco as a cargo port. There was now *no* way of bringing goods across the nation into southern California except those the Huntington group controlled. Counting the smaller lines and subsidiaries that passed into their grasp, *nineteen* rail systems, in all, came under their domain. It was not surprising that to the residents of California, the resulting unified system was known as "the Octopus" and that its average freight rate was the highest in the nation.

the omnipresent trust And it was not just the railroad industry that used economic power to create a monopoly position. In whiskey and in sugar, in tobacco and cattle feed, in wire nails, steel hoops, electrical appliances, tinplate, in matches and meat, there was an octopus similar to that which fastened itself on California. One commentator of the late 1890s pictured the American citizen as born to the profit of the Milk Trust and dying to that of the Coffin Trust.

If the robber barons milked the public as consumers (and to an even greater extent bilked them as stockholders), they also had no compunctions about cutting each other down to size. In the struggle for financial control of the Albany and Susquehanna Railroad, for instance, James Fisk and J. P. Morgan found themselves in the uncomfortable position of each owning a terminal at the end of a single line. Like their feudal prototypes, they resolved the controversy by combat, mounting locomotives at each end and running them full tilt into each other—after which the losers still did not give up, but retired, ripping up the line and tearing down trestles as they went. In similar spirit, the Huntington group that built the Central Pacific hired General David Colton to run a subsidiary enterprise for them, and the general wrote to his employers:

> I have learned one thing. We have got *no true* friends outside of us five. We cannot depend upon a human soul outside of ourselves, and hence we must all be good-natured, stick together, and keep to our own counsels.

Whereupon he proceeded to swindle his friends out of several millions.

With this buccaneering went as well another identifying mark of the times: what the economist Thorstein Veblen was to call Conspicuous Consumption. One repentant member of the Gilded Age recalled in his memoirs parties at which cigarettes were wrapped in money for the sheer pleasure of inhaling wealth; a dog that was presented with a $15,000 diamond collar; an infant, resting in a $10,000 cradle, attended by four doctors who posted regular bulletins on the baby's (excellent) health; the parade of fabulous chateaux stuffed with fabulous and not-so-fabulous works of art on New York's Fifth Avenue; and the collection of impecunious European royalty as sons-in-law of the rich.

The age was a rollicking, sometimes cruel, but always dynamic one. Yet our task here is not to recount its colorful social history as much as to understand its deeper economic consequences. It is impossible to consider the period with which we have been concerned without taking into account the social type of the robber baron and the milieu in which he operated. Bold, aggressive, acquisitive, competitive, the great entrepreneur was the natural agent to speed along the process for which the technology of the day prepared the way. But as yet we have only begun to sketch out the changes wrought by the joint impact of strong men and ever-more-complex machinery. Hitherto we have mainly looked at the direct technical effects of mass production. Now we must investigate its economic effects.

KEY CONCEPTS AND KEY WORDS

Technical progress

1. The Industrial Revolution brought not one but *successive waves of technical progress* and economic advance.

2. In studying the impact of these industrial discoveries, we must broaden our lens to look beyond the effect on productivity alone (although that was no doubt the single most important result). Industrialization brought:

Urbanization

- A vast increase in *urbanization.*
- A cumulative rise in the degree of *economic interdependence* of individuals within society.

Alienation

- A new climate for and character of work, including the disturbing problems of *monotonous industrial work* (alienation).
- A *sweeping redistribution of occupations* away from unskilled toward semiskilled, technical, and managerial labor.

Unions

- The rise of *unionism.*

Mass production

Economies of scale

3. The new technology brought as well a change in the character of both production and competition. Production became more and more a process of highly integrated subassemblies, making possible the *mass production* of goods. The large amounts of capital required for mass production led to very great *economies of scale.*

Destructive competition

4. With the advent of mass production, *the nature of competition also changed into a destructive force.* Economies of scale led to situations in which a leading firm could undersell all competitors and thus dominate a market.

"Robber barons"

5. The dynamic potential of the new technology was given further impetus by the *aggressive "robber baron" era* of business leadership.

QUESTIONS

1. Describe the social, as well as economic, repercussions of the following inventions: the typewriter, the jet airplane, television, penicillin. Which do you think is greater in each case—the social or the economic impact?

2. The philosopher Karl Jaspers has claimed that modern technology brings an "immense joylessness." Do you agree? Is factory work unpleasant, to your mind? office work, in a very large organization such as an insurance company? Do you think the nature of industrial work can be basically changed?

3. White-collar jobs have always proved harder to unionize than so-called blue-collar (factory-floor) jobs. Why do you think this is so? Do you think it might change?

4. Suppose that you have a business in which you hire five workers, to whom you pay $4 an hour; suppose further that you have overhead costs of $100

a day and that you pay $1 in materials cost for each item that your business manufactures. Assuming that you keep all five workers, what is your average cost per unit of output if your plant turns out 10 items per eight-hour day? 100 items? 1,000?

5. Which is more economical, a plant with a payroll of $400 a week, with $100 of overhead a week, and with an output of 100 units per week, or a plant with a payroll of $80,000 a week, an overhead of $100,000 a week, and an output of 50,000 units per week?

6. How do you explain economies of large-scale production? Why do certain businesses, such as cigarette manufacture, seem to enjoy them, whereas other businesses, such as barbering, do not?

6 THE CHANGE IN MARKET STRUCTURE

So far we have investigated the impact of the new technology of mass production mainly insofar as it exerted its pervasive influence on socio-economic life, and we have only glanced at its effects on the workings of the market system proper. Now we must look more carefully into this latter problem. For under the joint impetus of the drive of bold entrepreneurs and the self-feeding tendencies of economies of large-scale production, dramatic changes began to appear in many sectors of the economy by the end of the nineteenth century. A system originally characterized by large numbers of small enterprises was starting to give way to one in which production was increasingly concentrated in the hands of a relatively few, very big and very powerful business units.

By 1900, for example, the number of textile mills, although still large, had dropped by a third from the 1880s; over the same period, the number of manufacturers of agricultural implements had fallen by 60 percent, and the number of leather manufacturers by three-quarters. In the locomotive industry, two companies ruled the roost in 1900, contrasted with nineteen in 1860. The biscuit and cracker industry changed from a scatter of small companies to a market in which one producer had 90 percent of the industry's capacity by the turn of the century. Meanwhile, in steel, there was the colossal US Steel Corporation, which alone turned out over half the steel production of the nation. In oil, the Standard Oil Company tied up between 80 to 90 percent of the nation's output. In tobacco, the American Tobacco Company controlled 75 percent of the output of cigarettes and 25 percent of cigars. Similar control rested with the American Sugar Company, the American Smelting and Refining Company, the United Shoe Machinery Company, and dozens more.

From an overall view, the change was even more impressive. In the early 1800s, according to the calculations of Myron W. Watkins, no single plant controlled as much as 10 percent of the output of a manufacturing industry. By 1904, 78 enterprises controlled over half the output of their industries, 57 controlled 60 percent or more, and 28 controlled 80 percent or more. From industry to industry, this degree of "concentration" varied—from no significant concentration at all in printing and publishing, for instance, to the highly concentrated market structure of industries like copper or rubber. But there was no mistaking the overall change. In 1896, railroads excepted, there were not a dozen $10 million companies in the nation. By 1904, there were over 300 of them, with a combined capitalization of over $7 billion. Together, these giants controlled more than two-fifths of the industrial capital of the nation and affected four-fifths of its important industries.[1]

Clearly, something akin to a major revolution in market structure had taken place. Let us examine more closely the course of events that led up to it.

THE RISE OF BIG BUSINESS

change in competition

The initial impact of the trend to big business was an unexpected one. Rather than diminishing the degree of competitiveness of the market structure, it extended and intensified it. In the largely agricultural, handicraft, and small-factory economy of the early nineteenth century, "the market" consisted mainly of small, localized markets, each insulated from the next by the high cost of transportation and each supplied by local producers who had neither the means nor the motivation to invade the market on anything resembling a national scale.

The rise of mass production radically changed this fragmented market structure and, with it, the type of competition within the market. As canals and railroads opened the country and as new manufacturing techniques vastly increased output, the parochial quality of the market system changed. More and more, one unified and interconnected market bound together the entire nation, and the petty semimonopolies of local suppliers were invaded by products from large factories in distant cities.

Quickly, a second development followed. As the new production techniques gained momentum, aggressive businessmen typically not only built, but overbuilt. "As confident entrepreneurs raced to take advantage of every ephemeral rise in prices, of every advance in tariff schedules, of every new market opened by the railroads and puffed up immigration," write Thomas Cochran and William Miller in a history of these industrializing times, "they recklessly expanded and mechanized their plants, each seeking the greatest share of the new melon."[2]

[1] John Moody, *The Truth about Trusts* (Chicago: Moody, 1904). See also Ralph Nelson, *Merger Movements in American Industry, 1895–1956* (Princeton, N.J.: National Bureau of Economic Research, 1959).

[2] *The Age of Enterprise*, rev. ed. (New York: Harper, Torchbooks, 1961), p. 139.

The result was a phenomenal burst in output but, simultaneously, a serious change in the nature of competition. Competition now became not only more extensive, but more *expensive.* As the size of the plant and the complexity of equipment grew, so did the "fixed charges" of a business enterprise—the interest on borrowed capital, the depreciation of capital assets, the cost of administrative staff, the rent of land, and "overhead" generally. By the 1880s, for example, fixed costs averaged *two-thirds* of the total cost of railroad operation. These costs tended to remain fairly constant, regardless of whether sales were good or bad. Unlike the payment of wages to a working force, which dropped when workers were fired, there was no easy way to cut down the steady drain of payments for these fixed expenditures. The result was that the bigger the business, the more vulnerable was its economic health when competition cut into its sales.

The ebullience of the age, plus the steady growth of a technology that required massive investments, made competition increasingly drastic. As growing giant businesses locked horns, railroad against railroad, steel mill against steel mill, each sought to assure the coverage of its fixed expenses by gaining for itself as much of the market as it could. The outcome was the emergence of "cutthroat competition" among massive producers, replacing the more restricted, local competition of the small-business, small-market world. In 1869, for example, the New York–Chicago railway freight rate on a hundredweight of grain crashed from $1.80 on February 4 to 40¢ twenty days later, climbed back to $1.88 in July, and then plummeted to 25¢ in August when another "war" broke out. In the oil fields, the coal fields, among the steel and copper producers, similar price wars repeatedly occurred as producers sought to capture the markets they needed to achieve a profitable level of production. All this was unquestionably favorable to the consumer, as indeed competitive situations always are, but it threatened literal bankruptcy for the competing enterprises themselves—and furthermore, bankruptcy on a multimillion-dollar scale.

limitation of competition   In these circumstances, it is not difficult to understand the next phase of economic development. The giants decided not to compete.

But how were they to avoid competition? Since common law invalidated any contract binding a competitor to fixed prices or production schedules, there seemed no alternative but voluntary cooperation: trade associations, "gentleman's agreements" or "pools," informal treaties to divide the market. By the 1800s, there were a cordage pool and a whiskey pool, a coal pool, a salt pool, and endless rail pools, all calculated to relieve the individual producers from the mutually suicidal game of all-out competition. But to little avail. The division of the market worked well during good times; but when bad times approached, the pools broke down. As sales fell, the temptation to cut prices was irresistible, and thus began again the old, ruinous game of competition.

The robber-baron ethics of the day contributed to the difficulties. "A starving man will usually get bread if it is to be had," said James J. Hill, a great railway magnate, "and a starving railway will not maintain rates."[3] Typically, at a meeting of railroad heads called to agree upon a common freight schedule, the president of one road slipped out, during a brief recess, to wire the new rates to his road, so that it might be the first to undercut them. (By chance, his wire was intercepted, so that when the group next met, it was forced to recognize that even among thieves there is not always honor.)

trusts,
mergers, and
growth

During the 1880s, a more effective device for control became available. In 1879, Samuel Dodd, lawyer for the new Standard Oil Company, had a brilliant idea for regulating the murderous competition that regularly wracked the oil industry. He devised the idea of a trust. Stockholders of companies that wished to join in the Standard Oil Trust were asked to surrender their actual shares to the board of directors of the new trust. Thereby they would give up working control over their companies, but in return they would get "trust certificates" that entitled them to the same share in the profits as their shares earned. In this way, the Standard Oil directors wielded control over all the associated companies, while the former stockholders shared fully in the profits.

Eventually, as we shall see, the trusts were declared to be illegal. But by that time, still more effective devices had been created. In 1888, the New Jersey legislature passed a law allowing a corporation chartered in the state to buy stock in another corporation. This was a privilege that had not previously been available to corporations chartered anywhere in the United States. The result was the rapid appearance of the corporate merger—the coming together of two corporations to form a new, bigger one. In manufacturing and mining alone, there were 43 mergers in 1895 (affecting $41 million worth of corporate assets); 26 mergers in 1896, 69 mergers in 1897. Then in 1898, there were 303—and finally in 1899, a climactic, 1,208 mergers combined some $2.26 billion in corporate assets.[4] A further great wave of mergers occurred in the 1920s. In all, from 1895 to 1929, some $20 billion in industrial corporate wealth was merged into larger units.*

---

[3] Cochran and Miller, *The Age of Enterprise*, p. 141.

[4] *Historical Statistics of the United States*, Series V, pp. 30–31.

* We must take a footnote to call attention to a development that deserves a chapter in itself. This is the importance of the *corporation*, as a marvelously adaptive legal form of organizing production, in spurring on the growth of the economy. Unlike the personal

Another effective means of limiting competition was the *holding company*. Having passed a law permitting its corporations to buy stock in one another, New Jersey now allowed its corporations to do business in any state. Thus the legal foundation was laid for a central corporation that could control subsidiary enterprises by the simple means of buying a controlling share of their stock. By 1911, when the Standard Oil combine was finally dissolved, Standard Oil of New Jersey had used this device to acquire direct control over seventy companies and indirect control over thirty more.

Yet we must not think that it was only the movement toward trustification and merger that brought about the emergence of the giant firm with its ability to limit—or eliminate—competition. *Equally, perhaps more, important was simply the process of internal growth.* Ford and General Motors, General Electric and AT&T, du Pont and Carnegie Steel (later to be the core of US Steel) grew essentially because their market was expanding and they were quick, able, efficient, and aggressive enough to grow faster than any of their competitors. All of them gobbled up some small businesses along the way, and most of them benefited from agreements not to compete. But their gradual emergence to a position of dominance within their industries was not, in the last analysis, attributable to these facts. It was, rather, the dynamism of their own business leadership, coupled with a production technique that made enormous size both possible and profitable.

threat of economic feudalism
For the first time, business size began to rival the size of government units. By the end of the nineteenth century, some business units were already considerably larger than the states in which they were located. Charles William Eliot pointed out in 1888 that a single railway with headquarters in Boston not only employed three times as many people as the entire government of the Commonwealth of Massachusetts, but enjoyed gross receipts nearly six times that of the state government that had created it. But by comparison with the findings of the Pujo Committee of the U.S. Senate, not quite twenty-five years later, the railway was rather small. The committee pointed out that the Morgan banking interests held 341 directorships in 112 corporations whose aggregate wealth exceeded by three times the value of *all* the real and personal property of New England. And not only was the process of trustification

---

proprietorship or partnership, the corporation existed quite independently of its owners, survived their deaths, and could enter into binding contracts in "its" own name. Further, by limiting the liability of its owners to the value of the stock they had bought, it protected a capitalist against limitless loss. Much has been written, quite rightly, about the abuses of corporations, but it is important to recognize how valuable was this ingenious legal innovation in encouraging the accumulation of capital and in creating the organizational means to supervise and direct that capital into production.

eating away at the competitive structure of the market, but the emergence of enormous financially controlled empires posed as well a political problem of ominous portent. As Woodrow Wilson declared, "If monopoly persists, monopoly will always sit at the helm of government. I do not expect to see monopoly restrain itself. If there are men in this country big enough to own the government of the United States, they are going to own it."[5]

rise of antitrust legislation   Not surprisingly, from many quarters the trend to bigness was vehemently opposed. From the 1880s on, a series of state laws strove to undo the trusts that squeezed their citizens. Louisiana sued the Cottonseed Oil Trust; New York, the Sugar Trust; Ohio, the Oil Trust—but to little avail. When one state, like New York, clamped down on its trusts, other states, seeking the revenue available from a change in corporate headquarters, virtually invited the trust to set up business there. When the Supreme Court ruled that corporations, as "persons," could not be deprived of property without "due process of law," state regulation became almost totally useless.

It was soon clear that if something further were to be done, the federal government would have to do it. "Congress alone can deal with the trusts," said Senator Sherman in 1890, "and if we are unwilling or unable, there will soon be a trust for every production and a master to fix the price for every necessity of life."[6]

The result was the Sherman Anti-Trust Act, which, on its surface, was an effective remedy for the problem. "Every contract, combination . . . or conspiracy, in restraint of trade" was declared to be illegal. Violators were subject to heavy fines and jail sentences, and triple damages could be obtained by persons who proved economic injury because of unfair price rigging.

Indeed, under the Sherman Act a number of trusts were prosecuted; and in a famous action in 1911, the great Standard Oil Trust was ordered dissolved. Yet, despite the breakup of a few trusts, the act was singularly weak. Fines for violations were too small to be effective, and in any case, few were levied: not until Franklin Roosevelt's time would the Antitrust Division of the Department of Justice have as much as a million dollars with which to investigate and control the affairs of a multibillion-dollar economy. In fact, during the first fifty years of its existence, only 252 criminal actions were instituted under the Sherman law. And then, too, the prevailing judicial opinion of the 1890s and early 1900s was not much in sympathy with the act. The Supreme Court early dealt it a severe blow by finding, in the American Sugar Refining case, that manufacturing was

---

[5] Richard Hofstadter, *The Age of Reform* (New York: Knopf, 1955), p. 231.
[6] Cochran and Miller, *The Age of Enterprise*, p. 171.

not "commerce," and therefore the American Sugar Refining Company, which had bought controlling stock interests in its four largest competitors, was not to be considered as acting "in restraint of trade." It is not surprising that the concentration of business was hardly slowed in such a climate of opinion. As a humorist of the times put it, "What looks like a stone wall to a layman is a triumphal arch to a corporation lawyer."

These weaknesses led to further acts in 1914: primarily, the Clayton Anti-Trust Act, prohibiting specific kinds of price discrimination and mergers by the acquisition of stock in competing corporations; and the Federal Trade Commission, which sought to define and prevent "unfair" business practices. As we shall see later, these acts were not without their effect. Yet, undermining the entire antitrust movement was one critical and vitiating fact. The purpose of antitrust was essentially to restore competitive conditions to markets that were in danger of becoming monopolized by giant firms. Against this tendency, antitrust legislation could pose a deterrent only insofar as the monopolization process resulted from the outright *combination* of erstwhile competitors. Against a much more fundamental condition—the ability of large businesses to enjoy decisive advantages over small businesses in finance, merchandising, and research—it could offer no remedy. While antitrust effort concentrated its fire against collusion or amalgamation, it was powerless against the fact of spontaneous internal growth.

the Berle and Means study

And therefore growth continued. Through most of the first quarter of the twentieth century, the biggest corporations not only grew, but grew much *faster* than their smaller competitors. As Adolf Berle and Gardiner Means pointed out in a famous study in 1932, between 1909 and 1928, the 200 largest nonfinancial corporations increased their gross assets over 40 percent more rapidly than all nonfinancial corporations.[7] Looking into the future, Berle and Means concluded:

Just what does this rapid growth of the big companies promise for the future? Let us project the trend of the growth of recent years. If the wealth of the large corporations and that of all corporations should each continue to increase for the next twenty years at its average annual rate for the twenty years from 1909 to 1929, 70 percent of all corporate activity would be carried on by two hundred corporations in 1950. If the more rapid rates of growth from 1924 to 1929 were maintained for the next twenty years, 85 percent of corporate wealth would be held by two hundred huge units. . . . If the indicated growth of the large corporations and of the national wealth were to be effective from now until 1950, half of the national wealth would be under the control of big companies at the end of that period.[8]

---

[7] *The Modern Corporation and Private Property* (New York: Macmillan, 1948), p. 36.
[8] *The Modern Corporation and Private Property*, pp. 40–41.

Indeed, warned the authors, if the trend of the past continued un-checked, it was predictable that in 360 years, all the corporate wealth in the nation would have become fused into one gigantic enterprise, which would then have an expected life span equal to that of the Roman Empire.

BIG BUSINESS TODAY

Has the Berle and Means projection come true? The question brings to a climax our long survey of the changing market structure. We have been concerned with gathering up the various forces that created and shaped the market as a great system of economic control. Now we must see what the outcome of that process has been.

the world of small business

Let us begin by looking at the market system in the United States today. Immediately, we notice one thing: There is not one market system in America, but two. One of them, with which we are all familiar at first hand, consists of the millions of small enterprises that make up the large stratum of the population known as "small-business men." Here are the stores we pass every day on the avenues, the columns of names in the yellow pages of the phone books.

In the late 1980s, there were roughly 19 million business enter-prises in America, counting every firm from the smallest newsstand, through all the farms—2.1 million of them—to the biggest enterprises in the nation, such as General Motors or Exxon. Of these 19 million, we can designate 14 million as "small." This takes in 10.5 million proprietor-ships with annual receipts of less than $50,000, a million partnerships with receipts of $100,000 or less, and 2.5 million corporations that do a half million a year or less.[9]

Thus, in terms of sales (or assets), little business is little indeed. Yet, by virtue of their numbers, the small businesses of America are by no means unimportant in the national economic picture. Small business (defined as having fewer than 20 employees) collectively employs roughly a quarter of the American labor force. This compares with slightly over one-third of the labor force that works for the "not-for-profit" sector—state, local, and federal governments, hospitals, social-service agencies, clubs, etc.—and with the 13 percent that works for big business (over 1,000 employees).* Millions of small entrepreneurs constitute the

---

[9] *Statistical Abstract of the United States*, 1991, p. 525. The latest figures are for 1987, but the numbers grow slowly, and the percentages change even more slowly.

* The figures don't add to 100 percent. The difference (29 percent) is accounted for by employers who are bigger than "small" and smaller than "big."

very core of the American "middle class," and thus give a characteristic small-business view to much of American political and social life.

the world of
big business

At the other end of the scale are the enterprises that can be called "big." There are no proprietorships or partnerships among them; the world of big business is strictly corporate. Thus even though only one firm in seven is a corporation, corporations as a whole do about six times as much business as all the rest of the business world put together. But within the corporate world there is a sharp division between the small and big ends of the scale. Only one corporation in six does more than $1 million in sales, but these companies—505,000 of them—account for 92 percent of all corporate sales.

Yet even this description of the world of "big" corporations does not reveal the concentration of economic power in a tiny number of gigantic enterprises at the extreme end of the scale. For here, in a few hundred companies, is an economy within an economy—a system unto itself, controlling a third of all the tangible wealth in the nation.[10] This very small core of corporations, numbering about 600 firms, accounts for 84 percent of all industrial sales; and within that core is an inner core that by itself produces the main flow of industrial production on which the economy rests.

Table 6-1 gives us a first overview of the strategic position of the giant corporation within various divisions of the economy.

TABLE 6-1 Giant Corporations

RELATIVE SHARES OF LARGE CORPORATIONS IN VARIOUS SECTORS, 1987

	All corporations		Corporations with assets of $250 million or more	
Sector	Number	Total assets ($ billion)	Number	Percentage of assets in that sector
Mining	42,050	220.1	71	72.6
Manufacturing	294,211	3,111.7	922	82.8
Transportation, communication, utilities	147,893	1,352.5	324	90.6
Finance, insurance, real estate	521,136	8,732.3	2,951	85.1
Wholesale and retail trade	971,758	1,177.7	342	47.9

SOURCE: *Statistical Abstract of the United States*, 1991, pp. 530–31.

[10] *Statistical Abstract of the United States*, 1991, p. 526.

The table speaks for itself. Note that the giant corporation is much more dominant in some sectors, such as transportation and communication, than in others, such as retail and wholesale trade. The contrasts of size, however, stand out particularly in the latter sector, where we find well over three-quarters of a million corporate enterprises (note that we are not even counting the millions of proprietorships and partnerships), but where 200-odd giant companies, such as Sears Roebuck, A&P, Safeway, and others, nonetheless control over one-third of the total assets.

mergers   These figures do not yet give us a sense of the recent movement toward corporate concentration. The 1950s and 1960s saw a burst of merger activity comparable to the great merger movement of the late nineteenth century. Between 1951 and 1960, one-fifth of the top 1,000 corporations disappeared—absorbed within the remaining four-fifths. As a result of this and other growth, by 1971, the 100 largest manufacturing corporations owned 49.3 percent of the assets of all manufacturing corporations—*a larger percentage than the top 200 corporations had held in 1948!*

Moreover, the pace of this centralizing activity quickened all through the 1960s. Between 1963 and 1966, the value of assets acquired by the big mining and manufacturing companies averaged $4 billion to $5 billion a year. This rose to $10 billion in 1967 and to $15 billion in 1968, and then exploded in a phenomenal burst of activity in the 1980s, when companies spent almost a trillion dollars to acquire other corporations. In 1984 alone, 2,999 "big" mergers took place, involving $122 billion in assets. The number in 1985 was even larger, with at least five mergers (such as the $6.4 billion purchase of RCA by General Electric) larger than the total of *all* mergers in any year prior to 1967. Even the great stock market crash of October 1987 only put a momentary halt to merger activity. By the end of the decade, the value of the average merger had reached $67 billion, more than triple that of 1980.

behind the   Why the merger mania of the 1980s? Two principal factors underlie the
merger   great merger-and-acquisition boom of that decade. The first was eco-
movement   nomic. Twenty years of inflation had acted to raise the value of the plant and equipment that constituted the real assets of corporations, while serving to depress the general buoyancy of the stock market. As a result, many opportunities arose for aggressive-minded companies to buy out others (often with borrowed money) in order to acquire their assets for less than their full worth.

Equally important was a marked change in political attitudes. The Reagan administration looked approvingly on a merger movement that earlier administrations would have regarded with alarm. This was partly because the Reagan government generally favored permitting businesses to act freely in their own self-interest, and partly because it perceived in the merger movement a means for creating strong "survivors" *Survival Darwinist* who would be capable of better defending American business interests in the steadily worsening battle with foreign business.

We will come back to some of these matters in due course. But meanwhile a question may well have occurred to many readers. Did not the merger movement confirm the worst fears of Berle and Means? In *The Modern Corporation and Private Property* (p. 46), they wrote, "a society in which production is governed by blind market forces is being replaced by one in which production is carried on under the ultimate control of a handful of individuals." In the light of our historical study, we can rephrase that conclusion very simply. It means that the market as the basic control mechanism within capitalism is about to be replaced by another system, akin to a new economic feudalism. Is that the conclusion to which the statistics on corporate size now force us?

*con-
glomerates
and the
marketplace*
The answer is not a simple one. There is no question that a massive concentration of corporate power exists in America and that the degree of concentration within business as a whole is increasing. At the same time, rather surprisingly, the degree of concentration in the *marketplaces* of the economy does not seem to be getting significantly worse.

How can that seemingly contradictory state of affairs exist? How can corporations be getting bigger and not be increasingly monopolistic? The answer is that the merger wave of the last decades took place largely by the rise of so-called *conglomerates*—corporations that have grown by merging with other corporations not *within* a given market but in a *different* market. Consider the case of International Telephone & Telegraph. Originally a much smaller company wholly engaged in running foreign communications systems, ITT determined in 1961 to embark on a major acquisition and diversification program. During the next seven years, it acquired fifty-two domestic and fifty-five foreign companies with combined assets of $1.5 billion. In 1969 alone, the directors approved an additional twenty-two domestic and eleven foreign acquisitions. As a result, by 1973, ITT had jumped from thirty-fourth to ninth in industrial size, with sales and assets of $10 billion each and 438,000 employees— the third largest private employer in the world. More important, whereas it had once been a "one-product" company, selling and operating telecommunications systems, by the 1970s, ITT rented cars (Avis), operated motels and hotels (Sheraton), built homes (Levitt), baked bread (Continental), sold insurance, produced glass, made consumer loans, managed a mutual fund, and processed data—among other things.

We do not yet know the long-term consequences of the rise of such giant, diversified companies. Many of them have been put together more with an eye to realizing the profits that could be had from exchanges of shares than with any careful consideration of operating efficiencies, which accounts for the fact that a number of conglomerates have already come unglued. Others may indeed prove to be efficient combinations of diverse activities that will enjoy the advantages of access to a central pool of capital and a topflight supermanagement. Or, having made the leap, a conglomerate may simply struggle to hold onto its place: ITT, for example, was down to the 11th biggest corporation within four years of reaching its 1973 peak; and by 1990 had fallen to 324th in asset size!

stability of market shares

But as matters now stand, it seems unlikely that the conglomerates will be adding to their size by buying up *competitors*. Hence, it is likely that the structure of the individual markets in which they operate will show no more change than they have in the past. And here, in the critical area of the marketplace, we discover a truly surprising long-run stability. *For more than three-quarters of a century now, there has been no substantial increase in monopoly in the nation's markets, considered as a whole.* Going back to 1901, we find some industries—tobacco, chemicals, stone, clay and glass, transportation equipment—where industrial concentration has risen; but in others, no less important—textiles, pulp and paper, petroleum and coal products, rubber, machinery—concentration has fallen since 1901.

The same conclusion holds for more recent years. If we take the four largest companies in any industry and compare the value of their total shipments to the value of all shipments in the industry, we find a similar mixed trend over the years between 1960 and 1982. In the automobile industry, for example, there was a big shakeout following World War II, when a number of smaller manufacturers, like Studebaker and Packard, disappeared, and the top three increased their share of the market to 92 percent. Thereafter, their share of *domestic* output remained steady, but the big three as a whole were forced to give up over a quarter of the market to foreign intruders. In many other industries, the movement toward concentration has been either negligible or has actually declined. The top four companies were the source of 72 percent of all shipments of soaps and detergents in 1963, but only 60 percent in 1982; the top four electronic computer manufacturers shipped two-thirds of the industry's output in 1967, but only 43 percent fifteen years later.[11]

the debt problem

As we enter the 1990s, the trend toward the concentration of total assets seems to have slowed down or stopped. In its place, another problem has

[11] *Statistical Abstract of the United States*, 1981, pp. 793, 794.; 1988, p. 707.

come to the fore. The merger mania of the 1980s resulted in an enormous rise in corporate debt, as the acquiring corporations bought up the assets of other corporations by floating high-risk bonds—so-called "junk bonds"—to raise the cash needed for their multibillion dollar transactions. With this came a vast increase in corporate indebtedness, which in turn brought a corresponding rise in fixed costs. Unlike dividends, which can be cut when profits sag, interest must be paid under all conditions. Hence one end result of the merger mania has been a considerable *financial* weakening of corporate America. Whether there will be an offsetting gain in operating efficiency we will have to wait to see.

THE ECONOMIC IMPACT OF BIG BUSINESS

Now we must stand back a pace and once again look at the operation of the market system as a whole, seeking an answer to the questions we posed at the outset. What is the consequence of the giant corporation for American society as a whole? What are its effects on the operation of a market economy?

The second question is easier to cope with than the first. We will remember that a distinguishing feature of the market system was that the *power of control was vested in the consumer.* There were two aspects of this power. First, a market society enabled households to have the ultimate decision as to the allocation of the factors of production. *Their* desires arranged the productive pattern of society, not the desires of society's rulers, its keepers of traditions, or its producers. Second, the market society assured consumers that they would be able to buy the output of society at the lowest price compatible with a continued flow of production. While producers might wish to make exorbitant profits from consumers, they would be prevented from doing so by the pressure of competition from other producers.

the challenge to consumer sovereignty

Do consumers still exercise this economic sovereignty? In a general sense, they do. If the consumer does not choose to buy the goods produced by giant concerns, those concerns have no choice but to curtail the production of those goods. For example, in the mid-1950s, the Ford Motor Company poured nearly a quarter of a billion dollars into the production of a new car, the Edsel. The car was rejected by consumers, and after a few years its production was quietly discontinued. Familiar, too, is the effect of a swing in consumer tastes. From the mid-1950s on, imports of foreign sports and small cars rose steadily—from 57,000 vehicles in 1955 to 5 million cars and trucks in 1989. With the exception of American Motors, the major car manufacturers insisted that the trend to compacts was only a fad and that Americans "wanted" bigger cars.

But there was no brooking the contrary opinion of consumers themselves. Eventually, all the major manufacturers were *forced* into the production of small cars, and foreign manufacturers, who had specialized in small cars, increased their share of the U.S. market from a mere 6 percent in the mid-1960s to 25 percent by the end of the 1980s.

What, then, is the difference between this state of affairs and that of the "ideal" market system? One major difference lies in the fact that the great corporations today do not merely "fill" the wants of consumers. They themselves help to *create* these wants by massive efforts to interest the public in buying the products they manufacture. In 1989, for example, business spent some $124 billion on advertising its products—an expenditure nearly three-fourths as large as our total expenditures for public elementary and secondary education. By way of contrast, in 1867, we spent only $50 million on advertising; and in 1900, only $542 million. So while consumers still move the factors of production to satisfy their "wants," these wants are themselves increasingly influenced by the producers. In contrast to the ideal market where producers hasten at the beck of an imperious consumer demand, in the new market, consumers are to some extent themselves at the beck of an imperious producer demand.

We might note, for instance, that no sooner was the first small Ford placed on the market than the company announced a "luxury" small car, and this example was quickly followed by other producers. It may very well be that consumers prefer a large spectrum of sizes and shapes of automobiles. But it is difficult to square the original image of serving the consumers' uninfluenced wants with the process by which new models are designed and touted.

oligopolistic pricing   The second main attribute of the ideal market was that consumers' interests were satisfied as cheaply as possible because prices were forced down to the average cost of producing goods. Is this still true?

The question leads us to consider an aspect of the emergence of giant firms that we have not yet examined. We saw that the original rise of the big companies, with their heavy overhead costs, led to an intensification of competition. But the competitive situation changed significantly once the big companies came to dominate their respective fields. For the new pattern of a few large firms sharing the market with their rivals created a market structure called *oligopoly*, and oligopoly changed the way that competition worked.

Oligopoly means a market controlled by a few sellers. It is not *monopoly*, which is a market in which we find only one seller, but neither is it "pure" competition, in which markets are served by many sellers. Gas stations are examples of pure competition, but the oil companies are examples of oligopolies.

What difference does oligopoly make? The main points of the contrast are not difficult to grasp. Classical competition implies a situation in which there are so many firms (of roughly the same order of size) that no one of them by itself can directly influence market prices. This is the case—more or less—within much of the small business world. No single gas station, by lowering its price, can change the price of gas in a city. In oligopoly, by way of contrast, the numbers of firms are few enough (or the disparity in size among the few large ones and the host of smaller ones is so great) that the large firms cannot help affecting the market situation. If Exxon lowers its price, all its rival companies are likely to follow suit. As a result, whereas in classical competition, firms must accept whatever prices the market thrusts upon them, in oligopolistic markets, prices can be "set," at least within limits, by the direct action of the leading firms.

In many of the most important industrial markets, as we have seen, it is oligopoly rather than pure competition that is the order of things today. In industry after industry, economies of large-scale production have brought about a situation in which a few large producers divide the market among themselves. Often these markets are dominated by one very large firm that serves as "price leader," raising or lowering its prices as general economic conditions warrant, and being followed up or down by everyone else in the field. US Steel in the steel industry, and General Motors in the auto field, until the 1980s, "led" their industries in this fashion. By and large, as we would expect, these "administered prices" were considerably higher than the prices that a pure competitive market would deliver. General Motors, for example, traditionally priced its cars to earn 15 to 20 percent *after taxes*, on the assumption that the company would only utilize about two-thirds of its plant capacity.

deregulation   Until a decade or so ago, our analysis of the effect of oligopoly would have ended with these remarks. Economists generally viewed the change in market structure as creating a much less aggressive business world so far as price competition was concerned. Moreover, the general view was that the demise of old-fashioned price competition was not entirely to be lamented because product competition still kept the oligopolists on their toes. In fact, if economists fretted at all about the presence of administered prices, it was mainly because of the danger that they would serve as a transmission belt for inflation: one company's higher prices—raised, perhaps, because of a wage settlement—being "competitively" followed *upward* by its fellow oligopolists.

The experience of the 1980s has changed this view considerably. All-out competition has reemerged as a central fact of economic life. In part, the turnabout came because of the policy of the Reagan administration to deregulate certain oligopolies such as the airline industry, which soon found itself in price-cutting wars that greatly resembled those of the railroads in generations past. In the savings and loan industry, deregulation led to a scandal-ridden orgy that ultimately required a very expensive government rescue operation. For better or worse, there is no doubt that the staid oligopolistic climate of the past was over.

international competition

But by far the most important factor making for change was the advent of a new international aspect to competition. As a consequence of lagging American productivity and modernization, and because the international economic situation made it very cheap to purchase foreign commodities, a flood of German, Japanese, and other European and Asian products began to inundate the American market. General Motors found, by the 1980s, that its closest rival was no longer Ford, but Japanese car companies. United States Steel was so badly battered by foreign steel imports that it made strenuous efforts to sell off large amounts of its steel plants and to get out of the business in which, not so long ago, it had appeared to be an impregnable bastion. To emphasize that switch, it renamed itself USX.

The flood of Toyotas, VWs, Sonys, and made-in-Hong-Kong labels brought an unmistakable message: *The age of competition was not over.* By the mid-1980s, it had been estimated that over 70 percent of American industry operated in markets that were already, or could easily become, competitive international marketplaces.[13] It become clear that the comfortable stability of the 1950s and 1960s was gone, probably forever. Not just in the United States, but in all industrial societies, a new international aspect to competition was changing the face of industrial structures as rapidly and as painfully as did the rise of the national corporation a century earlier.

POWER AND RESPONSIBILITY

The rise of international competition opens a chapter in the making of modern economic society that goes beyond the immediate issue of market structure. We will return to that subject after we have traced other strands in the evolution of the market system. But before we turn to these, there is an aspect of the modern corporation that deserves to be followed a little further. We have learned something—not yet enough—about the effect of the giant corporation on the workings of the market mechanism. Now we must probe a little more deeply into its meaning for the larger society.

[13] Joseph Duffey "U.S. Competition" in *Global Competitiveness*, ed. Martin K. Starr (New York: W. W Norton, 1988), p. 80.

What can be done about the fortresses of power that have emerged in modern capitalism? Is there a way of imposing public responsibility on the big corporation? As we shall see, the question is exceedingly difficult. Let us discover this for ourselves by examining some frequently encountered proposals for increasing the social responsibility of the giant corporation.

1. *Profit as social responsibility.*

The first suggestion is most prominently associated with the name of Nobelist Milton Friedman, a philosophic conservative whose response to the question of what a corporation should do to discharge its social responsibility is very simple: *make money.*

The function of a business organization in society, argues Friedman, is to serve as an efficient agent of production, not as a locus of social improvement. It serves that productive function best by striving after profit—conforming, while doing so, to the basic rules and ethical norms of society. It is not up to business to "do good"; it is up to government to prevent it from doing bad.

Moreover, as soon as a businessman tries to apply any rules other than moneymaking, he takes into his own hands powers that rightfully belong to other parts of society, such as its political authorities. Friedman would even forbid corporations to give money to charities or universities. Their business, their responsibility to society, he insists, is *production*. Let the dividend receivers give away the money the corporations pay them, but do not let corporations become the active social-welfare agencies of society.[14]

The counterarguments to Friedman's position are not difficult to frame. They are two:

1. Friedman assumes that stockholders' moral claims to the earnings of the vast semimonopolies they "own" are superior to claims of the consumers or workers from whose pockets these profits are plucked. This is at least a debatable point: Since the stockholders are *not* active entrepreneurs, they make little or no contribution to the profits of the corporation. Why, then, should their claim exceed a reasonable compensation for the risk of their money?

2. Friedman assumes that the government, whose purpose is to set the rules and oversee the operations of business, acts *independently* of the corporations it regulates. But many studies show that the so-called regulatory agencies of the government usually act *on behalf of the big corporations* they "regulate," rather than on behalf of the consumer. For

[14] Friedman, *Capitalism and Freedom* (Chicago: University of Chicago Press, 1962), Chap. 8.

example, the Food and Drug Administration banned cyclamates as a dangerous food additive in 1969, *nineteen years* after the first warnings of their dangerous effects had been brought to its attention! In the long interim, it failed to act, largely because of its reluctance to incur the wrath (and political counterattack) of the industry it was supposedly "regulating."[15]

2. *The corporation as social arbiter.*

Quite a different approach to the problem of social responsibility has been widely espoused by many concerned corporate executives. This view recognizes that the corporation, by virtue of its immense size and strength, has power thrust upon it, whether it wishes to have it or not. The solution to this problem, as these people see it, is for corporate executives to act "professionally" as the arbiters of this power, doing their best to adjudicate equitably among the claims of the many constituencies to which they are responsible: labor, stockholders, customers, and the public at large. The executive of one of the largest enterprises in the nation said, three decades ago, "The manager is becoming a professional in the sense that like all professional men he has a responsibility to society as a whole."[16] This is a claim still commonly advanced by corporate managers.

There is no doubt that many top corporate executives think of themselves as the referees among contending groups, and no doubt many of them use caution and forethought in exercising the power of decision. But the weaknesses of this argument are also not difficult to see. Unlike the case with other professions, there are neither criteria for "qualifying" as a corporate executive nor penalties for failing to accept social responsibilities. The executive of a corporation who fails to act responsibly may incur the opprobrium of the public, but the public has no way of removing him or her from office or reducing his or her salary.

Nor is there any clear guideline, even for the most scrupulous executives, defining the manner in which they are *supposed* to exercise their responsibility. Is their concern for the prevention of pollution to take precedence over their concern for turning in a good profit statement at the end of the year, or giving wage increases, or reducing the price of their product? Is the contribution of their company to charity or education supposed to represent *their* preferences, or those of their cus-

---

[15] James S. Turner, "The Chemical Feast," in *The Report on the Food and Drug Administration*, ed. Ralph Nader and Summer Study Group (New York: Grossman, 1970), pp. 5–30.

[16] R. W. Davenport and *Fortune* editors, *U.S.A.: The Permanent Revolution* (Englewood Cliffs, N.J.: Prentice Hall, 1951), p. 79.

tomers or workers? Has Xerox a right to help the cause of public broad-
casting; Exxon to help finance Harlem Academy (a private school aimed
at assisting Harlem youths to go on to college); the makers of firearms
to help support the National Rifle Association?

3. *Antitrust: the dissolution of monopoly.*

These questions begin to indicate the complexity of the issue of "social
responsibility" and the problems implicit in allowing these extremely
important *social* decisions to be made by private individuals who are in
no way publicly accountable for their actions. Hence, a third approach
to the problem of responsibility takes yet another tack. It suggests that
the power of big business be curbed by dividing large corporations into
several much smaller units. A number of studies have shown that the
largest *plant* size needed for industrial efficiency is far smaller (in terms
of financial assets) than the giant firms typical of the *Fortune* list of the
top 500 industrial corporations (or for that matter of the next 500). Hence,
a number of economists have suggested that a very strict application of
antitrust legislation should be applied, not only to prohibit mergers, but
also to separate a huge enterprise such as General Motors into its natural
constituent units: a Cadillac Company, an Oldsmobile Company, a Chev-
rolet Company, and so on.

One major problem stands in the way of this frontal attack on corporate power. It is that size and social responsibility are by no means
clearly correlated. Indeed, small, competitive industry is typically beset
by low research and development programs, antilabor practices, and a
general absence of the kinds of amenities we associate with "big business."

Moreover, there is no reason to believe that smaller firms would
be more pollution-conscious (indeed, owing to competitive pressures,
they might be less inclined to minimize pollution) or that they would
be more conscientious in advertising, racial nondiscrimination, and other
practices. In other words, the loss of *political* power, which might well
accompany the fractioning of the largest firms, is apt to be offset by a
rise in certain forms of economic ruthlessness or even antisocial behavior.

Competition, it has been remarked more than once, is a social condition to which all parties in an enterprise economy pay homage, but
that only economists take seriously. Business and labor both spend much
of their energies trying to avoid competition or to minimize it, and the
attempt to intensify competition by breaking up large firms into smaller
ones might bring about worse problems than it alleviates.

4. *Nationalization.*

Then why not nationalize the large firms? The thought comes as rank heresy to a nation that has been accustomed to equating nationalization with socialism. Yet Germany, France, England, Sweden, Italy, and a host of other capitalistic nations have nationalized industries ranging from oil refineries to airlines, from automobile production to the output of coal and electricity. Hence, John Kenneth Galbraith has suggested that we should nationalize the giant armaments producers who are wholly dependent on the Pentagon, in order to bring such firms under public control.

But would nationalization achieve its purpose of assuring social responsibility? We have seen the Pentagon prevent one of its "ward" companies, Lockheed Aircraft, from suffering the fate of an ordinary inefficient firm by rescuing it from bankruptcy with special contracts and "loans." Outright nationalization would only cement this union of political and economic power by making Lockheed a part of the Pentagon and thus making it even more difficult to put pressure on it to perform responsibly.

The problem is that nationalization not only removes the affected enterprise *entirely* from the pressures of the market, but almost inevitably brings it under the political shelter of the government, which further removes the venture from any effective criticism. Experience in Europe suggests that nationalization may be useful for certain purposes, but that is no guarantee that nationalized firms will be responsible on other scores. It is not much in favor these days.

remaining possibilities All these difficulties make it clear that the problem of social responsibility will not be easy to solve (or for that matter, even to *define*), no matter what step we choose, from laissez faire to nationalization. And for each of these problems with regard to the corporation, we could easily construct counterparts that have to do with the control over labor unions or over the government itself.

What, then, is to be done? A number of lines of action suggest themselves. One is the widening of the *legal responsibility* of the corporation to include areas of responsibility for which it now has little or no accountability. Environmental damage is one of these; consumer protection is another. (The suits filed against Exxon for the *Valdez* oil spill and against the producers of the thalidomide sleeping pills are important steps in this direction.) Ralph Nader has further suggested that a top corporate official be legally charged with seeing to it that the company complies with the law in full, and that the top officers of noncomplying companies be suspended, as is now the penalty for certain violations of SEC regulations. He also strongly advocates the federal, rather than state, incorporation of big companies—a step that would greatly facilitate the establishment of tough national standards of corporate responsibility.*

A second step would be a widening of *public accountability through disclosure*—the so-called fishbowl method of regulation. Corporations could be required to report to public agencies their expenditures for pollution control, for political lobbying, and so on. Corporate tax returns could be opened to public scrutiny. Unions and corporations both could be required to make public disclosure of their race practices with regard to hiring or admission, advancement, and rates of pay. Public responsibility for advertising, with formal proofs submitted to back all claims, is yet another means of securing better accountability to the public.

Still another course of action would be to appoint *public members* [dislike] to boards of directors of large companies or to executive organs of large unions and to charge these members with protecting the consumers' interest and with reporting behavior that seems contrary to the public interest. Worker-members of boards of directors might also serve such a useful purpose (there are such members in Germany). The mobilization of the votes of concerned stockholders is still another way of bringing social pressure to bear.

Finally, there is the corrective action of dedicated private individuals such as Ralph Nader, who rose to fame on his exposé of the safety practices of the auto industry, and who has since turned his guns on pollution and other irresponsibilities of big business, and on poor performance in the federal bureaucracy. Such public pressure is necessarily sporadic and usually short-lived, but it has been a powerful source of social change.

advantages of bigness

Last, there is the other side of the coin: There are some arguments in favor of bigness—arguments anchored in the technological and social gains that large-scale enterprise can bring.

One of these is *research and development*. The momentum of capitalism depends to a large degree on the continuous "creative destruction" (as economist Joseph Schumpeter called it) by which the products of society are winnowed and replaced by new products. That process of winnowing and replacement, in turn, depends to a large degree on the ability of companies to invest large sums in experiments, in laboratory tests, and in pure and applied research. Only big companies can absorb the financial costs of such investments.

---

* Proposals for legislating responsibility are many; their rate of adoption is, however, slow. For a recent set of fifty suggested legislative changes, see Russell Mokhiber, *Corporate Crime and Violence* (San Francisco: Sierra Club Books, 1988), pp. 39–65.

A second advantage of bigness lies in the *amenities offered to employees* and the consideration shown to consumers by a significant number of big companies. Until recently, the best labor practices and the best records of consumer-mindedness have been found among the largest firms, not among the smaller corporations. The reason is not that big business is inherently more social-minded. It is that big business, by virtue of its large and relatively secure profits, can afford to indulge in enlightened employee practices and in solicitous relations with consumers. As Galbraith, so often an acerbic critic of the big corporation, has written, "The show-pieces [of the economy] are, with rare exceptions, the industries which are dominated by a handful of large firms. The foreign visitor, brought to the United States . . . visits the same firms as do the attorneys of the Justice Department in their search for monopoly."[17]

These arguments in favor of bigness must, however, be qualified. Recent advances in computerized manufacturing have made possible the economical production of relatively small "batches" of customized output instead of long uninterrupted streams of unchanging output. This has opened a window of opportunity for smaller, flexible firms to compete against large, bureaucratic giants. While USX has been unable to maintain its competitive place in the world steel market, small "mini-mills" have done a flourishing business. Thus, the technological edge that once gave a marked advantage to bigger plants may be eroding, although large size remains crucial in certain industries.

So, too, the edge enjoyed by big business in employee relations may also be changing. Under the pressure of international competition and intensified domestic rivalry, many of the social advantages offered by large firms have been lost. Plant closings and relocations have left communities stranded, and aggressive antiunion campaigns have disturbed the serene tenor of corporate life described by Galbraith in the 1950s. Not least, the reorganizations that have usually followed after giant corporate mergers have brought salary reductions and—unthinkable!—actual firings to the once-secure echelons of middle management.

It would be too much to say that big business no longer enjoys a technological advantage or no longer offers superior working conditions, but the advantage is not what it once was, and may narrow still further in the future.

power: the unresolved problem   How shall we summarize this situation? No single, simple judgment can be passed on the consequences of business size. Rather, it may help if we stand aside and view bigness in a historical perspective.

Then it can be seen that mass organizations are a seemingly ines-

---

[17] John Kenneth Galbraith, *American Capitalism* (Boston: Houghton Mifflin, 1952) p. 96.

capable concomitant of our age of high technology and increasing social interdependence. The roots of this fact were discussed earlier, and its broader consequences will be seen later. Here it should be noted that, depending on our interests, we stress different aspects of this universal phenomenon. To some, who fear the continued growth of very large scale business, the most significant aspect is that we have not managed to control business power. To others, concerned over the emergence of larger labor unions, it is labor power that most dangerously eludes effective control. And to still others, who are most worried by the growth of big government, it is the growth of public power that is the main problem.

What is common among these concerns is the awareness that enormous, only half-controlled organizations have come to dominate much of the market system. But the problem is bigger than that. For if we look to the failed socialist systems, we see the growth of ministries of production and administration that displayed much of the same bureaucratic indifference and mixed political and economic power as do our corporations, unions, and government agencies. This suggests that many of the problems of "big business" will plague any modern industrial society.

This is a problem that we will touch on again in Chapter 13. There we will see that the market system has huge strengths in bringing about the *efficient operation* of an economic society, and these strengths may be more important *at certain stages of historical development* than the weaknesses into which we have been looking. In other words, in a final appraisal of the market system—and of capitalist society that depends on a market mechanism—it is a historical perspective that we require rather than a static calculus of pluses and minuses. For that, let us return to our narrative.

KEY CONCEPTS AND KEY WORDS

Concentration
1. A combination of aggressive entrepreneurship and the economies of scale typical of industrial technology brought about a *concentration of economic power* in many markets in the late nineteenth and early twentieth centuries.

Merger
2. The emergence of large firms with massive capital structures led to "cutthroat" competition that was exceedingly dangerous for the firms concerned. Hence there were *many attempts to stabilize the competitive struggle* by means of pools, trusts, holding companies, and mergers.

Antitrust
3. As the great trusts and combines rose to power, there was a "countervailing" thrust of political *antitrust legislation*, culminating in the Sherman Anti-Trust Act (1890), later in the Clayton Anti-Trust Act (1914), and in subsequent amendments designed to make mergers more difficult.

Internal growth

4. None of these laws prohibited or interfered with *internal growth*. As a result, large businesses continued to expand. A famous survey by Berle and Means in 1933 predicted that if the rate of growth of the top 200 nonfinancial corporations continued, they would soon own virtually the entire economy.

Mergers and merger mania

5. This prediction has been partly borne out, especially through the *mergers* that have dramatically increased the concentration of manufacturing wealth. Recently, concentration has slowed down, but a "merger mania" financed by "junk bonds" has greatly increased corporate interest costs.

Consumer sovereignty

6. The rise of big business threatens the concept of *consumer sovereignty*, the most important rationale of a free market system. Consumer sovereignty nullifies the power of firms because all crucial decisions emanate from households deciding what they wish to buy, at what price. The rise of *advertising* as a massive force and of *oligopolistic pricing* undermines that household power.

Oligopoly

7. Oligopoly means a market dominated by a few sellers. In contrast to competitive markets with many sellers, here big firms can set the level of prices more or less at their own discretion, instead of having to accept the price established by the forces of supply and demand.

Renewal of competition

8. The stability of an oligopolistic marketplace has been interrupted by a reappearance of very severe competition. This stems partly from deregulation and partly from the pressures of a deep recession, but the main impetus has been a new onslaught of foreign competition.

9. A number of proposals have been advanced for assuring the responsible social conduct of large corporations. These include: (1) strict attention to *profit making only*; (2) *"professional" standards* of conduct and self-conscious attention to social needs; (3) *breakup of big business through antitrust legislation*; and (4) *nationalization*.

Corporate responsibility and its problems

10. Each of these proposals has its weaknesses. Social responsibility is likely to depend on the development of new *legal responsibilities* for business and labor, new areas of *public accountability*, *public representation* on executive boards, and the important power of *private investigation and publicity*.

11. The overall problem of power remains recalcitrant, not only in a market society but in all societies. This is a problem to which we will return in our subsequent investigation of the historical trajectory of the market system itself.

QUESTIONS

1. Can you name the chief corporate executives of these top industrial firms in the United States: AT&T, General Motors, Exxon, Ford, General Electric, IBM, Texaco? How many names of leading businessmen do you know? What does this suggest as to the character of business leadership today as contrasted with the 1890s?

2. Why does heavy overhead cost lead to "cutthroat competition"? Why is this kind of competition dangerous?

3. Suppose Congress decided to foster a return to classical competition in the United States. What changes would have to be wrought in the American business scene? Do you think this is a practical possibility?

4. Compare the situations of a farmer selling wheat to a grain company and an executive of a large auto company selling a new model. How much latitude does each have in pricing his product?

5. Do you believe that tastes are created by advertising? Have your own been?

6. What do you consider to be the most desirable characteristic of bigness in business? The most undesirable?

7. Suppose you wanted to measure concentration in an industry. What attributes of the firms in that industry would interest you: their respective sales? their assets? their number of employees? Might different measures give different concentration ratios?

8. What are the important differences between "pure" competition and oligopoly as regards the position of the consumer? the producer? On net balance, which do you think is preferable? Why?

9. Do you think businesses should be more socially responsible? How would you go about achieving a higher level of social responsibility in the following areas: (1) truth in advertising; (2) absence of political interference with government; (3) colorblind hiring and promotion; (4) high levels of antipollution performance? What measures would you propose for numbers 2 and 3 with regard to labor unions? How would you bring government agencies to a higher level of social responsibility?

10. Do you think corporations have a right to back right-wing groups? left-wing groups? centrist groups? modern art? old-fashioned art? universities? sports groups? political parties? How do you justify your answers?

11. Do you think it would help to nationalize the big arms companies? Could you imagine a situation in which you would favor the nationalization of any company? How about the railroads if they were about to go bankrupt and leave the nation stranded? How about GM if it defied a government regulation with regard to producing a pollution-free vehicle? How about the Boeing Company if that seemed the only way of keeping an American airframe manufacturer alive in the face of competition from other nationalized airframe makers?

7
THE GREAT DEPRESSION

In the preceding chapter, we concentrated on important aspects of the developing industrial economy—the swift rise in productivity, the impact of mass production, the thickening texture of the market. But we purposely ignored one effect of technology that, in retrospect, towers over the others. This effect was the tremendous impetus that technology gave to the process of economic growth.

In Chapter 4, "The Industrial Revolution," we commented on the importance of technology for growth. Prior to the Industrial Revolution, a chart of the well-being of the average person in Europe would have shown a distressingly horizontal profile, rising in some years or even centuries, falling in others, perhaps tilted slightly upward as a whole, but certainly displaying nothing like a steady year-by-year increase in the output of goods and services available per capita. We noted that even with the initial introduction of the new technology, the standard of living did not immediately improve. But starting in the third quarter of the nineteenth century, the accumulations of capital and the accretion of expertise began to display their hidden powers. In nearly every industrializing country, and most dramatically in the United States, the profile of economic well-being now began to show that steady and regular improvement that has become the very hallmark of modern economic times.

Figure 7-1 shows us the general path of this growth in the United States from the 1870s, when the process was in full swing, to 1929, when it reached a dramatic peak, to which we will shortly return. If we draw a line through the irregularly upward-moving graph to express the average rate of growth, taking good years and bad together, we find it to be about 3.5 percent (with all price changes eliminated), which means that the total volume of output was doubling about every twenty years. Since the number of people was also doubling, although more slowly, per capita shares in this mounting volume of goods obviously grew more slowly. Roughly, we can estimate that individuals improved their lot at

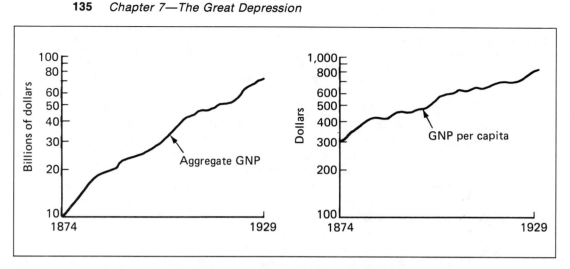

FIGURE 7-1   Real GNP (1929 Prices) Aggregate and Per Capita

a rate of about 1½ to 2 percent a year, doubling their real incomes about every forty years.* There is no doubt that the period as a whole was one of unprecedented progress and improvement. How strange, then, that it should have ended in the greatest disaster in the history of the market system—one that very nearly spelled the end of capitalism and that permanently altered the system in ways that we must now learn about.

---

* Note that Figure 7-1 shows aggregate well-being in terms of GNP, and per capita well-being as GNP per capita. GNP stands for *gross national product,* a term in the economist's lexicon that has entered the vocabulary (although not, perhaps, the clear understanding) of most Americans. Gross national product is the market value of all the final goods and services we produce over a year. The word "final" means that we do not include the market value of each and every item, but only of those that go into finished, or final, goods. For instance, government statisticians include in GNP the market value (the selling price) of all the automobiles made during the year, but they do not also include the value of the steel, the paint, the upholstery, rubber, etc., that have been bought by the auto companies. The selling price of the final good—the car—includes these "intermediate" goods, and it would therefore be double counting to add them into GNP on top of the value of the car.

Economists distinguish among four general kinds of final goods. One is the *consumption* goods and services that households buy—food, clothes, movie admissions. A second kind consists of the capital goods that business buys—their *investment* in plant and equipment, additional inventory, and the like. A third category consists of the goods and services bought by local, state, and federal *government*—police services, education, roads, the cost of defense, etc. The last item is made up of the goods we make at home and sell abroad, minus goods made abroad and sold here—*exports minus imports.* These four streams of output make up our aggregate gross national product. Per capita GNP is the aggregate sum divided by the population. Last note: We do not include in GNP the cost of "transfer payments" such as Social Security, unemployment insurance, and welfare. This is because these payments do not purchase any output. They simply redistribute the incomes that are derived from actual production.

America in 1929

We in America today are nearer to the final triumph over poverty than ever before in the history of any land. The poorhouse is vanishing from among us. We have not yet reached the goal, but, given a chance . . . we shall soon with the help of God be in sight of the day when poverty will be banished from this nation.

Thus spoke Herbert Hoover in November 1928, and indeed, by 1929, the American economy had shown extraordinary progress. Population had grown from 76 million in 1900 to over 121 million, and ten years had been added to the expectation of life at birth for whites and thirteen for nonwhites. To hold and feed and sustain its growing numbers, the nation had built up two new cities to a million each, five to over half a million, nearly 1,500 from rural to urban classification. Meanwhile, there were jobs for 48 million people—all save 3.2 percent of the labor force in 1929. Furthermore, these jobs holders had seen average weekly hours of work in manufacturing drop from nearly 60 in 1900 to 44. Average hourly earnings more than doubled, while consumer prices lagged sufficiently behind to allow a rise in real wages of some 10 to 20 percent. It was not surprising, then, that an atmosphere of optimism gripped America in 1929 and that President Hoover's official words only reflected an informal sentiment throughout the nation.

the stock market boom

Certainly few Americans suspected that a major economic calamity might be just around the corner. On the contrary, most people were concerned with quite another prospect of the American economy, and a highly attractive one. This was the great stock market boom—a boom that by 1929 had pulled perhaps 10 million people into "the market," where they had the pleasure of watching their money painlessly and effortlessly grow. As Frederick Lewis Allen, a social historian of the Twenties, described it:

> The rich man's chauffeur drove with his ears laid back to catch the news of an impending move in Bethlehem Steel; he held fifty shares himself on a twenty point margin. The window cleaner at the broker's office paused to watch the ticker, for he was thinking of converting his laboriously accumulated savings into a few shares of Simmons. Edwin Lefevre (an articulate reporter on the market at this time who could claim considerable personal experience) told of a broker's valet who made nearly a quarter of a million in the market, of a trained nurse who cleaned up thirty thousand following the tips given her by her grateful patients; and of a Wyoming cattleman, thirty miles from the nearest railroad, who bought or sold a thousand shares a day.[1]

It was, of course, admittedly speculative, and yet the risks seemed eminently justified. Someone who had put $1,000 each year, from 1921 on, into a group of representative stocks would have found himself worth

---

[1] Frederick Lewis Allen, *Only Yesterday* (New York: Bantam, 1946). p. 349.

over $6,000 in 1925, almost $9,000 in 1926, well over $11,000 in 1927, and an incredible $20,000 in 1928—well over $100,000 in today's terms. And that was just the beginning: During June and July of 1929, industrial stock averages went up nearly as much as they had during the entire year of 1928, which had been a year of unprecedented rise. By August 1929, the three months' summer spurt had already outdistanced the entire 1928 rise. In those three months alone, an investor who had bought 100 shares of Westinghouse would have almost doubled his money; even a buyer of staid AT&T would have been richer by a third. It seemed that everyone had but to beg or borrow money to buy shares in order to get rich.

the great crash
What pricked the bubble? No one knows exactly what final event was to blame. But when the boom did break, it was as if an enormous dam had suddenly crumbled. All the frenzy that had stretched out over two years in sending stocks up was concentrated in a few incredible weeks beating them down. On Tuesday, October 29, 1929, an avalanche of selling crushed the exchanges. On occasion there were *no* offers to buy stock at all—just to sell it. Goldman Sachs, a much-sought-after investment trust, lost almost half its quoted value on this single day. By the end of the trading session (the ticker, lagging behind, stretched out the agony two and a half hours longer than the actual market transactions), 16,410,000 shares of stock had been dumped, an unprecedented number for that time. In a single day, the rise in values of the entire preceding year had been wiped out. A few weeks later, $30 billion of "wealth" had *lost* vanished into thin air. Millions who had counted their paper gains and thought themselves well off discovered they were poor.

The great crash is in itself a fascinating chapter in the "madness of crowds." At first it seemed unconnected with anything bigger. In fact, the early weeks after the crash were regularly marked with expressions of confidence: The general cliché of the day was that things were "fundamentally sound." Yet things were *not* fundamentally sound. The terrifying crash ushered in the much more terrifying depression.

the Great Depression
Frederick Lewis Allen wrote:

It was an oddly invisible phenomenon, this Great Depression. If one observed closely, one might note that there were fewer people on the streets than in former years, that there were many untenanted shops, that beggars and panhandlers were much in evidence; one might see breadlines here and there, and "Hoovervilles" in vacant lots at the edge of town (groups of tar-paper shacks inhabited by homeless people); railroad trains were shorter, with fewer Pullmans; and there were many factory chimneys out of which no smoke was coming. But otherwise there was little to see. Great numbers of people were sitting home, trying to keep warm.[2]

However invisible to the casual observer, the depression was far from being a mere figment. To begin with, gross national product—the measure of the nation's total output—fell precipitously from $104 billion in 1929 to $56 billion in 1933. Almost one dollar's worth of final output out of every two simply disappeared. As a result, unemployment soared. In 1929, the unemployed had numbered 1.5 million. By 1933, the number had risen eightfold until *one person out of every four in the entire labor force was without a job*. In the nation as a whole, residential construction fell by 90 percent; there were virtually no houses built. Nine million savings accounts were lost as banks closed their doors. Eighty-five thousand businesses failed. In Pennsylvania in 1932, it was reported by the state Department of Labor that wages had fallen to 5 cents an hour in sawmills, 6 cents in brick and tile manufacturing, 7.5 cents in general contracting. In Tennessee, women in mills were paid as little as $2.39 for a fifty-hour week. In Kentucky, miners ate the weeds that cows ate; in West Virginia, people began to rob stores for food.[3]

causes of the depression: speculation

How did this tragedy come about?

An immediate, precipitating cause was, of course, the speculative fever that had engulfed the economy by 1929. The mania was not confined to Wall Street. Throughout the nation, a get-rich-quick philosophy had destroyed normal business and banking caution. Foreign bonds of the most dubious validity were eagerly (and sometimes ruthlessly) pushed by the banks into investors' hands or, worse folly, put into their own portfolios.* In addition, huge pyramided structures of investment trusts and holding companies erected a house of cards atop the operating base of enterprise. For instance, Georgia Power & Light Company was controlled by the Seaboard Public Service Corporation, which was controlled by the Middle West Utilities Company, which was controlled by Insull Utility Investments, Inc., which was controlled by the Corporation Securities Company of Chicago (which was controlled, in turn, by Insull Utility Investments, which presumably *it* controlled). Of these compa-

---

[2] Frederick Lewis Allen, *The Big Change* (New York: Harper, 1952), p. 248.

[3] Arthur Schlesinger, Jr., *The Crisis of the Old Order* (Boston: Houghton Mifflin, 1957), pp. 249–50.

* Many of these deals were unsavory to the point of malfeasance. The son of the President of Peru, for instance, was paid $450,000 by the securities affiliate of the National City Bank for his services in connection with a $50 million bond issue, which the bank's affiliate then floated for Peru. The President's son's "services" consisted almost entirely of an agreement not to block the deal. Eventually, of course, the bonds went into default. (John K. Galbraith, *The Great Crash, 1929.* Boston: Houghton Mifflin, 1955, p. 186)

nies, only one—Georgia Power—actually produced electricity. The rest produced only profits and speculative opportunities. And the Insull empire was only one of *twelve* holding companies that owned 75 percent of all the utility operating plants in the country.

All these manipulative activities helped to pave the way for the depression. When the stock market finally crashed, it brought down with it an immense flimsy structure of credit. Individual investors who had borrowed to the hilt to buy securities had their stock sold out from under them to meet their indebtedness to brokers. Banks and financial institutions, loaded with dubious foreign bonds, were suddenly insolvent. Meanwhile, to compound the terrible panic, the monetary authorities pursued policies that unwittingly weakened the banking system still further, greatly prolonging the length of the Depression.[4]

weakness on the farm

In the vulnerability of an economy bound up with a rickety and speculative financial superstructure, we have located one reason for the Great Depression—or, more specifically, one reason why the Wall Street crash pulled down with it so much business activity. But we have far from exhausted the explanations for the depression itself. For the crash, after all, might have been no worse than many previous speculative disasters. Why was it protracted into a chronic and deep-rooted ailment?

The question turns our attention away from the spectacular misfortunes of 1929 to a consideration of the state of the economy as a whole in the years preceding the collapse. We have already characterized the first quarter of the twentieth century as a time of unprecedented expansion. Could it be, however, that behind the overall figures of rising output and incomes there were concealed pockets of trouble?

There is no question that one such worrisome sector existed. This was the farm sector, especially the all-important grains. All through the 1920s, the farmer was the "sick man" of the American economy. Each year saw more farmers going into tenantry, until by 1929 four out of ten farmers in the nation were no longer independent operators. Each year the farmer seemed to fall further behind the city dweller in terms of relative well-being. In 1910, the income per worker on the farm had been not quite 40 percent of that of the nonfarm worker; by 1930, it was just under 30 percent.

Part of this trouble on the farm, without question, stemmed from the difficult heritage of the past. Beset now by drought, now by the exploitation of powerful railroad and storage combines, now by his own penchant for land speculation, the farmer was proverbially an ailing member of the economy. In addition, American farmers had been tra-

---

[4] See Milton Friedman and Anna Schwartz, *The Great Contraction* (Princeton, N.J.: Princeton University Press, 1965).

ditionally careless of the earth, indifferent to the technology of agriculture. Looking at the average individual farmer, one would have said that he was poor because he was unproductive. Between 1910 and 1920, for instance, while nonfarm output per worker rose by nearly 20 percent, output per farm worker actually fell. Between 1920 and 1930, farm productivity improved somewhat, but not nearly so fast as productivity off the farm. For the great majority of the nation's agricultural producers, the trouble appeared to be that they could not grow or raise enough to make a decent living.

inelastic demand

If we had looked at farming as a whole, however, a very different answer would have suggested itself. Suppose that farm productivity *had* kept pace with that of the nation. Would farm income as a whole have risen? The answer is disconcerting. The *demand* for farm products was quite unlike that for manufactured products generally. In the manufacturing sector, when productivity rose and costs accordingly fell, the cheaper prices of manufactured goods attracted vast new markets, as with the Ford car. Not so with farm products, however. When food prices fell, people did not tend to increase their actual consumption very greatly. Increases in overall farm output resulted in much lower prices but not in larger cash receipts for the farmer. Faced with what is called an "inelastic" demand—a demand that does not respond in proportion to price changes—sellers are *worse* off than they were before a flood of output.

That is very much what happened during the 1920s. From 1915 to 1920, the farmer prospered because World War I greatly increased the demand for his product. Prices for farm output rose, and his cash receipts rose as well; in fact, they more than doubled. But when European farms resumed their output following the war, the American farmers' crops simply glutted the market. Although prices fell precipitously (40 percent in the single year 1920–1921), the purchases of farm products did not respond in anything like equal measure. As a result, the cash receipts of the farmer toppled almost as fast as prices. Meanwhile, his taxes were up by some 70 percent, and his mortgage payments and his cost of living in general had approximately doubled. Matters improved somewhat during the later 1920s, but not enough to bring the crop farmers back to substantial prosperity.

There is a lesson here in economics as well as history. Had farmers constituted an oligopolistic market, the decline in farm income might have been limited. A few producers, facing an inelastic demand for their products, can see the sense in mutually curtailing output. Rather than flooding a market that does not want their product, they can agree, tacitly or otherwise, to hold back production to some amount that the market will absorb at a reasonable price. But the individual farmer is about as far from an oligopolist as one can imagine. When the price for his crop falls, it gains the individual farmer nothing to decrease his output. On the contrary, in his highly competitive situation, the best that he can do is to rush to sell as much as he can before things get worse—thereby unwittingly *making* things worse.

At its core, the trouble with the farm sector was that the market mechanism in this particular case did not yield a satisfactory result.* That might not have been so serious had it not been for another development: While agriculture remained static and stagnant, the manufacturing sector was growing by leaps and bounds. Yet its growth was undermined because a fifth of the nation—the agricultural sector—was unable to match the growing volume of production with a growing volume of purchasing power. As the farmers' buying power lagged, it pulled down the demand for tractors, cars, gasoline and electric motors, and manufactured consumers' goods, generally. Weakness on the farm was thus symptomatic of a weakness throughout the economy, a failure of purchasing power across the whole lower stratum of the nation to keep up with the tempo of national industrial production.

weakness in the factory Most economists of the 1920s, as we have said, would have agreed that there was a source of potential trouble on the farm. Had we suggested that there might be another potential breeding ground for trouble in the factory or the mine, however, few would have given their assent. Most people's eyes, during the 1920s, were fixed on only one aspect of the industrial sector—production—and here there was surely little reason for complaint.

Yet had scrutiny penetrated a bit deeper, very serious signs might well have been spotted in this presumably most buoyant section of the economy. For while production was steadily rising, *employment* was not. In manufacturing, for example, physical output in 1929 was up 49 percent over 1920, while employment was precisely unchanged. In mining, output was up 43 percent, while employment had shrunk some 12 percent. In transportation and in the utility industry, again output was higher— slightly in transportation, spectacularly in utility's electrical output—and again, employment had actually declined.

big profit not shared

---

* In theory, there is a cure for situations in which the producers of one commodity are undercompensated relative to other pursuits: Producers will leave the undercompensated field for more lucrative occupations. Indeed, the American farmer tried this cure. It has been estimated that twenty farmers left the soil to seek city work for every urban worker who came to the land. Unfortunately, the cure did not work fast enough. While the agricultural sector steadily diminished in relative size, it could not shrink its absolute numbers significantly. From 1910 to 1930, approximately 10 million farmers remained "locked" on the farm, perhaps half of them barely contributing to national output beyond their own meager livelihoods.

Overall employment had not, of course, declined. It was significantly up in construction, in trade and finance, in the service industries, and in government. But note that all these employment-absorbing industries were characterized by one common denominator: They were all relatively devoid of technological advance. Or to put it the other way around, all the employment-static or declining industries were singularly characterized by rapid technological advance. In other words, pressing against the overall upward tendency of the economy was an undertow of *technological displacement.*

more productivity w/ fewer employees

technology and employment

Heretofore in our frequent consideration of technology, we have never stopped to inquire what its effects might be on employment. Rather, we have implicitly assumed those effects to be positive, as we dwelt on the capacity of industrial technology to increase output. Yet it is not difficult to see that technology need not always be favorable for employment. When a new invention creates a new industry, such as the automobile, it is clear that its employment-creating effect can be enormous. Yet, even in such an instance there is an undertow, albeit a small one, as the growing automobile industry crowds out the old carriage industry. When we turn to inventions that do not create new *demands* but merely make an established industry more productive, it is clear that the initial impact of technical change can generate serious unemployment.

Technologically displaced workers may be reabsorbed eventually, particularly if the economy is growing rapidly. We will return to this problem later on in the chapter, but now we want to examine still further the effect of rapid technological change in the "displacing industries" themselves during the 1920s. And here we see an interesting fact. As production soared and employment sagged, the output per man-hour rose rapidly; in fact, between 1920 and 1929, it increased over 30 percent in transportation, over 40 percent in mining, and over 60 percent in manufacturing.* This much larger flow of production per hour meant that wages *could have* been raised substantially or prices cut sharply. But this is not what we find to have been the case. Only on the unionized railroads did wage rates rise (by about 5 percent). In mining, hourly earnings fell by nearly 20 percent, and in manufacturing, they remained steady. Since the hours of work per week were also declining, the average annual earnings of employees in these industries were far from keeping pace with the rise in their productivity. In mining, average yearly earnings fell from $1,700 to $1,481. In transportation and manufacturing,

cut costs increase profits

---

* These productivity indexes cannot be computed from our previous output and employment figures, since weekly hours changed. For the original figures, see *Historical Statistics,* Series W.

yearly earnings fell from 1920 through 1922 and did not regain 1920 levels until 1928 and 1929.

Thus, the gains from higher productivity were not passed along to the industrial worker in terms of higher wages. Were they passed along via lower prices? Yes, to some extent. The overall cost of living between 1920 and 1929 fell by about 15 percent. Part of this reduction, as we have seen, was due to falling food prices. Nonfood goods fell sharply in price from 1920 postwar peaks to 1921; thereafter they, too, declined about 15 percent up to 1929, but the fall was not enough to distribute all the gains from industrial technology. How do we know this? Because the *profits* of large manufacturing corporations soared between 1920 and 1929. From 1916 through 1925, profits for these companies had averaged around $730-odd million a year; from 1926 through 1929, they averaged $1,400 million. Indeed, in the year 1929, profits were triple those of 1920.[5]

maldistri-bution of income

Now we can generalize from what we have just discovered about the trend of wages and profits to state one further reason for the sudden weakness that overcame the economy, beginning in 1929. Income was distributed in such a way as to make the system vulnerable to economic shocks.

This does *not* mean that somehow the American economy was failing to generate "enough" purchasing power to buy its own output. An economy always creates enough *potential* buying power to purchase what it has produced.

There can, however, be a very serious *maldistribution* of the income payments arising from production. For not all the proceeds arising from production may be placed in the hands of people who will *exercise*

TABLE 7-1 Top Incomes

Percentage shares of total income received by the top 1 percent and top 5 percent of total population[a]		
Year	Top 1 percent	Top 5 percent
1919	12.2	24.3
1923	13.1	27.1
1929	18.9	33.5

SOURCE: *Historical Statistics.*
[a] The table shows the "disposable income variant"; i.e., income after payment of taxes and receipt of capital gains.

[5] *Historical Statistics*, V, 236.

their purchasing power. Incomes paid out to the lower-paid strata of the labor force do, indeed, return to the stream of purchasing power, for the worker tends to spend his or her wages quickly. But incomes that take the form of profits, or business accruals, or of very high individual compensations may not quickly turn over as purchasing power. Profits or high incomes may be saved. They may eventually return to the great stream of purchasing demand, but income that is saved does not "automatically" return via the route of consumption expenditure. Instead, it must find a different route—the route of investment, of capital building.

Returning to the economy in 1929, we can now see as well what was perhaps the deepest-seated reason for its vulnerability: the fact that its income payments were not going in sufficient volume to those who would surely spend them. We have already understood why farmers and workers, who were indeed possessed of a "limitless" desire to consume, were pinched in their *ability* to buy. Now we must complete the picture by seeing how the failure to distribute the gains of productivity to the lower-income groups swelled the incomes of those who were potential *non*spenders.

What we see here is an extraordinary, and steadily worsening, concentration of incomes. By 1929, the 15,000 families or individuals at the apex of the national pyramid, with incomes of $100,000 or more each, probably received as much income as the 5 to 6 million families at the bottom of the pyramid. And more was involved here than moral equity. This extraordinary concentration of incomes meant that the prosperity of the Twenties—and for the majority of the nation, it *was* a prosperity of hitherto unequaled extent—in fact covered over an economic situation of grave potential weakness. For *if* the nation's ongoing momentum should be checked, in this lopsided distribution of purchasing power lay a serious problem. So long as the high profits and salaries and dividends continued to be returned to the income stream, all was well. But what if they should not be?

CRITICAL ROLE OF CAPITAL FORMATION

The question brings us to a critical relationship that has gradually been emerging throughout these pages as the central dynamic process in determining the level of activity in a market society. The relationship is that between the savings that a society desires to make, on the one hand, and its opportunities for profitable investment, on the other. We cannot explain the main events of the Great Depression unless we have a general grasp of the central economic problem of a market society.

Actually, we have already understood half the savings-investment relationship. In our chapter on the Industrial Revolution, we saw that saving was an indispensable prerequisite for capital formation. Now we must complete our understanding by adding the next step in the growth process. *Unless we make large enough capital expenditures to absorb our saving, we will not be able to keep the economy moving forward.* If saving is essential for investment, investment is essential for prosperity.

Indeed, because investment expenditure is the way we return savings to the income flow, we can see that the rate at which we add to our stock of capital equipment will have a deep effect on our overall economic well-being. When spending for investment is sluggish, bad times are upon us. When spending for capital formation quickens, good times are again at hand. In other words, *the rate of capital formation is really the key to prosperity or recession.*

That does not yet tell us why the rate of capital expenditure should fluctuate. But a moment's reflection makes the answer clear enough. Spending for consumption purposes tends to be a reliable and steady process. Most consumer goods are quickly used up and must be replaced. The desire to maintain a given standard of living is not subject to sudden shifts or changes. As consumers, we are all to a considerable extent creatures of habit.

investment and profit expectations

Not so with capital expenditures. Unlike consumer goods, most capital goods are durable, and their replacement can therefore easily be postponed. Again in contrast to consumer goods, capital goods are not bought out of habit or for personal enjoyment. They are bought only because they are expected to yield a *profit* when put to use. We commonly hear it said that a new store, a new machine, or an additional stock of inventory must "pay for itself." And so it must. New investment increases output, and that additional output must have a profitable sale. If for any reason a profit is not anticipated, the investment will not be made.

This enables us to see that the *expectation* of profit (which may be greater or less than profits actually being realized at the moment) plays a crucial role in the rate of capital formation. But why—and this is the last and obviously the key question—should a profit *not* be expected from a new investment good?

The answers all bring us back to our point of departure in the early 1930s. One answer may be that a speculative collapse, such as the great crash, destroys "confidence" or impairs financial integrity and leads to a period of retrenchment while financial affairs are put in order. Another reason may be that costs shoot up and monetary troubles impede the boom: The banks may become loaned up and money for new capital projects may suddenly become "tight" and dear. Still another reason may be that consumption expenditures are sluggish, owing perhaps to a maldistribution of income, such as that of the late 1920s, thereby discouraging plant expansion. Or the rate of population growth or of family formation may decline, bringing a slowdown in the demand for housing. Or the boom may simply die a natural death—that is, the wave of technological advance on which it rode may peter out, the great investments needed to build up a tremendous industry may be completed, and no second wave of equal capital-attracting magnitude may immediately rise to take its place.

effects of falling investment

Many of these reasons, as we have seen, served to bring capital formation to a halt in the Great Depression. The crash itself, with its terrible blow to confidence and to the solvency of banks and holding companies, the weakness of the agricultural sector, the drag of technological displacement, and the maldistribution of income all combined to bring about a virtual cessation of economic growth. The figures in Table 7-2 for gross private domestic investment—the proper nomenclature for private capital formation—tell their own grim story.

Thus, the Great Depression can be characterized essentially as a tremendous and long-lasting collapse in the rate of capital formation. In housing, in manufacturing plant and equipment, in commercial building, in the accumulation of inventories, a paralysis afflicted the economy. Between 1929 and 1933, investment-goods output shrank by 88 percent in real terms—that is, after allowances for price changes. Although the capital-goods industries employed only one-tenth of the total labor force in 1929, by 1933, one-third of total unemployment had been caused by the shrinkage of these critical industries. Here is a major key to the depression.

multiplier effect

But the trouble did not end there. When savings are not returned to active purchasing power because of inadequate investment, the fall in buying begins to spread. Let us say that a steelworker is laid off because of the slump in building. He will certainly pare his family's budget to the bone.

TABLE 7-2 Gross Private Domestic Investment

Year	Residential nonfarm construction	Other construction	Producers' durable equipment	Change in inventories
	Billions of current dollars			
1929	$3.6	$5.1	$5.9	$+1.7
1932	6	1.2	1.6	−2.6

SOURCE: *Historical Statistics.*

But this in turn will create a further loss in income for the businesses where the steelworker's family ordinarily spent its income. Others will lose their jobs or have their wages reduced. In this way a kind of snowball effect, or to use the proper term, a *multiplier effect*, is brought about.

This helps us understand the mechanism of the Great Depression. As capital expenditures fell during the early 1930s, they pulled down consumption expenditures with them; and because of the multiplier effect, by an even larger amount than the fall in investment. From 1929 to 1933, consumption declined from $79 to $49 billion, nearly twice as large a drop as the absolute fall in investment. And the fall of consumption, in turn, pulled down still further the flow of capital expenditures.

To be sure, the process works the other way around as well. When capital expenditures again begin to mount, consumption expenditures typically climb by an even larger amount. For example, President Truman pointed out in a radio address in 1949 that $1 billion of new public expenditures, which gave initial income to some 315,000 people, also added to the incomes of some 700,000 more. In expansion as well as in contraction, there is a typical *cumulative* pattern to economic activity, as success breeds further success, and failure breeds further failure.

Our brief excursion into theory of economic fluctuations comes to an end at this point. But the understanding we have gained enables us to see the Great Depression not only as a historical phenomenon, but also as an instance of a more endemic problem of a market society. We have seen how that society paved the way for the Great Depression by its malfunctions in the 1920s. Now let us follow the struggles of the economy in the 1930s as it sought to escape from the deepest and most destructive depression it had ever known.

KEY CONCEPTS AND KEY WORDS

Growth 1. The outstanding economic fact of the hundred years prior to 1929 was the long trend of *economic growth*—a trend that doubled per capita incomes in the United States roughly every forty years and that brought U.S. prosperity in 1929 to unprecedented heights.

Depression 2. The long trend of growth came to a disastrous stop—for nearly a decade—with the advent of the *Great Depression*. The causes of the depression were many:

Credit structure
Technological unemployment
Distribution of income

- A *speculative and shaky credit structure* that was demolished by the *stock market crash* of 1929, and by *inept monetary policy*.
- A *steady deterioration of farm purchasing power* aggravated by the inelastic demand for farm products.
- A considerable undertow of *technological unemployment*.
- A bad and *worsening distribution of income*.

Capital formation

3. The joint effect of these causes was a tremendous *collapse in capital formation*. Between 1929 and 1933, investment (in real terms) declined by 88 percent.

National income

4. *A fall in investment is a prime cause of a fall in national income,* because investment is the route over which savings return to the flow of national spending. When investment fails to return savings, recession begins.

Investment spending

5. Investment is thus a critical element in determining the level of prosperity. It is, however, a highly volatile element, since *investment spending depends on expected profits.* When expectations are not optimistic, new capital will not be built.

Multiplier effect

6. A relatively small decline in investment spending can spread through the economy. This is called the *multiplier effect.*

QUESTIONS

1. Discuss the causes of the Great Depression in terms of what you know about the economy today. Do you think another Great Depression is possible?

2. Among the families you know, how many work for companies that provide goods or services for capital formation—that is, for investment purposes rather than for consumption?

3. Suppose that you were in business and intended to build a plant to turn out a promising new item—say, a pencil that would last twice as long as present kinds. What sorts of developments might discourage you from making this investment? How much would your final decision hinge on what you anticipated for the future, compared with what you knew to be the situation today?

4. How can the money you put into a savings bank get back into someone's hands as his or her income? the money you put into a newly formed business? the money you put into insurance?

5. If your income (or your parents') were suddenly reduced to half, by how much would your expenditures fall? What sorts of businesses would be hit by your reduced spending? Would they, in turn, curtail their expenditures?

6. Why is investment so critical in determining the level of prosperity?

8 THE EVOLUTION OF GUIDED CAPITALISM

"This nation asks for action, and action now. . . . We must act and act quickly."

The words are from the inaugural address of the incoming President, Franklin Delano Roosevelt. It is hard today to reconstruct the urgency, the sense of desperation, against which the words were addressed on March 4, 1933. A few hours before the actual inauguration ceremony, every bank in America had locked its doors. The monetary system was at the point of collapse. Nearly 13 million Americans were without work. A veterans' march on Washington, 15,000 strong, in the previous year had been dispersed with tear gas, tanks, and bayonets. On the farms, mortgage-lifting parties, at which a noose was tactfully displayed, served as powerful deterrents to any representatives of insurance companies or banks who might be thinking of bidding on foreclosed land. Meanwhile, a parade of business leaders before the Senate Finance Committee had produced a depressing sense of impotence. Said the president of a great railroad, "The only way to beat the depression is to hit the bottom and then slowly build up." "I have no solution," said the president of one of New York's biggest banks. "I have no remedy in mind," testified the president of US Steel. "Above all we must balance the budget," urged a long string of experts.[1] The crisis was a deep and genuine one; it is doubtful if the United States has ever stood closer to economic collapse and social violence.

the New Deal   The new President's response was immediate and vigorous: In the three months after Roosevelt's inauguration, writes Arthur Schlesinger, "Congress and the country were subjected to a presidential barrage of ideas and programs unlike anything known to American history." This was the famous Hundred Days of the New Deal—the days in which, half by

[1] Arthur Schlesinger, Jr., *The Crisis of the Old Order* (Boston: Houghton Mifflin, 1957), pp. 457–58.

149

design, half by accident, the foundation was laid for a new pattern of government relationship to the private economy, a pattern that was to spell a major change in the organization of American capitalism.

We begin to trace its general outline in the main measures of the Hundred Days. In all, some fifteen major bills were passed: the Emergency Banking Act, which reopened the banks under what amounted to government supervision;* the establishment of the Civilian Conservation Corps to absorb at least some of the young unemployed; the Federal Emergency Relief Act to supplement the exhausted relief facilities of states and cities; the Emergency Farm Mortgage Act, which loaned four times as much to farmers in seven months as all federal loans in the previous four years; the Tennessee Valley Authority Act, setting up TVA, a wholly new venture into government enterprise; the Glass-Steagall Banking Act, divorcing commercial banks from their stock- and bond-floating activities and guaranteeing bank deposits; the first of the Securities Acts aimed at curbing stock speculation and reckless corporate pyramiding.

The Hundred Days only inaugurated the New Deal; it did not by any means complete it. Social Security, housing legislation, the National Recovery Act, the dissolution of public-utility holding companies, and the establishment of a Federal Housing Authority were yet to come. So was the Wagner Act. Indeed, it would not be until 1938 that the New Deal would be "completed" with the passage of the Fair Labor Standard Acts, establishing minimum wages and maximum hours and banning child employment for interstate commerce.

It would take us beyond the boundaries of our survey of general economic history to investigate the content of each of these important pieces of legislation, but we can gain an overall view of the New Deal by summarizing its achievements against the backdrop of the problems and issues of economic history that we have already encountered. Then we will see that the New Deal marked a genuine change in the development of the market economy itself. With its advent we begin to trace the evolution of a new kind of capitalism, different in significant ways from that which we have heretofore studied. We must understand the nature of this evolution if we are to bring our survey of general economic history to its contemporary terminus in our own society.

the farm problem One general problem that confronted the New Deal we noted earlier, in the preceding chapter. It was the severe misfunction of the market mechanism in agriculture.

---

* Some idea of the desperation of the times can be gained from the fact that the act was passed by the House of Representatives *sight unseen*!

The problem, we will remember, arose in large part from two causes: the nature of the inelastic demand for farm products, and the highly competitive, "atomistic" structure of the agricultural market itself. The New Deal could not alter the first cause, the inelasticity of demand, for this arose from the nature of the consumers' desire for food. But it could change the condition of supply that hurled itself, self-destructively, against an unyielding demand. Hence, one of the earliest pieces of New Deal legislation—the Agricultural Adjustment Act—sought to establish machinery by which farmers, as a group, could accomplish what they could not as competitive individuals: curtailment of output.

The curtailment was sought by offering payments to farmers who agreed to cut back their acreage or in other ways hold down their output. In the first year of the act, there was no time to cut back acreage, so that every fourth row of growing cotton had to be plowed under, and 6 million pigs were slaughtered. In a nation still hungry and ill-clad, such a spectacle of waste aroused sardonic and bitter comment. And yet, if the program reflected an appalling inability of a society to handle its distribution problem, its attack on overproduction was not without results. In both 1934 and 1935, more than 30 million acres were taken out of production in return for government payments of $1.1 billion. Farm prices rose as a result. Wheat, which had slumped to 38¢ a bushel in 1932, rose to $1.02 in 1936. Cotton doubled in price, hog prices tripled, and the net income of the American farmer climbed from the fearful low of $2.5 billion in 1932 to $5 billion in 1936.

We need not here retrace the many later developments in the agricultural programs of the New Deal and its successors. Suffice it rather to make the point that the *central* idea of the AAA has remained. Farmers' incomes no longer reflect the extreme fluctuations characteristic of an inelastic demand, but are cushioned by government payments earned by adhering to some form of crop limitation. The uncontrolled competitive struggle to market crops has given way to a continuing effort to achieve a balance between supply and demand by limiting supply itself.

farm results Has the idea worked well? It might have, but for one thing. Belatedly, technology caught up with American agriculture. Starting in the years before World War II and continuing thereafter with accelerating effect, productivity on the farm began to soar—in fact, it rose faster than productivity in industry. Hence, despite the limitation of *acreage*, the actual output of *crops* increased steadily: between 1940 and the late 1960s, for instance, the amount of harvested acreage declined by 15 percent, but the yield per acre increased by *more than 70 percent*. The result was a flood of output, huge quantities of which had to be purchased and stored by the government under its support programs. Despite the gradual distribution of these surpluses to the underdeveloped lands during the 1960s and the emergence of a world food shortage in the 1970s, the surplus problem has been a recurrent national embarrassment.*

Thus the attempt to solve the farm problem has been a mixed success. It has not, for instance, succeeded in much improving the economic status of the million and a half least-productive small farmers. In addition, many middle-class farmers have been hard hit by the vagaries of the agricultural market. In the late 1970s, successful farmers who borrowed heavily to improve their farms found themselves saddled with crushing interest payments when crop prices fell in the early 1980s. In constant dollars, net farm incomes in 1983 were only *one-third* of their 1979 level! Farm foreclosures were once again headline news, and some of the heartbreaking drama of the 1930s was visible on TV, although on a smaller scale than in those desperate days. As we write, things are again changing—this time for the better.

In truth, farming has always been an economically difficult way of life, a fact that helps us understand the presence of farm support programs of one kind or another in all advanced capitalist nations, not just in the United States. Yet we must not lose sight of the larger picture even as we acknowledge the failure of social policy to remedy the problems of inelastic demand curves and dynamic technologies.† We get some sense of the longer trend when we realize that in 1940 only one-third of all farm families had electricity in their homes and only half that number had refrigeration. Today virtually all farms are electrified and refrigerator ownership is over 95 percent. Thus, despite the hardships that afflict the industry, the million-odd farmers who produce some 90 percent of our agricultural output have risen to enjoy an essentially middle-class standard of living, a parity with the urban middle class that was never achieved before.

the attempt to control markets   Our primary interest, however, is not to assess the relative success or failure of the farm programs from early New Deal days to the present. It is rather to note that all the programs spelled a fundamental change in the role of the government in a market society. *The essence of that change was that the government sought to alter the structure of certain*

---

* Technology had been catching up with—and creating problems for—the farmer for a long time. One of the reasons for the overproduction of the 1920s was that we were steadily cutting back on the acreage needed to sustain horses and mules as tractors came into general use. Before World War I, we used to devote over a quarter of our cropland to sustaining draft animals. After 1940, this fell to just over 10 percent. Much of the land not needed for animals went into production for the market, thereby adding its load of straw to the camel's back. I am indebted to Professor Eldon Weeks for this point.

† For inelastic demand, see pp. 140–41.

markets to allow the competitive process to produce socially acceptable results.

For it was not only in the agricultural sector that the government tried to ameliorate the functioning of the competitive process. In the industrial sector as well, a new policy of active intervention tried to bring about a better working of the economic mechanism.

In industry as in agriculture, during the first years of acute economic distress, intervention mainly took the form of an attempt to limit supply. Under the provisions of the National Industrial Recovery Act (NIRA), passed in 1933, business was permitted to make sweeping price-and-production agreements (in return for wage agreements designed to better the incomes of the poorest paid). In other words, recovery was aimed at by legalizing the partial oligopolization of business.

The NIRA was greeted with great enthusiasm, and nearly 800 industrial "codes" were elaborated under it. But as the demoralized markets of the early 1930s regained some degree of orderliness, a new source of complaint arose. Smaller producers within many industries claimed that the codes favored the large producer. By the time the experiment was declared unconstitutional by the Supreme Court in 1935, it had already become apparent that the problem was not too much competition, but too little.

There arose a radical shift in policy signaled by the vigorous prosecution of the antitrust laws, a development we traced in Chapter 6. Yet, although the angle of attack had changed completely, the objective was much the same: *to make the market work.*

regulating
the market

To what extent can the government make markets work? The answer, as we have seen, is far from clear-cut. Against the powerful forces of oligopoly on the one hand, and the self-defeating competition of "atomistic" industries on the other, the market-shaping powers of government may well prove to be inadequate. But in the formulation of the aim itself is evidence of a profoundly important change in the philosophy of the market society. No longer does laissez faire constitute the "ideal" relationship between government and the economy. Rather, there has arisen a recognition that there are many *different kinds of markets*, some of which require government intervention of one kind or another in order to function properly for the larger society. For instance, there is now a widely acknowledged need for government to intervene in markets where the processes of production normally generate bad "externalities"—that is, socially dangerous byproducts, such as poisonous wastes or other pollutants. There is agreement that government must insure that buyers be provided adequate information about products, whether these be medicines or stocks and bonds. There is unanimity that government should enforce standards of safety in markets such as air travel, and in products that can inflict violent damage, like automobiles and tires. There is a great deal of consensus that the government must intervene in labor markets to assure minimum standards of health and safety for men and women exposed to hazardous processes.

The questions of *how much* intervention and *what kind* of intervention remain disputatious matters: There is more than one way to make a market work better. And sometimes it is as difficult to decide on whether one should get the government out of markets as it is to decide on whether to get it into the market. Thus, the heritage of the New Deal is not a blank check for government to regulate whatever it wishes. It is, rather, a general, pragmatic recognition that markets do not always work best when left alone, and that government is willy-nilly the means by which a democratic polity must resolve the tensions between its economic activities and its noneconomic values.

countering the depression
The market system had broken down in a much more important way than was revealed in the farm glut, or even in the troubles of the manufacturing sector. Its real collapse in the 1930s was its inability to solve the basic production problem itself—its inability to put together human beings, capital, and land in order to produce a satisfactory level of output for the nation.

It is curious that the Roosevelt administration had little clear idea of how to remedy this situation when it first took office. Neither, as we have seen, did the business community. Indeed, for nearly everyone, economists included, the only "remedy" for the depression was thought to be a balanced budget for the government.

Yet there were emergencies to be faced that could not be deferred, even if they unbalanced the budget. Many of the unemployed were literally at the brink of starvation, and the resources of private, state, and local charities were in most instances exhausted. President Roosevelt, unlike his predecessor, did not believe that the receipt of federal relief would "demoralize" the unemployed any more than the receipt of federal loans from the Reconstruction Finance Corporation had "demoralized" business. By May of the inaugural year, a relief organization had been established; and a year later, nearly one out of every seven Americans was receiving relief. In nine states, one out of five families—in one state one out of three families—was dependent on public support. Not that relief did much more than keep these unfortunate families from starvation—the average grant per family was less than $25 per month—but it did provide an economic floor, no matter how rickety.

The immediate aims of relief were humanitarian. Shortly, however, they were followed by thoughts of the *useful* possibilities of relief expenditures. Soon the great bulk of relief spending was being paid for public works of various sorts: schools, roads, parks, hospitals, slum clearance—and even federal art, theater, and writing projects.

As the public-works program grew, however, the finances of the federal government took a turn for the worse, until, by the mid-1930s, it was clear that something like a chronic deficit of $2 billion to $3 billion a year had been achieved. Each year the government spent more than it took in through taxes—not only for relief, but for conservation, farm subsidies, veterans' bonuses, public housing, and aid to the states as well. To meet its bills, it borrowed the necessary money from the public through the sale of government bonds to private individuals, to corporations, and to the commercial banks. Obviously, as the total amount of bonds outstanding grew each year, so did the total debt of the nation. In 1929, the national debt totaled $16.9 billion. By 1935, it had risen to $28.7 billion, and each year it steadily rose: to $36 billion in 1937, to $40 billion in 1939, to $42 billion in 1940.

the economy   At first, the heavy spending of the federal government was greeted with
fails to   wary acceptance by the business and banking communities as a nec-
respond   essary temporary expedient. Before long, however, even within the administration itself, the mounting deficit was regarded with considerable misgivings. The recurrent excess of government expenditure over tax receipts was thereupon apologized for as "pump priming"—as an injection of government fuel which would, so to speak, start up the stalled motor of private expenditures, making further injections unnecessary. Thus, a few billions of government spending, it was hoped, would set into motion an upward spiral of spending and job expansion by the business sector.

But the upward spiral did not materialize. After 1933, helped by government spending, *consumption* expenditures began to rise, but private capital expenditures lagged behind. Although they, too, improved after 1933, by 1938, they were still 40 percent below 1929.

Why did private investment fail to rise? The answer lies partly in the fact that the very government deficits that were supposed to cure the depression only frightened business into a condition of economic paralysis that prolonged it. Coupled with the reform legislation of the New Deal, the new presence of government's large-scale economic activity caused business to lose its former "confidence." The businessman felt ill at ease in a changing economic and political climate and was in no mood to plan ahead boldly for the future. The general outlook stressed caution rather than promise; cycles rather than growth; safety rather than gain. And then, behind the psychological factors, real forces were also at work. A much slower rate of population growth in the 1930s depressed the important housing market. Even more serious, no major industry-creating technological breakthrough, comparable to the railway or the automobile, held sufficient promise of profitable growth to tempt private capital into a major capital-building boom of its own.*

Thus, for many reasons, the new federal expenditures did not prime the pump. Private investment did not spontaneously rise to take over its traditional propulsive function, now "temporarily" carried out by the government. This did not mean, however, that the economic influence of government was therefore relegated to a minor role. On the contrary, the failure of pump priming—conceived as an emergency measure—caused a widening in the conception of the government's role. Government now began to be envisioned as a *permanent stabilizing and growth-promoting agency for the market economy as a whole.*

compensatory government spending

The idea was slow in taking form and did not, in fact, receive its full-dress theoretical exposition until the middle 1930s. The most influential book setting forth the concept—albeit in highly technical terms—was John Maynard Keynes's *General Theory of Employment, Interest and Money*, published in 1936. Few books have roused such controversy or left so permanent a mark. As is often the case with new ideas, the book seemed at first complicated and difficult, and even among professional economists its basic concepts were the subject of murky discussion for a number of years. Yet, in retrospect, it appears as a very simple argument—the stuff of freshman economics courses!

The key to prosperity or depression, it had become increasingly evident, lay in the *total volume of expenditure* that a market society laid out for its goods and services. When that volume was high, employment and incomes were high; when it declined, output and employment declined as well. And what determined the volume of expenditure? As we have seen, the stream of consumption spending tended to be a passive factor, rising when individuals' incomes rose and diminishing when they fell. The volatile item, as both history and theory made clear, was the stream of capital expenditure.

From this starting point, it is not difficult to take the next step. If lagging private capital expenditures were responsible for lagging employment and output, why could not the government step in to make up whatever deficiencies arose from private expenditure? There had always been, after all, a fairly regular flow of public expenditure, much of it for capital-creating purposes, such as roads or schools. Why could not this flow of public spending be deliberately enlarged when the occasion

* Michael A. Bernstein has recently suggested that a transition to high-growth industries was dealt a crippling blow by the collapse of the financial structure. See his *The Great Depression* (New York City; Cambridge University Press, 1987).

demanded, to maintain the needed total volume of expenditure? True, this required the government to borrow and spend and thereby increase its debt. But did not much private capital spending also result in cor- porate debts? And why could not the debt itself be handled like corporate debts, which were never "paid off" in the aggregate but refunded, with new bond issues being sold to take the place of those coming due?

[margin handwritten: per- enmul debt]

To the economists of the Roosevelt administration, the answers to these questions seemed plain enough. The government not only could, but should, use its spending powers as an economic instrumentality for securing full employment. By this, they did not have in mind a "radical" revision of capitalism. Rather, they envisaged the evolution of a new form of *guided* capitalism—a market society in which the all-important levels of employment and output would no longer be left to the vagaries of the market but would be protected against decline and stimulated toward growth by public action.

fears of government intervention This was not how matters appeared to many members of the nation, however, and especially to the business community. They saw government spending as inherently "wasteful," and the mounting debt as evidence that we would spend ourselves into "bankruptcy." Beneath these arguments there lurked a deeper suspicion, a suspicion that government spending, whatever the protestations to the contrary, was the entering wedge for socialism or worse.

The controversy raged through 1940, and as we shall see, it still rages—or at least smolders—today. But in a sense, it was an empty debate in the New Deal years. At its peak, the annual deficit never touched $4 billion, and federal government purchases never contributed more than 6 percent to gross national product. Judged by the importance of government in the economy, probably no industrial nation in the world was *less* socialist than the United States. Yet if the fears of the conservatives were hardly realistic, neither were the hopes of the liberals. For in the prevailing atmosphere of distrust, the remedy of government spending could never be more than halfheartedly applied. Deficit spending in the 1930s was a holding operation and not an operation of growth. By 1939, although conditions had improved considerably over the levels of 1932, there were still 9.5 million people—17 percent of the labor force—without work.

impact of the war In the end, it was not theory that settled the history of compensatory government spending, but history that settled the theory. With the outbreak of World War II came a tremendous forced expansion in government outlays. Year by year, spending for war purposes rose, until in 1944 federal expenditures totaled just over $100 billion, and with this un-

[handwritten: expenditure & GNP ↑]

precedented rise in expenditure came an equally swift rise in GNP. By 1945, our gross national product had risen by 70 percent in real terms over 1939, and unemployment had dwindled to the vanishing point. The demonstration that public spending could impel the economy forward—indeed, could lift it beyond all previously imagined bounds—was unmistakable. So was the fact that a government could easily carry an enormously larger debt, a debt that now towered over $250 billion, provided that its gross national product was also much larger.

And with the war had come a marked change in attitude both toward the government and toward the economy in general. After four years of unprecedented effort, the American people looked to massive government action with a more accustomed eye; so, too, after four years of record output, they looked back upon the days of mass unemployment with a new feeling of shame. Perhaps most important of all, they looked ahead to the postwar period with considerable trepidation. Virtually every economist, contemplating the huge cutback in spending consequent upon a termination of hostilities, feared the rise of a vast new army of the unemployed. Even the most conservative opinion was uneasy at the political possibilities of such a return to the 1930s.

The upshot of the change in attitude was the passage of the Employment Act of 1946, which declared that it was "the continuing policy and responsibility of the Federal Government . . . to provide maximum employment, production, and purchasing power." It was, as we shall see, one thing to write such an act and another thing to implement it; but without question, the act marked the end of an era. The idea that the best thing the government could do to promote recovery was to do nothing at all, the belief that a balanced budget was in all cases the goal for government fiscal policy, and, beyond that, the trust in the blind forces of the market as inherently conducive to prosperity—all these once firmly held convictions had been abandoned. The debate within capitalism was no longer whether or not government should undertake the responsibility for the overall functioning of the market system. Now only the specific means were questioned: how best to achieve that end.

aftermath of the war   The war ended in 1945; within a year, federal spending dropped by $40 billion, and the nation waited tensely for the expected fall in employment, incomes, and prices.

Instead, it found itself confronting the least anticipated of all eventualities: a rousing inflationary boom. It is true that unemployment doubled, rising to 2 million, but this was still less than 4 percent of the labor force. Meanwhile, the number of people at work showed a steady rise: 54 million jobs in 1945; 57 million in 1946; 60 million in 1947; 63 million in 1950. Industrial production, after a brief postwar dip, was buoyant;

by 1953, it would surpass its wartime peak with no sign of more than a momentary turndown. Most striking of all was what happened to prices. Year by year, the cost of living rose: up a third between 1945 and 1948, up another 10 percent between 1948 and 1952, up still another 7 percent from then to 1957. In all, the purchasing power of the dollar declined by more than a third in the first twelve postwar years.

We will come back to study inflation in the chapters that focus on our current problems. First, let us fill in some more vital background before we turn to the issues of the 1980s. For out of the confrontation with the problem of inflation there emerged for the first time a general consensus on the nature of the mechanisms government was entitled to use in seeking to affect the overall operation of the system.

INSTRUMENTS OF POLICY

A full understanding of these mechanisms requires a study of technical economics. But it is not difficult to grasp the three basic means of control.

The first was *monetary control*, mainly centered in the Federal Reserve banking system. By easing or tightening the reserve requirements that all banks had to maintain behind their deposits, the Federal Reserve was able to encourage or discourage lending, the source of much economic activity. In addition, by buying or selling government bonds, the Federal Reserve was able to make the whole banking system relatively flush with funds when these were needed, or relatively short of funds when money seemed in excess supply.* This is just what the Federal Reserve failed to do in the early days of the Depression.

The second was *tax adjustment*. The pressure of consumer buying during the postwar boom served as a reminder of the fact that the largest fraction of the volume of total expenditure was always consumption spending. By raising or lowering taxes, particularly income taxes, the government could quickly increase or diminish this broad flow of purchasing power.

The third was *the federal budget*. By the 1950s, the great debate over the virtues of a balanced government budget had virtually come to an end. Among academic groups and in a widening circle of business leaders, the budget was recognized as a tool for regulating total national expenditure. In inflationary times, a budget surplus would serve to "mop up" part of the inflationary purchasing flow. In depressed times, a budget deficit (covered by borrowing) was a mechanism for generating a desired increase in that flow.

* See p. 139*n*. Perhaps even more important than active monetary policy is an institutional change introduced by the New Deal. This is the federal insurance of bank deposits. The familiar sign "Insured by FDIC" (Federal Deposit Insurance Corporation) has probably been the single most stabilizing force in modern captialism.

The idea of monetary controls was not new, but the general consensus on the use of taxes and budgets as deliberate instruments of economic policy to counter boom and recession *was* new. Once again, as in the case with government spending, it was not the force of theoretical argument that had won this historic agreement. Rather, it was the fact of historic change that had placed theory in a new light. For essentially, what commended the new means of influence over the market system were profound changes in the structure of that system. Let us see what those changes were.

redistribution of income   In our concentration on the functional problems of the economy in its years of depression, war, and inflation, we have omitted one very significant long-term development. This was a marked movement away from the extreme inequalities of reward that had so vividly marked the capitalism of the past.

In part, this was brought about by a decline in unemployment; in part, by aiding lower-income groups through the support of trade unions, through the enactment of minimum wage floors, and through the passage of welfare legislation. The change was not entirely due to public policy, however. The occupational shifts that we noted at the commencement of our previous chapter also played a powerful role, as workers shifted out of low-paid agricultural and unskilled labor into the semiskilled and skilled categories of the factory.

 skill

However varied the causes, the results were striking. Beginning with the New Deal, then receiving an even stronger impetus from the war, stiffer tax schedules and stricter enforcement had borne down upon the relative affluence of upper-income groups. Table 8-1 gives us some idea of the change.

What happened was quite extraordinary. From 1929 to 1988, we see a fall of almost half in the share of income going to the top 5 percent of

TABLE 8-1 Relative Affluence

Percentage shares of total income received by top 1 percent and top 5 percent of families

	1929	1941	1946	1989
Top 1% (after tax)	18.9	9.9%	7.7	n.a.
Top 5% (after tax)	33.5	24.0	21.3%	17.2

SOURCE: *Historical Statistics*, Series G135, 105 (1929, 1946); *Statistical Abstract of the United States*, 1988, p. 428; 1991, p. 651.

families. This does not mean that there has been smooth and steady progress toward greater income equality. During the years of the Reagan administration there was a movement against the long tide—the tax bill of 1985, for instance, hugely favored upper-income groups. During the 1980s, the lower 80 percent of U.S. families actually suffered a fall in real income; but the top 1 percent enjoyed an increase of 115 percent! In addition, as Table 8-2 shows, there has been a striking change since the great redistribution that followed on the New Deal and World War II. The top 20 percent of families in 1990 received almost ten times as much income, before taxes or transfers, as the lowest 20 percent. This is much the same as the ratio twenty-five years earlier. Nonetheless, comparing the distribution of income in the United States even in the last decade to its shape in the late 1920s leaves no doubt as to the long-term change our economy has undergone.

the growth of government This goes a long way toward explaining the predominantly middle-class viewpoint of American society (and may help explain as well our indifference to the plight of those who fail in the competitive struggle for incomes). If we now look at the extent and size of the "tax bite," as shown in Table 8-3, we can also understand the source of the powerful trend of sentiment against government taxing and spending that has emerged in recent years. When the New Deal first instituted its programs for social betterment, it was just "the rich" who paid income taxes. Today, it is more or less everybody.

Moreover, the change in the distribution of income is important not alone because of its social and political significance, but also because of its economic effects. The widening and deepening tax bite shown in

TABLE 8-2 Share of Total Income by Family Units

Income rank	Percentage of total income	
	1960	1990
All families	100.0	100.0
Lowest fifth	4.8	4.6
Second fifth	12.2	10.8
Third fifth	17.8	10.8
Fourth fifth	24.0	23.8
Highest fifth	41.3	50.0

SOURCE: *Statistical Abstract of the United States,* 1988, p. 428; 1990: U.S. Dept. of Commerce.
NOTE: Detail may not add to totals because of rounding.

TABLE 8-3 Impact of Individual Income Taxes

Year	Number of individual returns (millions)	Average income tax per return
1929	2.5	$17
1940	7.4	101
1988	109.8	4,784

SOURCE: *Statistical Abstract of the United States*, 1988, p. 303; 1991, p. 325; *Historical Statistics*, Series Y 292, 299, 303, 307.

Table 8-3 means that a much larger number of families is affected by a change in taxes, up or down. *This gives far greater leverage to govern-ment tax policy as a means of stimulating or holding back the economy than it had in the 1920s.*

A second development is of even greater consequence. This is the emergence of the public sector as a major component of the economy— a component larger in size, and more powerful in its impact, than the sector of private business investment. Table 8-4 shows us the change in ten-year jumps over the period. The magnitude of the shift can be summed up very simply: *In 1929, all government buying accounted for less than a tenth of gross national product. Since the 1960s, government purchasing has risen to a fifth of GNP.*

TABLE 8-4 Growth of Government Demand

YEAR	GROSS NATIONAL PRODUCT	GOVERNMENT PURCHASES:		FEDERAL PLUS STATE AND LOCAL PURCHASES AS PERCENTAGE OF GNP
		Federal	*State and local*	
	Billions of current dollars			
1929	103.1	1.3	7.2	8.2
1939	90.5	5.1	8.2	14.4
1949	256.5	20.1	17.7	14.7
1959	483.7	53.7	43.3	20.0
1969	930.3	98.9	111.2	22.4
1979	2,418.0	168.0	306.0	19.6
1989	5.244.0	401.4	570.0	18.5
1991	5.672.6	445.1	642.4	19.1

SOURCE: *Historical Statistics, Series F1–5; economic indicators.*

inside the
public sector

Two matters require our attention here. The first is the composition of government demand for output. Notice that state and local government is usually a much larger source of demand than the federal government. This is because most public services, such as education, sanitation, and police and fire protection, are bought at state and local levels. The importance of state and local government as a source of purchasing would be even more striking if we eliminated defense spending from the figures. This would reduce federal purchasing by about three-quarters, while not affecting state and local spending at all.

Second, we must understand that the impact of the federal government is much larger than it appears in Table 8-4, *where we see only the goods and services that government buys.* The federal budget also includes "transfer payments," which do not buy goods and services, but which directly affect the incomes of millions of households. The largest category of transfer payments is Social Security, but a very considerable amount of transfers goes as "grants-in-aid" to states and localities to support programs of various kinds, and for interest payments on the national debt.

If we add these transfer payments to government purchases, the impact of federal spending is much increased. In 1991, for example, the federal government bought $445 billion of goods and services, but it spent a considerably larger sum—$1.3 trillion. Total federal expenditures today amount to over one-fifth of GNP, and if we add net state and local purchases, the impact of all government spending rises to over one-third of GNP.*

As we shall see in later chapters, this does not make the United States an unusually government-oriented economy. On the contrary, compared with other capitalist nations in the world, we have a relatively modest public sector, and the impact of public spending is less than in West Germany, France, the Netherlands, and many other nations. *What we have described, in other words, is a change that can be seen in every capitalist nation—a change in government's role within the market sys-*

---

* The classification of government revenues and outlays is complicated, but we need to understand it in general terms if we are to make sense of "government spending." The federal government has three kinds of expenditures: (1) Purchases of goods and services, such as military spending or federal highways. These are part of GNP and are always included in the federal budget. (2) Transfers that involve "pass-alongs" of federal revenues to other government bodies, mainly states and localities, and also payment of interest on the national debt. These are not part of GNP, and are not in the budget. They are itemized under federal "expenditures and receipts." (3) "Off-budget" items administered by a federal agency whose revenues and expenditures are not included in most statistics of "government spending." These off-budget items include the very large flows of the Social Security system. There is a very important lesson to be learned from this: Before jumping to conclusions about "government spending," be sure that you know (1) if it is federal alone, or federal plus state and local; and (2) if it is federal, whether it includes transfers and off-budget items.

tem. Partly the outcome of a rising sense of public responsibility for individual well-being, partly the result of the urbanized, industrialized environment that besets us, a large and powerful public sector has emerged within every capitalist economy. The movement that we have traced within the United States as a consequence of the New Deal is part of a worldwide transformation of laissez-faire capitalism into guided capitalism.*

a new economic era?
Does the rise of guided capitalism mean that economic catastrophes such as the Great Depression cannot recur? The answer is a cautious yes. It is cautious because we know that very serious malfunctions can still befall us. We had a deep recession in the early 1980s, the worst since 1929. We had a devastating stock market crash in October 1987, even more precipitous than the crash of 1929.

But the answer is yes, however cautious, because it is much less likely that such malfunctions can give rise to the "free-fall" we experienced in the depression era. The recession of 1981 and the crash of 1987 did not generate the secondary and tertiary effects of former crises because the economic system now contains institutions, and is guided by a general understanding, whose main purpose is to prevent precisely such effects.

That is not to declare that modern capitalism no longer faces serious challenges. We will come to them in due time. But "another 1929" is not likely to be among them.

KEY CONCEPTS AND KEY WORDS

New Deal
1. The *New Deal* was a major effort to reverse the downward spiral of the Great Depression. A many-pronged attack, it sought both to correct the failures of the economy and to strengthen its workings.

2. The New Deal *interfered with the structure of markets* to a greater extent than had been tried by an American government before. Not only agricultural, but many industrial markets were regulated in an effort to bring about an orderly economic recovery. Although many of these efforts failed or were declared unconstitutional, the heritage of the New Deal has been a new concept of *government responsibility* and an effective end to the philosophy of laissez faire.

Pump priming
3. The most important of the New Deal policies was the deliberate initiation of *government spending*, first for relief, then for public works, as a means of stimulating private investment—so-called priming of the pump. Owing

---

* Modern capitalism goes by many names: welfare capitalism, state capitalism, late capitalism, and still others. Each title highlights some aspect of the system; for example, "guided capitalism" contrasts with "laissez faire."

to the small scale of the public spending and the prevailing business attitude of fear and suspicion of government intervention, the pump priming did not work.

Compensatory government spending

4. Out of the New Deal experience evolved a new conception of how the economy operated, and of how government might counteract depression. The key was now recognized to be the *total volume of expenditure.* And the new conception urged that whenever private expenditure was insufficient to maintain full employment, the government should add *compensatory spending* of its own.

Employment Act of 1946

5. The war provided convincing evidence that public expenditure could indeed bring about a high level of employment and output. After the war, the *Employment Act of 1946* recognized the role of the government in promoting "maximum employment."

Fiscal policy

6. Postwar experience brought inflation rather than the generally expected recession. But the period also saw the formulation of a general consensus on the tools of economic policy:

Monetary controls

Federal budget

• *Monetary controls* to encourage or discourage private spending.
• *Tax adjustments* to induce or to dampen consumer and business spending.
• The use of the *federal budget* as a balance wheel in the economy.

Public sector

7. These new tools were made more workable by the considerable *redistribution of income* that had taken place and by *the enlargement of the public sector.*

Guided capitalism

8. By no means a cure for all economic ills, *guided capitalism* nonetheless holds the promise of an end to the terrible depressions of the past.

QUESTIONS

1. What do you think is the prevailing attitude of big business to government today? of small business? farmers? students?

2. Even if the Hoover administration had wanted to take a more active role in combating the depression, it would have been difficult in those times for it to do so. Why?

3. Do you consider inflation to be as dangerous a condition as depression?

4. The farm problem will always be difficult to solve as long as agriculture is a highly competitive industry, faced with an inelastic demand and with a technology that continuously increases productivity. Explain why.

5. Do you think that all government spending is wasteful? some? all private spending? some? How does one measure "waste"?

6. In what ways has history provided the testing ground for the theory of government spending? Was World War II such a test? Was it conclusive? What would invalidate the theory that government spending can properly supplement private investment to cure a depression?

9

THE DRIFT OF EUROPEAN
ECONOMIC HISTORY

In the last several chapters, we focused our narrative of economic history on the rise of modern capitalism in America. But our initial narrative is not yet complete. For the central subject of our early pages was not just the rise of American capitalism, but also the emergence of the market system itself, and in describing its development in America, we have by no means described it everywhere. That will be our task in this final section of our book. We must follow the fortunes of the market first in Europe and then in the international economy. Then we will return to examine the problems of capitalism in America today, before concluding with a generalization about the market system in the long evolution of economic society.

EUROPEAN CAPITALISM

the feudal heritage Let us begin with Europe, for there are lessons to be learned in comparing the course of capitalism there and at home. The first is that the market system has developed differently there and here because it did not develop within the same social and political framework.

In the New World, capitalism developed with a population that had, to a large degree, spiritually and physically shed the feudal encumbrances of the Old World. In that Old World, many of the social outlooks and habitudes of the past lingered on. An awareness of class position—and more than that, an explicit recognition of class hostility—was as conspicuous by its presence in Europe as by its absence in America. In Vienna in 1847, writes one social historian:

At the top were the nobles who considered themselves the only group worth noticing. The human race starts with barons, said one of them. Then there were the big businessmen who wanted to buy their way into the human race; the little businessmen; the proud but poor intellectuals; the students who were still poorer and still prouder; and the workers who were poor and had always been very, very humble.[1]

The result was a totally different climate for the development of an economic society. Capitalism in America, building on a new and vigorous foundation, was, from the beginning, a system of social consensus. Capitalism in Europe, building on a feudal base, was deeply tinged with class conflict. It was without effort that American capitalism secured the loyal support of its "lower orders"; but in Europe, by the time of the revolutions of 1848, those lower orders had already turned their backs on capitalism as a vehicle for their hopes and beliefs.

national rivalries   Second, and no less important in explaining the divergence of American and European economic evolution, was the profound difference between the political complexion of the two continents. In America, save only for the terrible crisis of the Civil War, a single national purpose fused the continent; in Europe, a historic division of languages, customs, and mutually suspicious nationalities again and again prevented just such a fusion.

Accordingly, American capitalism came of age in an environment in which political unity permitted the unhindered growth of an enormous unobstructed market, while in Europe a jigsaw puzzle of national boundaries forced industrial growth to take place in cramped quarters and in an atmosphere of continued national rivalry. It is curious to note that whereas Europe was considered "wealthier" than America all through the nineteenth century, American productivity in many fields began to outstrip that of Europe from at least the 1850s, and perhaps much earlier. For instance, at the Paris Exposition of 1854, an American threshing machine was twice as productive as its nearest (English) rival and eleven times as productive as its least (Belgian) competitive model.[2]

These advantages of geographic space, richness of resources, and political unity were widened by subsequent developments in European industry. Not surprisingly, European producers, like those in America, sought to limit the destructive impact of industrial competition, and for this purpose they turned to *cartels*—contractual (rather than merely voluntary) agreements to share markets or fix prices. Unlike the case in America, however, this self-protective movement received the blessing, overt or tacit, of European governments. Although "anticartel" laws existed in many European countries, these laws were almost never enforced; by 1914, there were more than 100 international cartels, repre-

[1] Priscilla Robertson, *Revolutions of 1848* (New York: Harper, Torchbooks, 1960), p. 194.
[2] Thomas Cochran and William Miller, *The Age of Enterprise*, rev. ed. (New York: Harper, Torchbooks, 1961), p. 58.

senting the most varied industries, in which most European nations participated.*

Cartelization was undoubtedly good for the profit statements of the cartelized firms, but it was hardly conducive to growth—either for those firms or for new ones. By establishing carefully delineated and protected "preserves," the cartel system rewarded unaggressive behavior rather than economic daring; and together with the ever-present problem of cramping national frontiers, it drove European producers into a typical high-cost, high-profit-margin, low-volume pattern rather than into the American pattern of very large plants with very high efficiencies. The difference in economic scale is dramatically illustrated by steel. In 1885, Great Britain led the world in the production of steel; fourteen years later, her entire output was less than that of the Carnegie Steel Company alone.

the lag in productivity
As a result, by the early twentieth century, European productivity lagged very seriously behind American. A study by Professor Taussig in 1918 showed that the daily output of coal per underground worker was 4.68 tons in the United States, as contrasted with 1.9 tons in Great Britain, 1.4 tons in Prussia, and 0.91 tons in France. In 1905, the output of bricks per person employed was 141,000 in the United States and 40,000 in Germany; U.S. pig-iron production was 84.5 tons per worker in 1909, compared with only 39 tons in Great Britain in 1907.[3] Parts of these differences were attributable to geological differentials, but these, too, were made worse by restrictive business practices. The result was a steady falling behind in Europe as the twentieth century went on.

The divergence was strikingly noticeable in per capita incomes. In 1911, for example, when per capita income in the United States was $368, the corresponding figure for Great Britain was $250, for Germany $178, for France $161, for Italy $108. By 1928, American per capita income was $541 (in unchanged dollar values), while that of the United Kingdom was only $293; of Germany, $199; of France, $188; and of Italy, $96.[4] While American per capita incomes had grown by nearly 46 percent, English and French per capita incomes had increased only one-third as rapidly. German incomes rose only about one-quarter as fast, and Italian per capita incomes had actually declined.

---

* In 1939, an estimated 109 cartels also had American participation, since American companies were not prohibited by antitrust laws from joining international restrictive agreements.

[3] Heinrich E. Friedlaender and Jacob Oser, *Economic History of Modern Europe* (Englewood Cliffs, N.J.: Prentice Hall, 1953), p. 224.

[4] Friedlaender and Oser, *Economic History of Modern Europe*, p. 522.

crucial role of European trade

Still another consequence followed from the division of European industry and agriculture into national compartments. To a far greater extent than in America, it made the development of European capitalism subject to the expansion of international trade.

The division of the European continent into many national units made international trade a continuous and critical preoccupation of economic life abroad. For instance, a study has shown that in 1913, when manufactured imports provided but 3.6 percent of United States consumption of manufactured goods, they provided 9 percent of Germany's, 14 percent of England's, and 21 percent of Sweden's. Perhaps even more striking is the degree to which some nations in Europe depended on international trade for the foodstuffs on which they lived: In the five years preceding World War I, for instance, England produced less than 20 percent of the wheat she consumed and barely over 55 percent of the meat.[5] We find the same dependence on foreign trade in the export side of the picture. Whereas the United States in 1913 exported a mere fifteenth of its national product, France and Germany exported a fifth, and Britain nearly a quarter.

Thus, to a far greater degree than America, Europe lived by foreign trade. Here we see clearly the advantage to America of its enormous unbroken market over the fragmented national markets of Europe. All the gains from trade that were realized in the swift rise of American productivity were denied to Europe. To put it differently, in America, the division of labor was permitted to attain whatever degree of efficiency technology made possible, for in the end, virtually all products entered into a single vast market where they could be exchanged against one another.[6]

Obviously, there are lessons for our time in this story. But let us hold back until we finish our thumbnail history of European Capitalism. In Europe, international trade as a primary means for advancing productivity struggled against the retarding hand of national suspicions, rivalries, and distrust—and lost. A striking example was provided in the early 1950s by the great cluster of European steel and coal industry near the German-Belgian-Luxembourg borders. Here, in a triangle 250 miles on a side, was gathered 90 percent of European steelmaking capacity. But this natural geographic division of labor had to contend with political barriers that largely vitiated its physical productivity. Typically, German coal mines in the Ruhr sold their output to French steelmakers at prices 30 percent higher than to German plants; while, in turn, French iron-ore producers charged far higher prices in Germany than at home. As a

---

[5] *Der Deutsche Aussenhandel* (Berlin: 1932), II, 23. Friedlaender and Oser, op. cit., p. 206.

[6] For a fascinating analysis of different national "styles" of coping with technology, see Alfred Chandler, *Scale and Scope: The Dynamics of Industrial Capitalism* (Cambridge: Harvard University Press, 1990).

Δ % increase
is
low

result, while American steel production soared 300 percent between 1913 and 1950, the output of Europe's steel triangle rose but 3 percent during the same period.

breakdown of international trade

Our example itself poses a question, however. Prior to 1913, as we have seen, something like a great international division of labor did, in fact, characterize the European market, albeit to nothing like the extent seen in America. By 1913, we will remember, a very considerable flow of international trade was enhancing European productivity, despite the hindrances of cartels and national divisiveness. It was only the beginning of a truly free and unhampered international market, but at least it *was* a beginning.

What brought this promising achievement to an end? Initially, it was the shock of World War I, with its violent sundering of European trade channels and its no less destructive aftermath of punitive reparations, war debts, and monetary troubles. In a sense, Europe never recovered from its World War I experience. The slow drift toward national economic separatism, at the expense of international economic cooperation, now accelerated fatefully. Tariffs and quotas multiplied to place new handicaps before the growth of international trade.

The final blow was the depression of 1929. As the depression spread contagiously, nation after nation sought to quarantine itself by erecting still further barriers against economic contacts with other countries. Starting in 1929, an ever-tightening contraction of trade began to strangle economic life around the world. For fifty-three grim months following January 1929, the volume of world trade was lower each month than in the preceding one. Between the late 1920s and the mid-1930s, manufactured imports (in constant prices) fell by a third in Germany, by nearly 40 percent in Italy, and by almost 50 percent in France. As international trade collapsed, so did Europe's chance for economic growth. For two long decades, there followed a period of stagnation that earned for Europe the name of the "tired continent."

European socialism

Against this background of economic malfunction, it is easier to understand the growing insecurity that afflicted European capitalism. During the 1930s, serious rumblings were already being heard. In England, the Socialist Labour Party had clearly displaced the middle-class Liberals as the Opposition. In France, a mildly socialist "Popular Front" government came to the fore, albeit insecurely. Even in Italy and Germany, the fascist dictators repeatedly declared their sympathy with "socialist" objectives—and whereas their declarations may have been no more than a sop to the masses, they were certainly indicative of the sentiments the masses wanted to hear.

Note that the socialist movements were not communist—that is, they were pledged strongly to democratic political principles and envisaged a "takeover" through education and persuasion rather than by revolution and coercion. In addition, the socialists sought to convert only the strategic centers of production into public enterprises, not to "socialize" all of industry and agriculture. Thus, socialism was always a much more evolutionary program than communism. Nevertheless, to the European conservatives of the 1930s, the socialist leaders appeared every bit as dangerous as did the socialists' bitterest enemies, the communists.

By the end of World War II, socialist ideas were clearly ascendant throughout most of Europe. Even before the war was concluded, the Labour Party swept into office in England and rapidly nationalized the Bank of England, the coal and electricity industries, much of the transportation and communications industries, and finally steel. As the first postwar governments were formed, it was evident that a socialist spectrum extended across Europe from Scandinavia through the Lowlands and France to Italy (where the communists came within an ace of gaining power). To many observers, it seemed as if capitalism in Europe had come to the end of its rope.

RECOVERY OF EUROPEAN CAPITALISM

welfare capitalism   Yet, European capitalism did not come to an end. Instead, after the war, it embarked on a period of unprecedented economic growth. As we can see in Table 9-1, from 1948 to 1962, the nations of Europe not only doubled or tripled their pre–World War I rates of capital growth, but actually outstripped the contemporary performance of the United States economy by a margin almost as large.

Obviously, to bring about such results, important changes must have taken place in these economic societies. One of them, it is hardly

TABLE 9-1 Comparative Growth Rates

	Average annual rates of per capita increase				
	France	Germany	Italy	U.K.	U.S.
Pre–World War I (1870–1913)	1.4	1.8	0.7	1.3	2.2
Post–World War II (1948–1962)	3.4	6.8	5.6	2.4	1.8 (1950–1964)

SOURCE: M. M. Postan, *An Economic History of Western Europe* (London: Methuen, 1967), p. 17.

surprising to learn, was political. The postwar socialist governments quickly showed that they were not revolutionary but reform-minded administrations. Once in power, they instituted a number of welfare and social-planning measures, such as public health insurance, family benefits and allowances, and improved social security; but they did not engage in sweeping institutional changes. Despite its socialistic rhetoric during the 1960s and 1970s, Europe was still unmistakably capitalist.

Hence, when many of the socialist governments, facing the exigencies of the postwar period, were voted out again, they bequeathed to the conservatives the framework of a welfare state, *which the conservatives by and large accepted.* Harking back to one of the traditional weaknesses of European capitalism, we can say that this represented a conservative attempt to create a social-service state that would mend the historic antagonism of the working class. As a result, we find today that in most European states, welfare expenditures form a considerably higher proportion of government expenditures than they do in the United States. Social Security expenditures in most European Community countries run 50 to 100 percent higher than in our own.

The second reason for the survival of European capitalism was even more important. This was the rise of a movement within the conservative ranks to overcome a still more dangerous heritage of the past—the national division of markets. This great step toward creating a full-scale continental market for European producers is called the European Economic Community—or more familiarly, the Common Market.

the Common Market

To some extent, the Common Market was born out of the vital impetus given to postwar European production by the so-called Marshall Plan, under which Europe received some $12 billion in direct grants and loans from the United States to rebuild its war-shattered industry. Despite Marshall Plan aid, it soon became apparent that Europe's upward climb would necessarily be limited if production were once again restrained by cartels and national protectionism. To forestall a return to the stagnation of the prewar period, a few farsighted and courageous statesmen, primary among them Jean Monnet and Robert Schumann, proposed a truly daring plan for the abolition of Europe's traditional economic barriers.

The plan as it took shape called for the creation of a *supranational* (not merely an international) organization to integrate the steel and coal production of France, Germany, Italy, Belgium, Luxembourg, and the Netherlands. The new Coal and Steel Community was to have a High Authority with power to eliminate all customs duties on coal and steel products among members of the Community, to outlaw all discriminatory pricing and trade practices, to approve or disapprove all mergers, to order the dissolution of cartels, and to provide social and welfare services for all Community miners and steelworkers. The Authority was to be given direct power to inspect books, levy fines, and enforce its decrees—and, still more remarkable, it was to be responsible not to any single member government but to a multinational parliament and a multinational court, both to be created as part of the Community. A Council of Ministers was to act as a *national* advisory and permissory body, but even here, action could be taken by majority vote, so that no single nation (or even two nations) could block a decision desired by the Community as a whole.

By the fall of 1952, the Coal and Steel Community was a reality, and it lost no time going about its business. At mid-1954, customs duties and discriminatory pricing within the coal and steel "triangle" had been virtually eliminated, and roughly 40 percent more coal and steel was being shipped across national boundaries than had been shipped prior to the establishment of the Community. Cartels and secret agreements still remained, but their restrictive influence on production was much less than it was formerly.

The success of the Coal and Steel Community led, in 1957, to the next two organizations: Euratom, a supranational atomic power agency, and the Common Market itself, an organization that was to do for commodities in general what the Coal and Steel Community had done for its products. Under the Common Market treaty, a definite schedule of tariff cuts was laid down, envisaging within slightly more than a decade an entirely unimpeded continental market for Common Market members, with a single "external" tariff vis-à-vis the world. In addition, there was to be a single agricultural policy and, perhaps most imaginative, full freedom for the intermember mobility of both capital and labor.

unem-ployment problems Now the story takes an unexpected twist. The postwar boom lasted, albeit with waning momentum, into the 1970s when OPEC (Organization of Petroleum Exporting Countries) quintupled the price of oil and dealt all industrial nations a staggering blow. Yet, whereas the United States and Japan soon regained momentum (despite a second oil price hike in 1979), Europe did not. From 1973 on, its performance was as poor as it had been exceptional in the prior period. In the European Community as a whole, by 1986, unemployment rose from 3 percent of the labor force to 11 percent—and in poorer countries like Ireland and Spain, to 17.5 and 22 percent, respectively.

What was the cause of this slowdown? A number of explanations have been offered: European monetary authorities, more fearful of inflation than their U.S. counterparts, kept a tighter rein on money and thereby inhibited growth; an array of social obligations imposed by welfare-oriented governments deterred employers from hiring new workers;

a dwindling "work ethic" made well-cushioned unemployment seem attractive. All of these (and yet other) reasons may shed some light on the problem, but none clears it up. For example, the countries with the most generous welfare systems, such as Norway or Sweden, are the countries that have shown the *best*, not the worst, unemployment records. This suggests, although it certainly does not prove, that unemployment and slow growth in the European Community reflected a breakdown in the social consensus that emerged in the postwar decade, and a failure in the high-unemployment nations to create a new framework for labor-business-government cooperation.[7]

a new resurgence
That brings us to the present—indeed, to the very edge of the future. For one more chapter of European economic history is about to be written, a chapter certain to affect the level of European growth and employment. This is the next audacious step in the realization of a true Common Market. Although tariffs have largely been eliminated in intra-Community trade, a multitude of nontariff barriers remain, preventing the free shipment of goods manufactured in one country to points of sale in another. One example is the differences in emission levels required of automobiles; another is the differing standards required for the pre-market testing of drugs. In all, some 300 such trade-inhibiting barriers have been identified. At this writing, 83 have been eliminated and work is under way on another 100.

Many economists believe that the impetus given this last stage in market unification may be enough to raise Europe's rate of growth from a sluggish 2 percent to a robust 4 percent. Already a vast merger movement, resembling that in the United States, has begun to put together "continent-sized" firms to take advantage of opportunities in what will be the largest single market in the world, a third larger than that of the United States. By 1992, a degree of unity unimaginable in the early postwar years had already been achieved. Perhaps the most astonishing achievement was the agreement to create a single currency for Europe by 1999. With it will come a new chapter in European capitalism.

modern European capitalism
Thus after its time of trial, European capitalism again hopes for a high degree of success. But what happened to the socialist ideas and programs that emerged so strongly after the war? That brings us to the last, and in some respects most interesting, aspect of the European story. This is what happened to European capitalism after the communist system toppled, like the Berlin Wall itself, at the end of the 1980s. Oddly enough,

[7] See Andrew Glyn and Bob Rowthorn, "West European Unemployment: Cooperation and Structural Change," *American Economic Review*, Vol. 78 (1988), No. 2, pp. 194–98.

the downfall of socialism in Russia and its former satellite states did not mean a change in the generally "socialistic" drift of European capitalism. When we examine the Soviet system in Chapter 13, we will see that centralized planning in the USSR had no relation to the objectives that characterized the socialist movement in the West. Hence, renewed optimism in Europe did not mean an abandonment of the combination of social support systems and economic guidance that had become a firmly entrenched aspect of European capitalism. Indeed, these aspects were extended and accepted to such a degree that we can now speak of European capitalism as a distinct form of capitalism—in many ways resembling capitalism in America, but in some decisive aspects departing from it.

CORPORATIST CAPITALISM

The new form of capitalism is often called "corporatist," which does not mean that corporations dominate the system, but that the organization of the economy has become a formally shared responsibility, with business, labor, and government seeking to coordinate their respective policies to promote the interests of the nation.

The new corporatism varies from nation to nation, but generally features two institutional developments. The first is an effort to avoid the inflationary pressures that have damaged capitalist economic performance since World War II. Here corporatism takes the form of a kind of "social contract" aimed at giving expansionary economic policies a chance of succeeding, rather than self-destructing in higher costs and prices. In Germany, for example, trade unions now sit, by law, on the boards of large corporations, thereby becoming privy to the crucial decision-making process of business. In turn, unions agree not to seek wage settlements that maximize wages in the short run but imperil employment in the longer run, and to press for noninflationary, growth-promoting contracts.

The second aspect of corporatism is to work toward agreements that strengthen the nation's place in world production. For example, with labor and government sanction, the steel producers of the Ruhr have agreed to pool skilled labor forces and specialized capital equipment in the production of highly specialized anti-pollution equipment, thereby avoiding the prohibitive expense that would result if each producer tried to seize the market for itself.[8] Another institutional departure has been

[8] See Gernot Grabher, "Against De-Industrialization," in *Beyond Keynesianism: The Socio-Economics of Production and Full Employment*, Egon Matzner and Wolfgang Streeck, eds. (Brookfield, Vt.: Gower Publishing Co., 1991).

the combination of government financing and private management to create international high-tech, high-finance ventures of which the best known and most successful has been the Airbus, now a formidable competitor of the Boeing Company.

Will this new "corporate" amalgamation of energies become the dominant form of capitalism in the 21st century? Perhaps. We do not yet know. What is clear is that corporatism is clearly identifiable today in Austria, Denmark, Finland, Germany, the Netherlands, Norway, Sweden, and Switzerland, and that aspects of it are recognizable in France and Italy as well.[9] Meanwhile, halfway around the world, Japan has worked out a form of corporatism in which a close working relation between government agencies, banks, and large enterprises has earned it the name of Japan Incorporated. For better or worse, that appears to be a state of affairs with which the United States will have to contend over the coming years or decades.

But that takes us ahead to our next chapter. Here we should end our overview of the history of capitalism in Europe by reflecting on what we have seen. Capitalism in Europe today bids fair to assert its claim to world leadership. To no small degree that astonishing recovery has been the consequence of a political flexibility that has allowed European capitalism to extract from its own internal rival—socialism—those elements that could be most useful to it. To its irreducible core of the profit motive and the market mechanism, European capitalism has added a concern for those who have not found a productive niche in society, and a recognition that the profit motive and the marketplace may not suffice to guide society to the goals its peoples set for themselves.

KEY CONCEPTS AND KEY WORDS

1. The development of European capitalism was considerably hampered by a number of factors absent from the American scene. Among these were a *feudal heritage* that brought serious political problems, and *severe national rivalry* that prevented economic unification. As a result, productivity in Europe lagged behind the United States. Compounding the problem of slow growth was the *breakdown of international trade* following World War I.

Socialist opposition

2. Capitalism in Europe was seriously threatened by the rise of a *socialist opposition*. However, following World War II, conservative parties generally accepted the reformist ideas of socialism and backed large programs of *social welfare and a commitment to national economic guidance*.

[9] See John Cornwall, *The Theory of Economic Breakdown: An Institutionalist Approach* (Cambridge, Mass.: Basil Blackwell, 1990).

Common Market

3. Equally or more important was the creation of the European *Common Market*, a successful attempt to revive European trade and production.

Corporate capitalism

4. Capitalism in Europe has moved in a "corporatist" direction since the collapse of the Soviet Union and its East European satellites. Corporatism has generally taken two forms. It has attempted to lay the basis for a noninflationary expansion of output by assuring labor unions of their political security, in exchange for union agreement to seek noninflationary wage contracts. In addition, corporatism has encouraged public-private ventures like the Airbus, and new means of improving industrial efficiency through sharing labor and capital.

A changed environment?

5. Corporatism takes many forms, both in Europe and elsewhere—Japan "Incorporated" is an example. It may become a widespread form of capitalism in the decades to come.

QUESTIONS

1. Discuss how the fragmentation of a continent can affect the gains from trade. Does the experience of Europe illustrate that the bias of nationalism constitutes the main source of international economic difficulties?

2. What is the difference between economic guidance, as we find it in Europe, and the kind of planning we used to see in the USSR? (You might sneak a look at Chapter 13.)

3. Do you think it makes any sense to interpret the function of a nationalized company as being a kind of "public works," necessary for the success of the economy as a whole? Think about this in terms of Rolls-Royce, or British Petroleum, or Swiss Air.

4. Do you think that the general acceptance of the market framework by European socialist parties means that the historic antagonism between capitalism and socialism has come to an end? (More on this, too, in Chapter 13.)

10 THE NEW INTERNATIONAL ECONOMY

International economics used to be a subject that Americans could afford to ignore. Weren't we the leading nation in the world? Weren't we virtually independent of what went on elsewhere—importing less than 5 percent of our GNP, exporting about the same?

That has changed, and changed drastically, in the last two decades. America has been deeply affected by her failing capacity to compete successfully in key world markets. We know from everyday experience that foreign companies like Honda and Volkswagen, SONY and Panasonic, have become as familiar as Ford and GM, Westinghouse and GE. In the United States, the one-time trickle of imports and exports has grown to a river. In 1991, when the GNP was around $5.6 trillion, the value of imports and exports combined was around $1.4 trillion, over a quarter of our total output. All this is testimony to the extraordinary degree to which international trade today permeates our economy, as it permeates all advanced economies.

the growth of world trade

One way to locate America in the world economy is to place ourselves in an imaginary satellite far above the Earth and look down on the volume and characteristics of what might be called "global" economic activity.

What sorts of activity does this include? First we note the flows of goods and services from one nation to the next. The international economy is largely—although, as we shall see, by no means exclusively—built on the modern-day equivalent of those pack trains of goods we saw a thousand years ago, when the market economy was starting to appear from behind the natural manorial economy of early medieval Europe.

The measure of the importance of the global economy is the volume of this international flow of raw materials, foodstuffs, textiles, machines, automobiles, microchips, and munitions. Table 10-1 shows us the size and growth of these modern pack trains of goods and services. Note that the value of world exports skyrockets over the period. The rise is exaggerated because inflation boosts the prices of exports, along with all

TABLE 10-1 Value and Growth of International Trade

	1965	1970	1980	1989
Value of world exports ($ billion)	186	312	1,393	2,902

	1966–1980	1980–1989
Annual rate of growth of exports (percent)	6.7	4.1
Developed economies	7.3	4.1
LDCs	3.3	5.4

SOURCE: World Bank, *World Development Report*, 1991, pp. 230–31.

other goods, but other data show that the volume of trade also increased remarkably.

the composition of world trade

Next we take note of two main divisions in the overall flow. The first consists of the exchange of goods among the wealthy capitalist nations of the world. Rich countries trade primarily with other rich countries— no wonder, for that is where "the market" lies. Of the total of $2,907 billion of world exports in 1989, $2,174 billion consisted of the exchange of goods and services among the developed market economies (America, Europe, Australia, and Japan), which account for only one-sixth of the world's population.

A second trade flow of very great importance takes place between the less-developed countries (LDCs) and the rich ones. Not many years ago, this flow could have been described with considerable accuracy as the exchange of raw or semifinished commodities against manufactured goods or specialized services—Africa, Asia, and Latin America exporting their copper, manganese, and coffee against the tractors, typewriters, and engineering services of the nations of the North and West. Today that description is not so generally valid. Although commodities still play a very important role in their trade, a few LDCs have become exporters of considerable volumes of high-technology goods, such as radios and electronic equipment and subassemblies of automobiles. Much of this new aspect of international trade is the consequence of the search of advanced capitalist economies for low-wage areas where cheap labor can be combined with modern high technology. The result has been the extraordinary growth of areas such as South Korea, Singapore, Taiwan, and Hong Kong—the so-called Four Little Dragons (Japan is the Big Dragon)—as well as parts of Brazil, Mexico, and India. Although their volume of output is still small compared with that of the industrialized world, their rate of growth has been rapid—up some fourfold since the 1970s. This suggests that the age-old pattern of world trade—in which the "peripheral" underdeveloped regions produced raw materials and the "core" industrial nations produced manufactures—may be in the first stages of a great convulsive change.

THE UNITED STATES IN THE WORLD ECONOMY

This initial overview is enough to give us a sense of the extent and importance of the web of trade that binds countries and continents. Now let us see how the United States fits into this setting.

a historical turnabout

exports >
imports

We begin by tracing our overall volume of imports and exports for the last two decades. If we turn to Table 10-2, we see that total exports in 1970 came to $69 billion—about 6 percent of that year's GNP—and imports amounted to $61 billion. This gave us a small positive balance in what is called our current balance on goods and services. Such a positive balance has been a feature of American history almost without interruption since its earliest days. We have been net sellers to the world, using our earnings from foreign trade to become the world's largest and most powerful creditor.

If we now look to 1991, the picture changes dramatically. In that year, our exports came to $591 billion—up eight times in dollar amounts. Although much of that rise was the consequence of inflation, our exports as a percentage of GNP had doubled, from 6 to 10.4 percent. This was a testimony to our increased involvement in the world economy.

Equally striking was the change in imports. In dollar figures, the volume of goods and services purchased abroad rose from $61 billion to $622 billion. As a percentage of GNP, it also rose, from 6 to 10.9

TABLE 10-2 U.S. Balance on Goods and Services (billions of current dollars)

	Exports	Imports	Net balance
1970	69	61	8
1980	351	319	32
1983	353	359	−6
1984	384	442	−58
1985	370	449	−79
1986	397	494	−97
1987	450	564	−114
1991 (est.)	591	622	−31

SOURCE: *Statistical Abstract of the United States*, 1991, p. 431; *economic indicators*, 1991.

percent. As we have already mentioned, exports plus imports now amount to over one-fifth of GNP, over double their historic level.

But we have not yet considered the most striking and important development. As Table 10-2 shows, our exports were steadily falling behind our imports during the early 1980s. The deterioration came to a halt in 1987 and slowly improved after that, but not until 1991 did our exports finally cover the value of our imports—and even then, the very small balance in our favor resulted in considerable part from payments made to us by our allies in the Gulf War. Taking the decade as a whole, we see the disquieting spectacle of an economy that had long enjoyed a regular surplus of exports over imports suddenly unable to pay its way in the world of international trade.

deeper difficulties   Two disquieting comments must be added to this already alarming picture.

The first is that *the imbalance is mainly the result of a failure to maintain our favorable trade account with regard to goods, rather than goods plus services.* Our adverse merchandise (goods) balance in 1987 was $160 billion—larger than our balance on goods plus services; in 1991, the merchandise balance was minus $74 billion. Thus, the most threatening aspect of the historic turnabout has been the inability of U.S. manufacturers to defend their home markets against imports or to gain export markets abroad.

The second comment reinforces the first. *The collapse of the U.S. trading position has come despite a sharp fall in the price of the dollar since 1985.* As any country's currency becomes cheaper, the goods of that country also become cheaper for foreign buyers—if American dollars can be bought for fewer marks or francs or yen, it is obvious that American goods, which are priced in dollars, become cheaper for foreign buyers. It also follows that falling exchange rates discourage imports—French wine becomes more expensive for Americans when it takes more dollars to buy a given number of francs. Yet despite an unprecedented fall in the dollar, our balance on merchandise account has remained negative. This suggests that American goods are losing out in the world market because of their quality as well as their price.

BEHIND THE TURNABOUT

What lies behind this startling change?

oil   One culprit in the matter is easy to spot. It is America's dramatic rise in oil dependency. In 1960, we imported only 17 percent of U.S. petroleum consumption; in 1977, we imported 47 percent. Meanwhile oil prices skyrocketed from $1.60 to $30 per barrel as a consequence of the formation of OPEC (Organization of Petroleum Exporting Countries). Our oil bill alone gave us a negative balance on foreign trade account.

Oil prices have fallen sharply in recent years, and our foreign petroleum bill has therefore shrunk from $77 billion in 1980 to less than half that by the end of the decade. But our need for foreign petroleum has not diminished substantially, and many experts think it may double over the next decade. That single troublesome commodity is therefore likely to play a substantial role in our balance-of-payments problems for many years to come.

productivity

increases but not as much as in Asia

A second culprit is much more significant. It is the mysterious but pronounced decline in the rate at which U.S. productivity has improved, compared with its rate of increase in competitor nations. All during the 1950s and 1960s, the value of output per hour in the United States was far higher—and growing faster—than in any other nation, a crucial factor in enabling us to undersell the world despite our much higher wage levels. Things began to change in the next decade. From 1976 to 1981, productivity at home increased a mere 0.2 percent per year, compared with annual average increases of 7.1 percent per year in Japan, 3.9 percent in Germany, and 3.4 percent in France. As a result, the volume of manufacturing output per hour in the advanced nations of Europe nosed ahead of ours, and in Japan was rapidly catching up to U.S. levels.

Despite rising wage levels abroad, this loss of our advantage in productivity contributed heavily to the American turnabout. As our advantage disappeared, so did our ability to protect our domestic market against imports, or to hold onto or increase our market shares abroad. Two commodities stand out as the most dramatic instances of this decline in American competitive capability. In 1950, as the world's most efficient steelmaker, America produced half the world's steel. By 1980, that share had dropped to 14.2 percent; by 1988, to 12.3 percent. Almost as horrendous was the competitive fate of the automobile industry. In 1960, we produced three-quarters of the world's motor vehicles. Today we make less than one-quarter of them.

because of product quality

Equally disturbing, as the dollar fell from its very high levels of the early to mid-1980s, our balance of payments did not improve—that is, we did not buy less imports, although they became more expensive, or sell enough more exports, although they became cheaper for foreign buyers. This suggests, as we noted earlier, that the trouble lay as much in the quality of American goods as in their price.

the unsolved puzzle

Can we explain this distressing fall in productivity? The disconcerting fact is that we cannot. Edward Denison, perhaps the leading student of the causes of economic growth, has examined seventeen suggested hypotheses that might account for declining productivity—for example, the shift of the labor force into service occupations—and concluded that none of them, alone or in combination, accounts for more than a fraction of the slowdown.

As is often the case, in the absence of a clear-cut understanding of causes, we settle for a laundry list of complaints. Here are a few:

- Of the 77,251 patents issued in the United States in 1986, 45 percent went to applicants from other countries.
- A recent study has shown that the United States has dropped from second to seventh place among industrial nations in the skill level of its workers.
- In a comparative international test of education levels among twelve nations, our national average was in the lower third. In mathematics, American students ranked last.
- Japan graduates ten times as many engineers as lawyers; the United States graduates ten times as many lawyers as engineers.
- Until 1990, America was spending 6 percent of GNP on defense, Japan less than 1 percent.[1]

Such facts suggest that something is wrong with the social and political structures on which our economy rests. They imply that our structures of government and business and labor, as well as our deeply ingrained way of life, channel entrepreneurial activity away from constructive activities and discourage the bold, "transformative" technological ventures from which productivity growth ensues, especially in manufacturing. The decline in productivity has even led to the speculation that the fundamental problem may be that the United States is undergoing a kind of climacteric—a decline in its historic momentum that has often been the fate of world-dominant powers that protect their empires to the neglect of their civilian economies.

the limits of prevision These are discomfiting possibilities for Americans, brought up in an economy that seemed impregnable but now seems almost in a state of siege. Hence it is well to conclude on a note of caution. The decline of the United States may turn out to be only a passing phase—part of a rough but ultimately successful process of creative adaptation. (As we write these pages, there are signs that the trade balance is slowly—but only slowly—mending.) Finally, we should note that in the eyes of most European nations, as well as Japan, the United States economy still appears to be the most powerful and vigorous on earth.

Thus we face a challenge, not a predestined defeat. Perhaps the most disconcerting aspect of that challenge is that economics sheds only

[1] See Richard Lamm, "Crisis: The Uncompetitive Society" in *Global Competitiveness* (New York, W. W. Norton, 1988).

a limited amount of light on its outcome. This is because the forces that ultimately shape our destiny are political and social rather than economic. The economic processes of market society, however powerful, unfold within legal and institutional channels, some established by government, others by the spontaneous determinations of the community. The future of America in the world economy, like its future at home, cannot be predicted—it will be made. This is a reflection to which we will often have reason to return as we consider the options before America.

INTERNATIONAL PRODUCTION

But in this chapter, we have still to complete our acquaintance with the world economy. Let us therefore turn from the problems of world trade to another aspect of modern international economic relationships—not the exporting and importing of goods and services, but the international *production* of goods and services.

This introduces us to a hitherto unmet actor on the economic scene—the multinational corporation.

the multi-national corporation
What is a multinational corporation? Essentially it is a corporation that has producing branches or subsidiaries located in more than one nation. Take Pepsico, for example. Pepsico does not ship its famous product around the world from bottling plants in the United States. It *produces* Pepsi-Cola in more than 500 plants located in over 100 countries. When you buy a Pepsi in Mexico or the Philippines or Israel or Denmark, you are buying an American product that was manufactured in that country.

Pepsico is a far-flung, but not particularly large, multinational corporation. More impressive by far is the Ford Motor Company, a multinational that consists of a network of sixty subsidiary corporations, forty of them foreign-based. The Ford Escort—advertised as the "world car"—is manufactured in sixteen countries from Australia to Ireland.

If we studied the corporate structure of GM or IBM or the great oil companies, we would find that they, too, are *international* companies with substantial portions of their total wealth invested in productive facilities outside the United States. Indeed, if we broaden our view to include the top 100 firms in the United States, we find that two-thirds had such production facilities in at least six nations as of the early 1980s.

In 1990, assets of foreign affiliates of U.S. firms (which means their wholly or partially owned overseas branches) came to roughly $400 billion. Thus, between a quarter and a half of the real assets of our biggest corporations are located abroad. Hence, it is not surprising that many top companies depend on foreign operations for a large share of their profits.

Uniroyal, Gillette, Coca-Cola, and IBM all earn over half their profits abroad. So do most of the oil companies.

the globalization of multinational production

The movement toward the internationalization of production is not strictly an American phenomenon. If the American multinationals are the most imposing (of the world's biggest 500 corporations, over 300 are American), they are now closely challenged by non-American multinationals.

No one knows the exact dimensions of the multinational economic world, but the prestigious Brandt Commission reported that in 1976 the total sales of foreign affiliates of all big corporations (of all nations) were almost as large as the total volume of exports of all kinds (which includes huge flows of foods and other materials that are not produced by MNCs). According to the Commission's findings, MNCs control between a quarter and a third of total world industrial production.[2]

emergence of multinational production

Why did the multinational phenomenon arise? The initial reason lies in a characteristic of the firm to which we have heretofore paid only passing attention. This is the drive for expansion that we find in all capitalist enterprises. In our overview of the rise of American big business, we saw the emergence of giant enterprise as a consequence of the pull of markets and the push of mass production.[3] Much the same logic has driven firms, from early times, to expand their markets overseas. Samuel Colt, the inventor of the first "assembly-line" revolver, opened a foreign branch in London in the mid-1850s, and by the 1880s, the Singer Sewing Machine Company was gaining half its revenues from overseas production and exports.

motives for overseas production

But what drives a firm to *produce* overseas rather than just sell overseas? One possible answer is straightforward. A firm is successful at home. Its technology and organizational skills give it an edge on foreign competition. It begins to export its product. The foreign market grows. At some point the firm begins to calculate that it would be profitable to organize an overseas production operation. By doing so, it would save transportation costs. It might be able to evade a tariff by producing goods behind a tariff wall. It may be able to take advantage of lower wage rates. Finally,

[2] The Brandt Commission, *Common Crisis North-South: Cooperation for World Recovery* (Cambridge, Mass.: MIT Press, 1983).

[3] Alfred Chandler has shown in a brilliant book, *Strategy and Structure* (Cambridge, Mass.: MIT Press, 1962), that the typical domestic firm goes through a series of "logical" changes in organization, growing from a single-product, single-plant firm (in which every operation is supervised personally by the founder-owner) to a multidivisional, multiproduct enterprise in which a tiered organizational structure becomes necessary to superintend the strategic requirements of national geographic scope and increasing technical complexity.

it ceases exporting its products and instead exports capital, technology, and management: It becomes a multinational.

Calculations may be more complex. By degrees, a successful company may change its point of view: First it thinks of itself as a domestic company, perhaps with a small export market; then it builds up its exports and thinks of itself as an international company with a substantial interest in exports; finally its perspective changes to that of a multinational, considering the world (or substantial portions of it) to be its market. In that case, it may locate plants abroad *before* the market is fully developed, in order to be firmly established there ahead of the competition.

the international challenge at home

If we look at the world picture of production today, we find European and Japanese firms expanding their production overseas as rapidly as, or even more rapidly than, American firms. The rate of expansion of foreign-owned assets in the United States is especially startling. We get some sense of its pace in Table 10-3. The table shows that between 1981 and 1989 foreign ownership of productive (largely manufacturing) assets in our country increased almost fourfold, whereas American direct investment overseas rose only by about 63 percent.*

consequences of overseas ownership

We tend to bristle at the idea of foreigners "buying up" American firms. Should we? Does it make any difference if a company making cars in Tennessee is owned by Japanese rather than Americans? If such a company were a vehicle of Japanese political policy, it might make a vast

TABLE 10-3 Overseas Productive Investment: U.S. and Foreign ($ billions)

	1981	1989
U.S. direct investment abroad	228	373
Foreign direct investment in U.S.	109	401

SOURCE: *Statistical Abstract of the United States*, 1988, p. 758, Table 1330.

* There is a very important caveat to be added here. When the Department of Commerce calculates the value of the assets owned by Americans abroad, or those owned by foreigners here, it counts those assets at their value *on the date they were acquired.* Thus, in 1989, the total value of assets abroad owned by Americans amounted to $1,412 billion, while the value of assets owned by foreigners here came to $2,076 billion. This made the United States seem like a debtor nation. But was it? Much of the assets in American hands were acquired ten or even twenty or more years ago. They are carried on the books at values that may be five or ten times *less* than they would be worth today! Thus, the fact that foreigners have been acquiring assets in the United States more rapidly than Americans have been acquiring them abroad does not mean that we are in hock to the world. The real value of our overseas wealth—the value we would realize if we sold all our foreign-located assets—still makes us a formidable creditor, not debtor, nation. See Robert Eisner, "Issues for the Next President," *Challenge*, July–August 1988, p. 29.

difference, but the Japanese firm (just like its American counterpart in Yokohama) must obey the laws of the country in which it resides—and above that, the laws of the market. Honda has to compete for American buyers just the same as Ford.

Then what difference does it make? One answer involves styles of management. The Japanese, for example, have been very successful in getting their workers to work *for*, not merely *at*, their companies. Hence, foreign investors might be able to improve U.S. productivity if they were able to instill higher plant morale here. That is, however, an iffy question. Foreign ownership cannot be counted on to change the workways of the country to which it moves.

What of the effect on the balance of international payments? This is a much more complicated matter. To begin, multinational production obscures the traditional meaning of "exports." We think of an export as a good made by the firm of one country and sold to buyers in another. But in 1985, *American* companies sold $80 billion of goods to foreigners that were not counted as exports! Why? Because these goods were made by American companies *located in Japan*. In similar fashion, goods made by Japanese companies in America are not counted as part of Japan's exports. Both production flows count as part of the GNP of the nations in which they occur.

How, then, does multinational production affect trade balances? The answer is that the *repatriated profits* earned by a multinational firm are recorded as part of the overseas earnings of the nation the MNC is headquartered in and show up on the positive side of trade balances, like exports. More complicated yet, almost 20 percent of the imports into the United States are goods produced abroad by *American* firms.[4] We are thus "importing" our own production!

the politics of international economics

All these factors greatly change the meaning of international "trade." In addition, they bring an element of political decision to what would otherwise be strictly business calculations. Take the case of the treasurer of a large MNC like IBM. He is likely to have tens or, on occasion, hundreds of millions of dollars of company cash to deposit. Where is he supposed to park his funds? If he puts the interests of his company first, he will seek the highest-interest-yielding account or security, regardless of its national identity. If he puts patriotism and public policy first, he will probably deposit his funds only in U.S. banks or securities. Which is he—a capitalist without citizenry, or a citizen without concern for capitalist efficiency?

There are no answers to these questions as yet. In all likelihood the tension between the pull of economic and of political life will go on

[4] Kenichi Ohmae, "No Manufacturing Exodus," *Wall Street Journal*, April 25, 1988, p. A3.

without a satisfactory resolution for a long time. The big corporations are certain to continue their multinational thrust. As global producers, they will be the main international carriers of efficiency and development, especially in the high-technology areas for which they seem to be the most effective form of organization.

But if the power of the nation-state will be challenged by these international production units, it is not likely to be humbled by them. There are many things a nation can do that a corporation cannot, including, above all, the creation of the spirit of sacrifice necessary both for good purposes, such as development, and for evil ones, such as war.

international finance

We have seen how in recent decades an international economy of trade and production has risen to major global proportions and major significance to the United States. Now, briefly, we must see how the world's financial and monetary systems have also become much more unified through the growth of an international banking system.

The ancient predecessors to today's international banks are the merchants and bankers who helped make possible medieval trade. But banking today dwarfs any possible comparison with the past. If we rank the companies of the world on the basis of their market value (the value of their shares quoted on their national stock exchanges), ten out of the top twenty-five are banks—all of them Japanese.[5]

American banks are smaller, largely because of U.S. banking laws, but they too are globe-encircling. In 1965, the 20 biggest U.S. banks had a total of only 211 branches around the world; by 1972, the number had grown to 672; today it is well over 1,000. This same multiplication of banking facilities has taken place for foreign banks. In New York City alone, there are telephone listings of over 100 foreign banks with branches there.

The world's banks create an international credit system that ties together the economies of all nations. Using electronic techniques, banks lend money literally around the world, sometimes only for a few hours at a time: Money not working at Citibank in New York during night hours, for example, is loaned out to Hong Kong to put in a full working day there. A thousand years ago, money moved across the face of Europe at mule pace. Today it travels around the globe at the speed of light.

Moreover, the volume of international finance is enormous, many times larger than the value of all the goods and services plus all the actual investment capital that moves from nation to nation. New York, Zurich, Tokyo, and London handle hundreds of billions of dollars' worth of currency transactions each day, as money flits across oceans in search of higher interest rates or for reasons of security. Many observers are

[5] *Business Week*, July 18, 1988, p. 137.

made uneasy by the possibility that such vast flows could destabilize the world's banking system and precipitate a world financial crisis. High on the agenda of the coming decade will be the need to introduce new safeguards into the world of unrestrained international finance.

America in the world economy

These problems of international finance are too ramified to be analyzed in this book. But the upshot of our brief introduction in surely clear: The United States is no longer the enormous "island" economy it once seemed to be. More and more, the American economy has become interwoven with a much larger, truly transnational economy. In part, this interweaving affects the flows and patterns of our exchanges of goods with the rest of the world. In part, it affects the location of our industry abroad and of foreign industry here. And tying together the whole, we find the American monetary system extending beyond America proper to become part of an international credit reservoir in which "the dollar" becomes a monetary unit that is American in name, but not in nationality.

UNDERDEVELOPED SYSTEMS

Let us turn now to the underdeveloped world, sprawling across most of Africa and the Near East, Central and South America, the Asian land mass and the archipelagos. It is difficult to describe this world in terms of a simple stereotype because it encompasses so many different kinds of societies, geographic settings, and prospects for the future. Saudi Arabia is an underdeveloped country that has one of the highest per capita incomes in the world because its average income is derived from adding the incomes of 300,000 members of the royal household and 9 million members of a society that is barely out of the Middle Ages. Hong Kong is the home of the manufacturing enterprises established by multinational corporations, although its crowded tenements and squalid back streets bespeak another level of existence from that of the shiny corporate headquarters along Kowloon Road. Upper Volta is an underdeveloped country in which ragged herdsmen and peasant farmers battle against the encroaching desert; Nepal is an underdeveloped country in which the melting snow carries off the topsoil; India is an underdeveloped land with giant steel complexes and 500,000 villages, tens of thousands without a single paved road leading to them. Not to be forgotten, nearly all have severe population problems, even though birthrates are (finally) declining. By the year 2000, the population of Central America and the Caribbean will exceed that of the United States!

mass poverty

Thus, there is no single kind of underdevelopment, no single diagnosis for underdevelopment, and certainly no single cure. There is, however, a single ailment. It is mass poverty. The average per capita income of the developed nations of the West is around $10,500; of nonmarket planned economies, about $4,700; of the LDCs, taking the successful Hong Kongs and Singapores along with the Bangladeshes and Sudans, about $1,800. In the favellas of Rio de Janiero, along the klongs of Jakarta and Bangkok, in the barrios of Mexico City, in the palm groves of East Africa, the face of underdevelopment is the same: Men and women who look old at forty and who have never reached Western stature because they have not had enough food; children with diarrhea and skin disease and other infections that will make the first five years of life a hazardous period; mangy animals; dust; despair.

raising capital How are we to enfold this vast problem into the pattern of the international economic order? Let us start with an important generalization: *All the underdeveloped countries need capital.* Without more steel, electric power, machine capacity, and education, they cannot hope to escape from their chronic and endemic poverty.

But how to get capital? There are four ways.

1. *Trade.*

Trade has been the traditional source of earnings for the LDCs. In the past, however, this avenue for earnings was subject to the same difficulties that have always beset sellers of raw commodities—remember the woes of American farmers (page 139). Today a new channel for trade is opening for the New Industrializing Nations, like the Asian "tigers," that have found a place in the export of manufactured goods. This new development is bound to place strains on the industrialized world—our apparel industry, for instance, has been very hard hit by imports from Taiwan and Hong Kong—but it may nonetheless offer the best long-run chance for the LDCs themselves.

2. *Direct investment by private firms.*

A second avenue for capital is direct investment abroad. This increased from about $7 billion in 1970 to $46 billion in 1984—to be followed by a collapse in the following years, as international banking went through a severe crisis. Here the difficulties are two: First, the flow of private investment is inherently unstable; and second, it is largely carried on by multinationals which build factories that fit into *their* plans for growth, not necessarily into the plans of the nations in which the plants are located.

3. *Foreign aid.*

A third avenue is direct aid from the industrialized world. Over the years, world aid has slowly risen, but U.S. aid has not. In 1989, we gave about

$9 billion to various programs to help development, considerably less than what we had given five years earlier. For this and other reasons (development programs have not been very successfully carried out), foreign aid today is not likely to set into motion anything like a major industrialization process.

4. Borrowing.

Last, an underdeveloped country in need of capital can borrow funds from foreign private banks or from international agencies such as the World Bank, one of the institutions of the United Nations.

the international debt problem

During the early 1970s, spurred by hopes of a worldwide boom, the underdeveloped world began to borrow heavily from private banks in the developed world, as well as from governments and international agencies. Their total external debt rose from around $100 billion to about $600 billion. For a time this was regarded as a boon to lender and borrower alike. But with the OPEC price rises of 1973 and 1979, the LDCs found that their projected trade receipts, on which their creditworthiness had been based, vastly exceeded reality. More and more of their trade receipts had to be used to pay the interest on their borrowing, leaving less and less to be spent on bringing in capital equipment. In the mid-1980s, Brazil was using a third of her export earnings for debt service, Peru over 40 percent.

Under these burdensome conditions the network of international lending itself began to totter. Mexico defaulted on a loan; Peru declared that she was unwilling to pay any further interest. These actions had a double effect: They closed off these LDCs from any further access to the world's capital markets, and they imperiled the solvency of the big lending banks themselves. Frantic negotiations managed to prevent the bankruptcies of crucial countries or banks, although both suffered severe losses. Many of the borrowing countries were forced to agree to programs of austerity, despite the social cost of these programs, in order to assure that interest payments—somewhat reduced and stretched out over time—would be met. Many big banks "wrote off" their worst loans, reporting unprecedented losses.

At this writing, the debt crisis is no longer aflame, but it smolders. It will continue to smolder until the essential transfer of capital from the rich to the poor world finds a more reliable and secure route. To date, none has appeared.

coping with the future: three outlooks

Can we generalize as to the outlook for development? As we have emphasized, every LDC is a separate, individual case. Taken as a whole, however, we can see that three overall strategies are available to the underdeveloped world.

First, there are those regions of the world that have not even begun the process of modernization. Here we find a number of nations of Central Africa; parts of the remote interior of South America; backward regions and nations of the Far East such as Bangladesh and Afghanistan. In many ways, the collision with the West has not yet happened in these areas, and we can expect a great deal of disruption when it does. What is needed most in these areas is not capital. It is, rather, the foundation on which capital can eventually be built: a population that accepts birth control, a school system that brings literacy to the young, the end of oppressive regimes, and reliable government. Alas, these are difficult, perhaps even impossible, accomplishments to achieve overnight. In all likelihood, these poorest regions will have to endure a long period of turmoil and anguish before we can speak realistically of their entrance into the process of development.

Infrastructure

A second group of LDCs is made up of large, politically important nations that have made the leap into modernization—halfway. All of them have industrial sectors, sometimes large and impressive ones, but all also have vast backward areas where illiterate peasants live in a wholly separate world. Hence these countries are often described as "dual economies." The strategy here is easier to describe than to prescribe. It is to knit the two sectors together, bringing the backward regions into closer economic and social contact with the industrialized core. Effective social and economic planning is likely to hold the key here, but that, too, is not an easy aim to achieve. In addition, the dual economies must cope with trade and financial relationships with the capitalist West that are often unfavorable. Still, there is hope here— provided that the West has patience and understanding.

Finally, a number of smaller LDCs are parlaying political, social, and economic stability at home into successful ventures in the international economy. These LDCs have absorbed much of the shock of modernization, and are in fact new capitalisms with highly expansive market systems. We have noted South Korea, Singapore, Hong Kong, and Taiwan as examples of such Newly Industrializing Countries—NICs, in the current economic vocabulary. Their future growth is likely to hinge primarily on their continued ability to ride the currents of world trade, finance, and international production. Their success during the past twenty years has been remarkable and it seems possible that this success will continue.

If it does continue, the consequences for the international order may be very great. One possibility is that the relationship between the industrial "core" countries—the United States, West European nations, and Japan—and the nonindustrialized "peripheral" nations—mainly in Asia and Latin America and Africa—may experience a deep-seated change. The industrialization that has transformed the successful LDCs almost overnight might take root elsewhere. Why should not Turkey follow in South Korea's footsteps? Or Thailand in those of Singapore? It is already clear that modern production methods can be made to work in regions that have barely progressed beyond the stage of peasantry. Such a combination of high technology and low wages would represent a formidable challenge—not only to the United States, but also to the entire industrial world. It may well be the challenge that lies ahead.

KEY CONCEPTS AND KEY WORDS

International trade, production, and finance

1. This has been a long chapter, full of complex ideas. Let us try to sort it out in this review. The essential theme is the rising importance of an international economy, binding together the national economies of the world. The international economy has three main aspects: (1) powerful international flows of trade; (2) the rise of international production; and (3) a web of international finance.

Industrial countries vs. LDCs

2. Most international trade takes place among rich nations, but there are also important flows between rich and poorer nations (the less-developed countries, or LDCs). Some LDCs have begun to export manufactures.

Causes of the U.S. trade gap

3. In the world of international trade, the United States, long a net exporter of goods and services, has suffered a dramatic change to become a net importer. Its large trade gap is the consequence of at least three separate causes: our dependency on foreign oil, laggard productivity compared with that of Europe and Japan, and the troubling evidence of social underperformance. The last factor is the most important, but the least understood. We do not know if our decline in productivity is a passing phase or evidence of social change at home or in the world that may prove difficult to cope with. Economics throws very little light on such questions.

Role of multinational corporations (MNCs)

4. International production is a second aspect of the international economy. It is largely carried on by multinational corporations (MNCs) that do not export their products, but manufacture them in other nations. MNCs are a major element in the American economy, tying it into other economies. A quarter to a third of the assets of large U.S. firms lie abroad; and much the same degree of foreign penetration is true of the big firms of other nations.

Political and economic problems

5. MNCs have complicated political and economic effects. They change the meaning of exports and imports when these activities are undertaken by foreign branches of domestic concerns. And they may pose conflicts of business vs. national interest for corporate policy. There exists no answer, as yet, to the problems posed by the MNCs, or by the explosion of international finance.

Under development

6. Underdevelopment constitutes the economic environment for the vast majority of humankind. It is ascribable in part, perhaps, to bad climates and poor resources, but in the main, we have come to realize, it is the result of a collision between static ways of life and the force of emergent capitalism.

Capital formation

7. Development requires that capital equipment be obtained from the developed world—through trade, aid, investment by foreign companies, or by borrowing. In recent years, a splurge of borrowing, followed by high oil prices and a world recession, has saddled the LCDs (and the banks of the developed world) with a debt crisis. Until it is resolved, the pace of development will be slow, except perhaps in the Newly Industrialized Nations.

QUESTIONS

1. How many products *produced in America* can you identify as "foreign"? (You might start with the detergents and soaps produced by Lever Brothers, the office machinery produced by Olivetti-Underwood, the gas and oil refined by Shell.)

2. Can you draw up a plan for a company that would be privately owned and managed but *not officially headquartered in any one nation?* From whom would it receive its charter? Under what laws would it operate so far as the top management is concerned?

3. Do you think the rise of international production and finance opens the way for a more rational world, or a more divided one?

4. In what ways do you think underdeveloped economies differ from the American colonies in the mid-1600s? Think of literacy, attitudes toward work, types of work, and other such factors. What about their relationship to more advanced nations in each case?

5. Once upon a time, during the early and mid-nineteenth century, the American economy was well behind the developed world—mainly England—in its capital resources. How did America catch up with England? There was no foreign aid in those days. Did America earn part of its capital from exports? Do you remember from your history courses *which* exports? (Try cotton as a starter.) And what about borrowing? It may surprise you to know that the English were major builders of the American railways so far as the money was concerned. Is there a lesson from all of this with respect to the LDCs? What are the differences, which are equally important?

11 THE DYNAMICS OF CAPITALISM

We must be eager to pick up the threads of American experience and prospects, especially in light of the challenges of international competition. In our next chapter, we will focus entirely on economic policy, looking into the possibilities for locating America in the world economy, for redressing its unemployment, and for controlling inflation. But it would be premature to turn to policy before completing a diagnosis of America's situation—not only in the international economy, but also in the sweep of the economic history that is the real theme of our book.

a look at history

Let us begin by talking about depressions. How are they different from recessions? There is no formal criterion that marks one off from the other. A depression is simply a very deep or long-lasting recession. Recessions are relatively mild phenomena—depressions are something else again.

Some economists and historians would say that we move from recession into depression in the United States when unemployment crosses the double-digit line. In 1873, for example, the United States experienced unemployment and widespread business failures that much resembled the slump of the 1930s. Statistics are scanty for that era, but we have the word of the *Commercial and Financial Chronicle*, writing six years after the depression began, that "Business since 1873 has been like a retreating army on the march."[1] Twenty years later, in 1893, another depression blew in like a typhoon. We have better statistics for this one: Unemployment leaped from 3 percent in 1892 to almost 12 percent in 1893, then to over 18 percent in 1894. For the next four years, unemployment hovered around 14 percent, dropping below 10 percent only in 1899.

So there were at least two major depressions before 1930. Have we had one since? That depends on whether we want to call the slump of

[1] N. S. B. Gras and H. Larsen, *Casebook in American Business History* (New York: F. S. Crofts and Co., 1939), p. 718.

1980 to 1983 a recession or a depression. Measured in terms of unemployment, it was certainly a depression: Unemployment rose above 10 percent, a far cry from the 1890s or 1930s, but still very serious. Measured in terms of output, it was only a recession. The GNP did not plummet as in the early 1930s, but simply failed to grow. And measured in human terms—in actual physical deprivation or psychological and social disruption—it was far less traumatic than the Great Depression, when there was no unemployment insurance, no Social Security, and no welfare.

long waves in capitalism Reflecting on these historical bouts of depression, some economists have hypothesized that an underlying wavelike impulse can be discovered deep within capitalism. The ordinary business cycle of seven to eleven years' duration can be thought of as an economy rocking back and forth, while it is also rising or falling on a great ocean swell. While the economy is rising, we experience an era of vitality; while it is falling, we enter a period of stagnation.

Advanced first by Soviet economist N. D. Kondratieff in the 1920s, the idea of "long waves," lasting roughly fifty years from crest to crest, has attracted a considerable amount of attention. A recent compilation, presented in Table 11-1, shows the wavelike motion for four leading capitalist countries.[2]

Long swings of roughly fifty years' duration can be seen in this table. Note, however, that the German "downswing" from 1914 to 1938 shows a *higher* growth than the previous "upswing," perhaps because of Hitler's spending on rearmament.

TABLE 11-1 Long Swings in Four Industrial Nations
(average percent growth in real output)

Movement	Years	U.S.	Great Britain	Germany	France
Upswing	1846–1878	4.2	2.2	2.5	2.8
Downswing	1878–1894	3.7	1.7	2.3	0.9
Upswing	1894–1914	3.8	2.1	2.5	1.5
Downswing	1914–1938	2.1	1.1	2.9	1.0
Upswing	1938–1973	4.0	2.4	3.8	3.8

SOURCE: David Gordon, Richard Edwards, and Michael Reich, *Segmented Work, Divided Workers* (New York: Cambridge University Press, 1982), p. 42.

[2] For varied discussion of the Kondratieff cycle, see Joseph Schumpeter, *Business Cycles* (New York: McGraw-Hill, 1939); Ernest Mandel, *Late Capitalism* (London: NLB, 1975); W. W. Rostow, *The World Economy* (Austin: University of Texas Press, 1981); and David Gordon, Richard Edwards, and Michael Reich, *Segmented Work, Divided Workers* (New York: Cambridge University Press, 1982).

The pattern of long swings is reinforced if we look into the behavior of the normal business cycle—the rocking of the boat—over the entire period. Economists Gordon, Edwards, and Reich have shown that the seven-to-eleven-year cycles tend to have longer recoveries and shorter contractions during the quarter-century periods of vitality, and, as we would expect, shorter booms and longer contractions during the roughly twenty-five-year periods of stagnation. A similar confirmation of the long-wave hypothesis appears in indexes of world trade, which expanded more vigorously during the periods of vitality than in periods of stagnant tendencies.[3]

Does this mean that in the early 1980s we were caught in the downdraft of a Kondratieff cycle that will act as an undertow against recovery until it comes to an end in the 1990s? That seems a very unreliable proposition. Scholars of the long-wave pattern all stress that each of its periods has its own peculiar causes. No one has suggested any mechanical timing mechanism in the capitalist system that could enable us to predict with assurance that the 1990s will be a boom period, or if it is, what its duration will be.

Nevertheless, it is useful to know about the Kondratieff waves for two reasons. First, it brings home the realization that periods of extended sluggishness are not exceptions in capitalist history but, rather, a familiar pattern. Second, the long cycle emphasizes the worldwide nature of these periods of vitality and stagnation. To understand them, once again we have to take into account the world economy, not just our own.

CAPITALIST DYNAMICS

What could be the cause of these long booms and deep slumps that mark capitalism's history? What makes some recessions turn into dangerous depressions?

Here we enter a field within which very little agreement exists. The classical economists—Smith, Malthus, Ricardo, Marx—held widely varying views as to the dynamics of the system. And contemporary economists are equally at odds with one another about underlying processes and long prognoses. They do not agree, for instance, whether the natural tendency for a capitalist system is to expand at a satisfactory pace under the impetus of its search for profit or to sink into a kind of chronic stagnation. Nor do they agree whether policy measures can affect these tendencies, if they do exist.

[3] Gordon et al., *Segmented Work*, pp. 42–46.

the
accumulation
of capital

All economists do agree, however, that the motive force of capitalist growth is capital accumulation, to use Adam Smith's term for the saving-and-investing process by which the system works. But what determines the volume of accumulation? What makes capitalists eager to risk vast sums in one period, and unwilling to do so in another? One explanation lays the basic cause for vitality and stagnation at the doorstep of technology. Economists such as Joseph Schumpeter (1883–1950) attribute the momentum of long booms to technological breakthroughs that create entire new horizons for expansion.[4] The era of railroad building in the mid-nineteenth century was one such achievement that literally required the building up of an entirely new underpinning for the economies of the West. Railroadization was thus, in Schumpeter's view, the basic cause of the buoyancy of the 1850 to 1870 period, and the completion of the railroad network was the fundamental cause for the absence of momentum that lengthened the downturns of 1873 and 1893 into full-scale depressions.

That same argument provides a cogent explanation of the upswing that followed in the early twentieth century. Now the technological stimulus came from two sources: the introduction of electricity into the home, with the consequent building of huge utility systems; and the perfection of the gasoline-driven internal combustion engine that gave us the automobile, perhaps the most capital-generating invention ever made. And as before, the "completion" of the first huge wave of utility and automotive investment helps us account for the stagnant tendencies that dragged out the depression of the 1930s.

is technology
the cause?

Technology can thus undoubtedly shed light on the nature of long booms and help explain their petering out. In the case of the serious recession of the 1980s, the villain is at least partly the saturation of the European and Japanese market for automobiles which, in the first decades of the postwar boom, served to propel these economies forward with the same vigor that it had imparted to America in the 1920s. A second candidate for investment saturation is the jet plane, with its vast complementary investments in airports and hotels—also a prime economic mover in the earlier years of the boom and a gradually declining force in later years.

Nevertheless, an emphasis on the important role that technology always plays in opening new markets, which eventually get filled up, does not quite suffice to make "technology" the open sesame to the puzzle of depressions. For one thing, the explanation makes the appearance of technology a mysterious, spontaneous force rather than a social activity that takes place within the system. There is undoubtedly an important element of self-generation in technology, but there is also

---

[4] Joseph Schumpeter, *Business Cycles* (New York: McGraw-Hill, 1939).

evidence that much technological progress *follows* demand. For example, many technical advances in railroads came only after it was clear that there existed a strong demand for rail transport.[5] So, too, an emphasis on technology does not explain why some clusters of technology seem to dynamize the whole economy, whereas others do not. Nor does it tell us why some countries are quick to introduce new technologies, while others delay.

Technology provides at best partial illumination for our concern. Perhaps its greatest shortcoming as an explanation of long booms and deep slumps is that it does not tell us, before the event, whether an existing technological capability will suffice to bring forth a massive volume of capital investment. Take today's array of brilliant scientific and technological achievements—computerization in its still burgeoning aspects, genetic engineering, solar and nuclear energy, space exploration. Will these and other remarkable achievements impart the same momentum to the system as the machine tools of the Industrial Revolution or the railroads of the mid-nineteenth century? Will they transform the system, thereby creating whole new fields of employment? We have not the faintest idea.

is under-consumption the reason?

A second search for explanation starts from the demand rather than the supply side of things. It asks whether deep depressions, or long periods of undertow, may not be accounted for by shortfalls in purchasing power. It suggests that the reason capitalists do not build equipment rapidly enough is simply because the demand is not there to justify the risk.

Might there be some element within the workings of the system that would exert a dragging, braking effect, even though the undertow could be overcome from time to time when investment prospects were unusually promising? Karl Marx proposed such an explanation for chronic drag based essentially on the tendency of capitalists to substitute machines for labor, wherever that was profitable, thereby cutting down the volume of wage payments. Marx wrote that this created a condition in which the "restricted consumption of the masses" acted as a continuous depressive force bearing against accumulation.[6] Investment, therefore, had to take place in a market whose mass-purchasing base was constantly being eroded by the labor-displacing processes of capitalist accumulation itself!

[5] For a discussion of the self-generating aspect of technology through individual search and discovery, see Jewkes, Sawers, and Stillerman, *The Sources of Invention* (London: St. Martin's Press, 1960). For inventions following demand, see J. Schmookler, *Invention and Economic Growth* (Cambridge, Mass.: Harvard University Press, 1966).

[6] Karl Marx, *Capital* (New York: International Publishers, 1967), III, Chap. XV. For a masterful overview of technology in history, see Joel Mokyr, *The Lever of Riches: Technological Creativity and Economic Progress*, (New York: Oxford University Press, 1990).

propping up consumption

We cannot trace here the long history of underconsumption theory, but we should note two aspects of the argument. One is that the willingness of individual capitalists to go on investing in the face of a chronically weak market depends very much on their abilities to "capture" demand through new kinds of products or through cheaper means of creating old products. This supplies us with a better understanding of the powerful motive for technological improvement that capitalism creates.

Second, we must ask whether underconsumption could not be remedied by measures to raise demand, whether through direct government purchases of goods and services or by transfer programs such as Social Security. This would explain the upward German "downswing" we saw in Table 11-1, and it is, of course, the direction in which Keynes's policies were aimed, as we saw in Chapter 8.

Could not such programs effectively remove any threats that a tendency to underconsumption might bring? The experience of the 1960s and 1970s has been sobering in this regard. These were years in which wages rose and very large scale programs of transfer payments were first introduced under capitalism. Table 11-2 shows this trend for the United States, a trend that would be even more prominent in the capitalist nations of Europe.

wages and growth

Why did not the policy of high social wages (wages plus transfer payments) prevent the serious recession of the 1980s? One answer is that perhaps it *did* prevent that recession from turning into a full-scale depression by placing a floor under consumption. The second answer is that high wages tend to squeeze profits, unless their pressure is offset by rising productivity. But we saw in Chapter 10 that productivity growth lagged during the 1970s. Thus, underconsumption helps us understand the source of a drag on capitalist growth, but it does not explain why that drag is sometimes effective—and sometimes not.

the "social structure of accumulation"

For that, it may help to focus again on profits, the key element in all explanations of growth. And the key to the key, perhaps we recall from reading about Adam Smith and Karl Marx, is the relationship between wages and profits—the very relationship we have just looked at. Re-

TABLE 11-2 Wage and Transfer Payments (as a percent of U.S. national income)

	1950–1965	1965–1980
Compensation of employees	69.5	74.3
Transfer payments	6.4	13.3

SOURCE: Calculated from Department of Commerce data.

member that Smith explained the growth-sustaining properties of the system as resulting from the fact that any undue rise in wages would be met by an increase in the supply of labor in the marketplace. Marx also introduced a wage-regulating mechanism to sustain profits, although he thought it would operate through laborsaving machinery, not by the number of children that a prospering labor force would self-defeatingly rear to working age.

Modern-day economists do not seek for such an internally generated wage-and-profit–regulating mechanism within the system. But a broad approach to this classical problem has recently been put forward by labor economist David Gordon.[7] Gordon suggests that the ability of the system to yield adequate profits depends on a successful *social structure of accumulation.* By such a structure Gordon means, first, the manner in which employers organize and utilize their work force—a relationship that is the immediate determinant of the productivity of labor and its profitability. But he extends the concept outward from the factory floor to include the relationship of business to government, equally important in establishing a milieu in which profits can be successfully sought, and from the government out into the general relationship between business and the public, and thence into the world economy itself.

Note that this is not a hypothesis that identifies a specific cause of a slowdown in accumulation. Rather, it directs our attention to the complex of institutions characteristic of different historical settings, in search of relationships—perhaps political or even ideological, rather than economic—that serve to encourage accumulation for a time, and then gradually become a deterrent to it. Like a river that becomes silted up, a given combination of labor, government, public, and world relationships will eventually lose its capacity to serve as a conduit for the accumulation process. When that happens, accumulation comes to a halt, and we enter a period of malfunction during which business and government leaders alike seek new ways of making the system work.

the 1930s in retrospect   One of these turning points occurred during the depression of the 1930s. We recall that the immediate cause of that depression was the stock market crash that triggered a wave of bankruptcies and a general collapse of confidence. This was worsened by Federal Reserve policy that tightened credit rather than loosening it, and by a general belief that the remedy for a slump was "budget balancing."

Underneath these immediate causes, as we have seen, were deeper weaknesses such as lagging wages and a lagging farm sector which give support to an underconsumption view. But the inability of the economy to regain its former momentum was testimony to a still deeper-lying

[7] See Gordon et al., *Segmented Work.*

problem. This was the vulnerability of an economic system that had embarked on a long accumulation boom of private growth *without laying in any support system in the event that growth failed.* In the nineteenth century, America was still a small-town, small-business, heavily rural economy where economic setback was self-limited by virtue of the remaining high degree of independence of so many of its citizens. By the culmination of the great upswing that ended in 1929, small-business America had become big-business America, small-town America was dwarfed by big-city America, and farming America had been decisively displaced by factory and office America.

When the crash came, therefore, it toppled a vast interlocked structure of business and finance in a social setting that was no longer even modestly self-sufficient. With no underpinning under the banks, no dependable stream of expenditures for business, no floor under household income, the economy simply went into free-fall.

From the wreckage, business and government leaders gradually assembled a structure of institutions that significantly altered the way in which capitalism worked. Beginning with the New Deal and ending with its endorsement in the mid-1950s by Republican President Dwight D. Eisenhower, a new form of capitalism came into being, distinguished from its previous form by the much larger role played by government as a provider of demand. This is a development we are familiar with. But we can now see the evolution of the "mixed economy" and the "welfare state" as a process of transformation whose purpose was to create a milieu in which the accumulation drive would once again take place.

the long boom   Did the new social structure of accumulation create a setting in which investment would again flourish? For a long time it did. The period of economic growth from 1950 to 1973—the year in which the OPEC oil shock dealt the first destabilizing blow to the long boom—was the most buoyant, least interrupted, and most widely shared period of economic expansion that capitalism had ever known. In the United States, deviations from the central trend were only half what they had been in the years from 1900 to 1929. Throughout the world, capitalist nations were consciously aware that they had left behind a long history of financial insecurity and meager comforts for the majority of their populations, and entered upon an era in which something like a modest affluence was attained by perhaps three-fifths of their citizens. A degree of well-being and social assurance unimaginable in the 1920s (not to mention the nineteenth century) became generalized throughout the West. During the 1950–1973 boom, modern capitalism virtually eliminated dire poverty and provided a previously unknown level of material comfort to its citizens, including its older people and, most important of all, its working classes.

The rise in the general standard of well-being was both the cause and the effect of the rising social wage we previously discussed. The increase in real output made possible higher real wages and a larger volume of welfare transfers, and these in turn helped to sustain the buying power that supported the boom.

INFLATIONARY CAPITALISM

What, then, went wrong? Did technology falter? Did markets become saturated? Did the rising social wage eventually squeeze too hard against the sources of profit? We have no clear answers. The underlying causes of the bad recession of the 1980s remain obscure.

But one aspect of the long upswing preceding it is beyond dispute. The thrust of the system, which in the 1950s and 1960s resulted mainly in economic growth, changed over the years, so that by the 1970s, the result was mainly inflation. Here is where the idea of a social structure of accumulation is useful. It enables us to ask what elements in our institutional milieu were at first indispensable for generating growth, and then became more and more responsible for generating inflation.

inflation in history First, however, we must gain some historical perspective on the problem.* Let us begin by looking at the United States' experience in the century before 1950, shown in Figure 11-1. Two things should be noted about this chart. First, major wars are regularly accompanied by inflation. The reasons are obvious enough. War greatly increases the volume of public expenditure, but governments do not curb private spending by an equal amount through taxation. Invariably, wars are financed largely by borrowing; and the total amount of spending, public and private, rises rapidly. Meanwhile, the amount of goods available to households is cut back to make room for war production. The result fits the classic description of inflation: too much money chasing too few goods.

Second, we should note that the peaks of wartime inflation are followed by long valleys of peacetime stability or even falling prices. The reason is that mass-production technology was constantly lowering prices. In the century and a half before 1939, prices declined in the United States during as many years as they rose. *There was no inflationary trend.* Our parents and grandparents regularly put their savings

---

* Inflation before capitalism is different from inflation after capitalism. Ancient inflations—and we can trace the phenomenon back to the Roman emperors—were usually the consequence of monetary adulteration or of unusual accessions of treasure. When Roman emperors found their imperial reserves dwindling, it was common to stretch things by lowering the gold or silver or copper content of their coinage. The public rapidly responded to this debasement by lowering their appraisal of what money was worth. That is only another way of saying that prices rose. They rose also when gold was discovered: The influx of treasure into Spain as a consequence of the gold taken from Mexico and Peru in the sixteenth century touched off a fourfold inflation throughout Europe.

into twenty- and thirty-year bonds that paid 3 or 4 percent interest. They would never have done that had they not believed that the money they would get back when the bond came due would be worth as much— perhaps even more—than the money they invested.

chronic inflation That has obviously changed. In the United States, prices rose during forty-six of the forty-eight years after 1940, increasing sevenfold during the period. This was a new kind of inflation, seemingly built into the system—an inflation that surfaced in bad years as well as good, that persisted despite high rates of unemployment, and that dimmed the very memory of a time when prices fell as often as they rose, or when people bought thirty-year bonds without a thought of losing any of the buying power of their money.

Moreover, the change was not only evident in the United States. On the contrary, endemic inflation was visible in every capitalist nation (and in most noncapitalist ones, too). It is worthwhile to follow the columns of figures in Table 11-3 for the leading economies of the West.

The figures show that inflation has become a fact of life in every capitalist nation—more severe in some than in others, but present in all. What the table does not show is that this tendency has been visible for at least thirty years, and that it has accelerated over that period. During

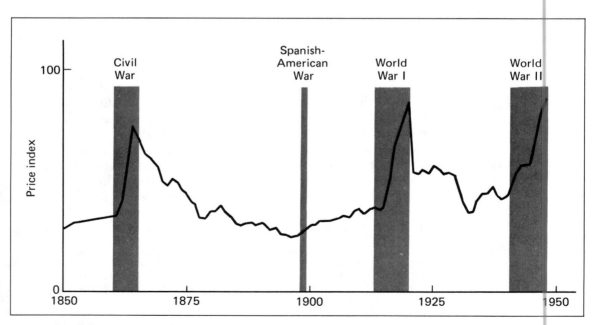

FIGURE 11-1   Inflation in Perspective

TABLE 11-3 Annual Rate of Growth of Consumer Prices 1970–75—1989

Year	U.S.	Japan	France	W. Germany	Italy	U.K.
1970–1975 (avg.)	6.7	11.5	8.8	6.1	11.3	13.0
1975–1980 (avg.)	8.9	6.5	10.5	4.1	16.3	14.4
1980–1985 (avg.)	5.5	2.7	9.6	3.9	13.7	7.2
1985–1986	1.9	0.6	2.5	−0.1	5.9	3.4
1986–1987	3.7	0.0	3.3	0.2	4.7	4.1
1987–1988	4.0	0.7	2.7	1.3	5.0	4.9
1988–1989	4.8	2.3	3.5	2.8	6.2	7.8

SOURCE: *Statistical Abstract of the United States*, 1988, p. 453; 1991, p. 847.

the decade of the 1950s, the price level of the ten leading industrial countries rose by 2.5 percent per year. During the 1960s, it rose almost 50 percent faster, at a rate of 3.5 percent per year. During the 1970s, as we can see, the momentum continued to gain: The average for the ten leading nations in that decade was 9 percent per year.

Only in the 1980s, as a consequence of the global recession of the early years of the decade, did the inflationary wave slow down—and no one is willing to state that it will not reappear if the years ahead see the resumption of a long boom such as the one we enjoyed up to the mid-1970s.

roots of inflation How can we explain this new attribute of capitalism? Its appearance in so many countries suggests that we have to look for changes in the social structure of accumulation typical of modern society—changes that impart an inflationary bias to the way the market system works.

The first worldwide change is obvious. It is the growth of large and powerful public sectors in all capitalist countries. Looking across the face of Europe, we find that governments typically account for 30 to 50 percent of all expenditures, and in some countries over 60 percent. In the United States, the total of government buying of goods and services (such as schools, roads, and defense), plus government provision of Social Security and the like, comes to about one-third of the GNP—three times what it was in the early 1930s.

Public expenditure is not inflationary in itself. There is nothing about a government purchase or expenditure that is inherently more inflation-producing than a private purchase. The difference is that the presence of a large flow of public spending effectively places a floor under economic activity. That in itself is enough to tilt a formerly depression-prone world toward an inflation-prone status.

increased private power
A second aspect of the sea change that has come over capitalism in the last century is the rise in private power. We see it in vast organizations—the icebergs—that dominate the waters of business and labor alike. The emergence of massive institutions of private power makes an important contribution to our inflationary propensity.

The rise of large institutions brings an inflationary impetus because prices tend to become less flexible in a downward direction when oligopoly replaces competition. As we have seen, sharp recessions bring price "warfare," but normal times are characterized by administered prices. Hence the drift from a largely rural, small-scale economy to a largely urban, big-scale industrial system has introduced what economists describe as a "ratchet tendency": Prices and wages go up easily, but down hard. These tendencies are as characteristic of corporate pricing behavior as they are of union wage demands. They help explain why modern capitalism is more inflationary than earlier capitalism by virtue of its social structure.

indexing
Next we find yet another change in most capitalist nations. This is the *indexing* of many public payments, especially for social insurance. As the cost of living goes up, so does the check that goes out to the retiree or the unemployed family. This also changes the way the economy works. When the price of oil jumps—as it did during the 1973 and 1979 oil crises—these families do not find that they have to cut down on other expenditures to keep their homes heated or their gas tanks full. After a little while, the higher price of oil shows up in the cost-of-living index, and shortly thereafter the green Treasury checks that go out to 40 million families a month also rise. All this serves the obvious purpose of preventing hardship, but it also greases the skids of inflation.

expectations
With this inflation-transmitting change in institutions comes an even more dangerous change in the way we think. The adage in the old depression-prone days used to be: "What goes up must come down," reminding families and businesses alike not to bet on the future as a one-way track. Nowadays the adage is more like: "What goes up will probably continue to go up."

These changes help us understand why we live in a world which, in distinction to that of our fathers, has become inflation-prone. We "catch" inflation the way capitalism of the late nineteenth and early twentieth centuries caught deflation. But contemporary experience differs from that of the past in a vital way. Peaks of inflationary rises have not been followed by long, gradual declines. Instead, modern-day capitalist inflation seems to feed on itself.

UNEMPLOYMENT

What can we do about inflation? We will consider that in our next chapter, but one further aspect of modern-day capitalism also belongs in this general overview. This is the rising trend of unemployment, another global fact of modern life. In Table 11-4, we show the rise of unemployment, averaged across the same major countries as before.

the causes of unem-ployment
What lies behind this rising trend of joblessness?

The essential reason we have already covered. It is the cresting of the long boom, the slowing down that makes the late 1970s, and perhaps the 1980s, look like the downside of another long swing. During all recessions, and especially those that occur when the worldwide state of capitalism is depressed, unemployment climbs above its norm.

As to *why* the boom crested, we recall that the answers are many: saturation of demand in the auto and jet-related industries, the shock of OPEC price rises in 1973 and 1979, the undertow of lagging productivity, the instability introduced by accelerating inflation. And there were still other causes to which we have not paid heed, the most important of which was the steady erosion of jobs, especially in factory employment, because of automation and "robotization."

inflation vs. unemploy-ment
Given the recession, then, it is not difficult to explain why unemployment presented itself as a global problem. But why must we take recession as "given"? Why did not the governments of the West apply vigorous measures to expand demand, along the lines pioneered in the 1930s? Why was not the recessionary slackening of the private economy countered by an expansionary thrust of the public sector?

The answer follows from what we have just considered about the inflationary propensity of the system. *Essentially, the Keynesian rescue*

TABLE 11-4 Percent of Total Labor Force Unemployed

	1970	1975	1980	1988
Six major capitalist economies (avg.)	3.0	4.7	5.3	7.5

SOURCE: Calculated from *Statistical Abstract of the United States*, 1988, p. 812; 1991, p. 848.

strategy was held back by the fear that additional government demand would mainly result in more inflation. The effect of government spending, it was generally held, would undoubtedly create some additional employment, but much higher prices. That was a trade-off that no Western government was willing to make.

Instead, virtually all nations concentrated on bringing inflation, not unemployment, under control. In the main, the medicine they used was *tight money*—central bank policies that constrained the lending abilities of commercial banks, bringing about very high rates of interest. The result of high interest rates, which touched 20 percent in the United States, was indeed a fall in inflation, but a fall that was effected by a general collapse of business. As small-business bankruptcies mounted to record heights, and as even large firms tottered, we began to see distress selling, a resurgence of old-fashioned price competition, and an emphasis on bringing down costs—all of which reduced the U.S. inflation rate from over 13 percent in 1980 to under 4 percent in 1983. But the cost was a leap in unemployment, the other side of inflation-reducing policies. By the early 1990s, there were *30 million* unemployed in Western Europe and America.

is unem-
ployment
unavoidable?

Thus, there are two explanations for the unemployment that has plagued worldwide capitalism. One of them is the historical fact that capitalism always generates unemployment as part of its accumulation process—bumping labor before the entrance of new technologies, and giving rise to unemployment during its recurrent business slumps. Some unemployment is probably necessary to ward off a squeeze on profits.

But unemployment in modern capitalism is also created by the policies it has chosen to control inflation. The character of the present-day social structure of accumulation largely banishes the old fear of self-feeding depression, but brings instead the fear of self-feeding inflation. To prevent that disaster, unemployment is deliberately induced by public policy because that is the only way we know to make the system "work"! Hence it seems likely that until we devise better anti-inflation measures than we now possess, unemployment will be a chronic problem for capitalism—partly created by its own dynamism, partly by the public authorities.

But how much unemployment? That is a much more interesting question because, as we will see in our next chapter, different countries have determined their "necessary" levels of unemployment very differently. That sets the stage for the question that has hovered in the background for many chapters: How well has the United States handled the inflation/unemployment dilemma? How much better could it do? What are the options before us?

KEY CONCEPTS AND KEY WORDS

Depressions and recessions

1. *Depressions* are only long-lasting *recessions*. There is no formal difference between them. (An old quip goes that you recognize a recession when your neighbor loses his or her job; a depression when you lose your own.)

Long waves or Kondratieff cycles

2. Industrial capitalism has experienced regular bouts of deep depression, which lead some economists to speak of a fifty-year "long wave." This wave is named after Russian economist N.D. Kondratieff, who first spotted it in the statistics of prices and trade. One of its earmarks is that the normal seven-eleven–year business cycle has longer upswings and shorter downswings during the rising phase of a long wave and vice versa.

The accumulation of capital

3. Whether or not there are fifty-year swings, it is important to learn what we can about the causes of recessions and depressions. Here we begin with Smith and Marx in stressing the central importance of the *accumulation of capital*. Recessions and depressions represent interruptions to that crucial process.

Technological breakthroughs and growth

4. One powerful explanation for these interruptions emphasizes to the presence of *technological breakthroughs* in creating fields for accumulation. In the absence of such industry-creating fields, accumulation slows down.

Under-consumption

Social wages

Profit squeeze

5. A second broad explanation lays stress on an undertow of insufficient consumption. Marx especially stressed *underconsumption* as a key element in dampening the accumulation process. Our experience in the 1950–1980 period shows that a rising *social wage* (transfers plus wages) helps to prevent cumulative falls in consumption, but is not enough to generate a boom in investment. High social wages, moreover, may serve to *squeeze profits*.

Social structure of accumulation

6. A third approach to the phenomenon of depression lays emphasis on the general milieu in which accumulation proceeds—a milieu that begins with the way in which labor is deployed and disciplined, extends into government-business relations, and even touches on the social climate in which business operates. The *social structure of accumulation theory* does not identify any single element as the cause of depression, but impels us to examine how a given social setting can support—or undermine—the savings-and-investment thrust.

Inflation-prone capitalism

7. This directs our attention to a pervasive aspect of the social structure of modern capitalism—its tendency to generate inflation. This has been a universal and accelerating tendency of the system, beginning in the 1950s and reaching a crescendo in the early 1980s. Something about modern capitalism seems to have rendered it *inflation-prone*.

Government floors

8. To what can we attribute this changed attribute of the system? A likely candidate is the new importance of large government expenditures that prevent recessions from developing into depressions. This sets a *floor under eco-*

Indexing and ratchet effects

nomic activity. In addition, the widespread use of indexing prevents shocks, such as the oil crisis of 1973, from exercising a recessionary effect. Aggravating the inflationary potential of the system are the combined power of big business and big labor to create *ratchet effects* in which wages and prices continuously rise, except in very severe recessions. These and other institutional changes create a milieu in which the inflationary expectations are "normal," much as depressionary ones were before the advent of the mixed economy.

Unemployment as a chronic problem

9. Modern capitalism has also been plagued by a steady and rising stratum of unemployment, the consequence of the severe recession of the 1980s. *A main reason for the persistence of unemployment has been the difficulty of applying remedial measures because of their inflationary effect.* In effect, the lurking presence of inflation precludes launching an all-out attack on unemployment. Some degree of unemployment may be necessary to prevent wages from *squeezing profits* so hard that accumulation could not go on. But, as we will see, the evidence shows that different countries manage to live with very different levels of "necessary" unemployment.

QUESTIONS

1. Think about what different elements might play important causative roles in a regular (seven-eleven–year) business cycle and in a long wave. Would you look to inventory buildups (or rundowns) in both? To population growth or urbanization? Can you think of other elements that might affect one kind of economic movement but not the other?

2. If you were prescribing the "best" situation for a fast-growing capitalist economy, would you urge high consumption or low? If high, how would you answer people who claimed that consumption was squeezing out savings, the source of accumulation? If low, how would you answer those who asked, "Where is the market demand going to come from?" Do you think that there is a middle way that may be best suited for steady growth?

3. How would you describe the social structure of accumulation in America today compared with the era just before and during the Great Depression? Do you think the most significant changes are economic or political—or both?

4. Can you describe how expectations of inflation help create inflation? Suppose that you were a union leader and read in the *Wall Street Journal* that economists expected a 6 percent inflation rate next year. Suppose you wanted to get a 4 percent net gain for your members, based on their increased productivity. What wage increase would you ask for? If you got it—and many other leaders did likewise—how would this affect the rate of price rise?

5. Can you devise a plan for gradually removing "indexing" without injuring the neediest recipients of Social Security?

6. Which is worse—a 10 percent inflation rate or a 10 percent unemployment rate? Think carefully about how widely the impact of each is experienced, and also how intensely. Are you not, in the end, balancing a lesser hurt experienced by many against a greater hurt experienced by a few? How should a democratic leader decide which is socially preferable?

12

THE OPTIONS BEFORE AMERICA

This is not a book about economic policy, a subject that requires a more complete grounding in both economic facts and theory than we have had. But our historical overview of the evolution of economic society has brought us into the present, where the United States faces an array of problems of a kind we have been looking into in our last two chapters. Before we attempt to sum up a final perspective on our theme, we ought to give some attention, however brief and incomplete, to the options before America.

CONTROLLING INFLATION

Let us begin by thinking about inflation, not only because it is a serious issue in itself, but also because, as we have seen, controlling inflation is a necessary precondition for taking effective steps to control unemployment and recession.

A good place to begin is with a rapid look at recent U.S. experience. In our last chapter, we saw how the deliberate pursuit of a tight money policy broke the back of the inflationary wave of the early 1980s. At the cost of a deep and painful policy-made recession, the rate of inflation was cut from 9.7 percent in 1981 to 2.6 percent in 1986. Thus, we demonstrated beyond a doubt that a serious enough slowdown, by intensifying competition on both labor markets and product markets, will bring inflation under control.

The trouble with the cure was twofold. First, the cure itself, with its double-digit unemployment and record-breaking rate of small-business bankruptcies, was in some degree as bad as the ailment. Second, the cure was like a powerful medicine that broke the patient's fever but did not get rid of the underlying infection. For once the money policy was eased, the rate of inflation ceased to fall; in fact, it once again showed signs of edging up. After having touched 2.6 percent in 1986, the inflation rate rose to 3.0 percent in 1987 and has stayed around 4 to 5 percent thereafter. These were much less alarming figures than we had to deal with before the tight money pill was swallowed, but they made it clear that even bitter medicine would not get rid of the virus whose several causes we have already become familiar with. Hence the question faced by the United States (and all market economies) today is whether some better policy cannot be devised.

wringing inflation out of the system

This brings us once again to consider the political limits of economic behavior. Speaking only as economists, it is not difficult to spell out measures that would probably remove the inflationary propensity of modern capitalism. Here are three of them:

1. *Eliminate the indexing of Social Security and the general practice of cost-of-living adjustments.* Otherwise, as we have seen, increases in cost become inflationary because they are automatically matched by increases in income.
2. *Limit the ability of big corporations and unions to raise prices or wages unless productivity also rises.* This would prevent wages from outpacing costs.
3. *Administer the federal budget as a national balancing force.* This would require the imposition of higher taxes, mainly directed against consumption, as soon as inflationary signs appeared.

What this list is intended to make clear is that there is little point to speaking "only as economists" about wringing inflation out of the system. The reason is that these measures could not get the public backing necessary to pass them. The suggestion that Social Security payments be allowed to fall behind the cost of living would be met by a great public outcry. Unions and corporations would protest if the government proposed to intervene into wage negotiations or price structures. Few in Congress would be willing to raise taxes when inflation threatened. Hence the problem of eliminating inflation is political rather than economic. It is to devise measures that will be as severe as needed—without rousing the opposition to prevent their effectiveness.

problems of inflation control

Are there such measures—steps that could be taken not merely to *control* or to *limit* inflation, but to *eradicate* it? It seems unlikely, for reasons that we shall now look into carefully.

voluntary measures

One of the easiest and least intrusive anti-inflation measures is to institute a *voluntary* incomes policy—an agreement, freely entered into by unions and corporations, to limit their wages and dividend payments in accord with some standard such as a productivity index. Thus, if national productivity showed an increase of, say, 3 percent, wages or dividend payments would rise by no more than that amount. In addition, corporations would have to agree not to raise prices unless they could demonstrate that costs had increased for reasons beyond their control.

The idea of a voluntary incomes policy is very attractive. If everyone would agree to limit his or her increase in income to, say, 3 percent, the inflation-producing forces would immediately drop *and no one would be any worse off.* Such a collective decision would halt the escalator but would not change our respective positions on it.

But the difficulty of such a policy is obvious. It is to make the policy stick. For if everyone does not cooperate, the scheme will not work. Just as it helps everyone see the game on the football field if all remain seated (and just as no one sees better if everyone stands), so an incomes policy will only work if everyone "sits," by abiding by the productivity standard. But again, just as at a football game, where the few who stand *will* see better, thereby tempting others also to rise, anyone who disregards the voluntary limitations on income will gain—so that soon everyone will be leaving his or her seat.

mandatory controls   At the opposite end we have compulsory controls, such as legal ceilings on prices or administered wages. Such controls would require two attributes to be effective: (1) They would have to be permanent, or at least standby, so that they would not be on-again, off-again; and (2) they would have to be backed up by heavy taxes. Controls alone are just sandbags holding back a rising river. The necessary sluiceway to bring the river under control can only be provided by taxes.

If war broke out, we could undoubtedly impose such mandatory controls and sluiceway taxes with good results—they were very successfully applied during the Korean War, for instance. This is because war provides the necessary spirit of compliance, as well as allowing the government to take whatever other measures the economy requires. If controls result in insufficient investment, for instance, a government in wartime builds or subsidizes the plant and equipment itself.

All that is much more difficult during peacetime. Then the attitude is not one of willing compliance, but reluctant obedience or outright evasion. In addition, controls are onerous. The Korean War system worked, but it required 18,000 inspectors. Even with modern computers, we would have to expect to raise a similar army to enforce mandatory wage or price ceilings today.

Thus the objection to mandatory controls is twofold. They are certain to cause a great deal of public irritation: We can all imagine the headlines they will produce. And they will pose an endless series of difficult questions in deciding how this or that price or wage rate should be adjusted as the economy grows and changes and faces new challenges. On the other hand, controls have one major benefit. More effectively than any other measure, they *will* halt the inflationary spiral. The halt may be only temporary, but it will provide a breathing space in which a really effective anti-inflationary tax policy can be formulated, and in which the dangerous indexing and COLA (cost-of-living adjustment) arrangements can be trimmed way back. If other measures fail, therefore, and if inflation continues its threatening assault on our sense of psychological security, we may yet turn to this last remedy.*

other policies— and problems
There are of course, other kinds of policies. There are schemes to levy taxes on corporations that sign union contracts above a general guideline rate. There are suggestions that all union contracts expire on the same date, to enable us to conduct a national wage policy instead of the present free-for-all. There are important "rifle shot" policies aimed at strategic cost elements, such as health care and food prices.

Would these, or similar kinds of policies, work? Perhaps. As we may have said too many times by now, everything depends on how willingly such measures are supported by the public. That is a matter about which economists have no special expertise. If there is a formula for a successful political economics, we do not know what it is.

Moreover, in two ways the United States may be at a disadvantage vis-à-vis its sister capitalist economies in the search for a solution. The first is that we are a large, regionally divided nation, in which unity and consensus are hard to come by. The secret of Japan and Austria in controlling their inflations may partly lie in their much higher degree of social unity compared to ours.

Second, the United States does not have a national labor organization and a national employers' federation as most other nations do. Therefore it lacks the institutional arrangements that may be necessary to hammer out "corporatist" policies that will be acceptable and enforceable. It has been suggested that nations with strong labor unions may be *less* inflation-prone than nations with weak ones because "la-

---

* One problem with mandatory income policies is that they will not gain the support of those whose incomes are controlled if large sections of the community escape from controls. Even controlling wages, dividends, and interest would leave untouched the incomes of proprietors, for example. Suppose, then, that we introduced a mandatory incomes policy that affected *all* income receivers, by imposing a tax of, say, 95 percent on all incomes, as reported to the Internal Revenue Service, *in excess of the previous year's income.* This would effectively bring every taxpayer into the same income discipline that we might urge for union members or for the government bureaucracy. Of course, there would have to be appeals boards and procedures to allow incomes to rise by more than 5 percent if individuals changed jobs, got promotions, etc. Clearly, such a universal income policy approach would be a very powerful measure against inflation. The question is: How frightened of inflation would we have to be before we agreed to a measure of this kind?

boristic" governments are often in a position to win cooperative action from their unions, whereas "capitalistic" governments may not be.[1]

the outlook   *Realistically, then, it is probable that some degree of inflation will continue to plague America for a long time.* If we are unable to devise solutions that have the support of the public, we will be forced to rely on tight money, with the sad consequence of unemployment. The challenge before the country, then, is to find a policy that imposes its restraints in a manner that seems fair and right. Once that challenge has been met, inflation will lose its latent threat—but not until then.

COMBATING UNEMPLOYMENT AND RECESSION

Can we mitigate unemployment and recession? As with inflation, the answer is yes—if we are willing to pay the price. A massive program of government spending on the scale of the World War II armament effort would soon employ every man, woman, and child in the nation and would raise GNP to altogether unprecedented levels. But what would be the rate of inflation? How severe would the controls over the economy have to be? How long would we be willing to put up with this kind of forced-march economy?

It is useful to begin with such a scenario for creating employment because it confronts us immediately with the realization that generating employment, like controlling inflation, is a political problem before it is an economic one. The crux of the problem is to discover the limits of government spending or intervention that are acceptable to the public, and thereafter to design policies that are compatible with these limits.

1. *Encouraging business.*

The first policy is as far removed from our scenario as anything could be. It is to *decrease* the role of government by lessening regulations on business, by cutting taxes, and by trimming government expenditures. As an overall approach, this has been called "supply-side" economics. It is based on the belief that there is a vast potential for expansion stored up in capitalism that has only to be encouraged by supply-side policies to manifest its effects.

Is supply-side policy, in fact, a means to full employment? This is not an easy question to answer. All through the 1980s we relied on the expansive forces of the marketplace to bring about employment growth,

[1] See John Cornwall, *The Conditions for Economic Recovery* (Armonk, N.Y.: M. E. Sharpe, 1983), pp. 17–18 and passim.

and on the face of it, the results were impressive. In sharp contrast to Europe, where, as we saw in Chapter 9, unemployment rose, in the United States it fell sharply. From its double-digit levels at the worst of the 1982 recession, the economy embarked on the longest uninterrupted rise in its history, and unemployment declined by almost half to a level of 5.5 percent in mid-1988. This was as close to "full employment" as any advanced nation was able to get in the decade of the 1980s. Between 1980 and 1988, over 17 million jobs were created in the American economy.

But two considerations mar this otherwise impressive achievement. First, the supply-side measures of the Reagan administration were largely confined to a dismantling of welfare or public investment. Spending on defense, and on Social Security and Medicare, continued to increase, thereby imparting an old-fashioned Keynesian impetus to the economy.* Second, the quantity of additional employment was a good deal more impressive than its quality. Over 17 million jobs were gained, but not the right jobs. Employment in the manufacturing sector, vital for our exports and for our productivity, actually declined over the decade. The big gains were registered in areas that added little to our economic dynamism—retail and wholesale trade, finance, and miscellaneous services.

Thus, many observers found the employment surge less reassuring than it appeared on the surface. A tentative assessment of supply-side policies must therefore be very cautious. First, we do not know whether encouraging business through lower taxes and less regulation will encourage employment in the absence of strong government spending. Second, we do not know whether the employment will be located in those industries that are most strategic for economic growth.

2. Building human capital and infrastructure.

A quite different approach to the employment problem involves government investment in national capital. This capital is of two kinds. One is our *human capital* of skills and knowledge. In the long run, this is probably the ultimate source of a country's productivity and inventiveness—one reason for the superior performance of the Japanese economy is very likely its far greater commitment to education than we have in America. Hence government investment in schools and schooling constitutes an indirect, but very important, means of raising the level of economic operation and employment.

---

* The government spending that propelled the economy also led to a rapid rise in government debt. This is not the proper place to examine that issue. The interested reader might look into R. Heilbroner and Peter Bernstein, *The Debt and the Deficit* (New York: W. W. Norton, 1989).

No less useful than investment in human capital is the use of government spending to build up the *infrastructure of public capital*—the physical plant owned by government on which so much private activity depends. In the absence of a modern infrastructure, it is impossible to build a modern economy.

We have already mentioned that it is America, not Europe, that is quaint and old-fashioned these days. It is common knowledge that the highway system in the United States, once the world's best, is now one of the Western world's worst. Lack of irrigation facilities poses serious obstacles to our agricultural future in many parts of the country. The absence of a single adequate port means that we must export most of our coal through Canada. Much of the nation's rail system, like the subways of New York City, needs to be rebuilt almost from scratch—not just to assure the amenities that one expects from a rich nation, but also to provide the services without which the private economy cannot work well.*

Much infrastructure is highly labor-intensive—it takes gangs of workers to build and maintain roadbeds and sewer systems and the like. What is important to bear in mind, however, is that infrastructure can also be highly stimulative for private industry. Like programs to strengthen human capital, programs to strengthen infrastructure can generate employment *and* economic growth.

3. Reducing structural unemployment.

A further way to reduce unemployment is to follow the lead of many European nations in matching jobs with workers. For unemployment is not solely a matter of people losing jobs; it is also a matter of people not being able to find new jobs. Unemployment can result from a mismatch between existing skills and required skills, or because workers looking for jobs do not have the characteristics (such as literacy) that employers want.

This kind of unemployment is called *structural unemployment*. Because it is lodged so strongly in specific attributes of the individual, it resists the "easy" cure of higher aggregate demand. An employer may prefer to pay his existing work force overtime rather than take on a new labor force that does not meet his specifications.

The remedy for structural unemployment is more difficult than for general lack-of-demand unemployment. Expensive programs of reloca-

---

* A very useful way of creating employment is to enlarge labor-intensive programs for health services, old-age care, rehabilitation programs, and the like. Unlike programs to build human capital, however, in the main these transfer expenditures do not increase productivity. They carry a higher inflationary cost than programs whose recipients are future job holders. That does not make them less useful—only more costly.

tion or retraining may be required to enable workers who lose jobs in, say, Michigan to move to Georgia, or to teach computer skills to a laid-off autoworker. Remedial schooling is expensive—and so is remedial relocation. Since most workers cannot afford to move before they are assured of steady employment, someone must be willing to foot the bill for unemployed workers who want to scout the woods, but lack the wherewithal to do so. Sweden is probably the most advanced country in the world in creating such a network of labor information and in underwriting the costs of job retraining and relocation. The results for the Swedish economy have been impressive: From 1980 to 1989, while unemployment in the rest of Europe soared, Swedish unemployment remained under 3 percent.

a commitment to high employment

Both building human capital and infrastructure and improving the operation of the labor market call for a commitment to high employment as a top national priority. What has been lacking in the United States to date is the willingness to place the benefits of employment at the top of the nation's economic goals, even at the price of incurring a mild degree of inflation. That is the political decision that must be made if we are to reduce unemployment in the United States to the levels that some capitalist mations have demonstrated to be possible.

AN INTERNATIONAL ECONOMIC POLICY

We have looked at two political and economic options facing America—inflation and unemployment. Now we must glance at the policy choices affecting a third great problem area—fitting the United States economy into the world scene.

motorcycles, cars, steel

Faced with a mounting trade gap, with two political bastions—autos and steel—laid low by foreign competition, and with an uneasy awareness of "falling behind," the United States wonders how to secure its place in a rapidly changing world economy.

So far it has not decided on a general policy. Consider three cases of response to foreign competition. The first is outright protectionism—putting high tariffs on competitive foreign goods. In 1982, for example, the Reagan administration raised tariffs on large motorcycles from 4.4 percent of their value to 49.4 percent. There was only one American producer, Harley-Davidson, that would benefit from this tariff. Harley-Davidson in a good year made 50,000 motorcycles. The nation most affected, Japan, made 7.1 million motorcycles and exported 900,000 of them to America.[2]

[2] *Newsweek*, April 25, 1983, p. 63.

Was it worth charging hundreds of thousands of American buyers of Hondas and Kawasakis the amount of this tariff in order to keep Harley-Davidson in business? Most economists would vehemently declare that it was not. Protectionism has traditionally been viewed by them as a means of propping up inefficient industries by penalizing customers who would prefer to buy better and/or cheaper foreign merchandise.

Next consider the automobile industry. The American car companies are not protected by any tariffs, but the U.S. government has negotiated "voluntary" agreements which limit the number of cars that the Japanese will export to this country. Meanwhile, GM, Ford, and Chrysler have all begun to build "American" cars abroad, assembling parts in low-wage areas such as Mexico. As a result of the movement of American production abroad, combined with the inflow of Japanese, Swedish, German, French, and Italian vehicles, 150,000 American autoworkers have lost their jobs, probably forever. Is this less costly than protectionism?

Finally, take the case of steel. Here the market has steadily eroded for two reasons. One of them is the fault of the industry itself. After World War II, American steel management was the last, not the first, to modernize its plant and equipment: From 1975 to 1980, it spent less than 1 percent of its revenues on research and development. Meanwhile, American steelworkers won union contracts that made them the most highly paid steelworkers in the world, with double the wages and fringe benefits paid to Japanese workers. Unfortunately, they were not also the leaders in world productivity.

A further reason for the debacle in steel was the active part taken by foreign governments in protecting the fortunes of their steel producers. In the 1970s, for example, British steel undersold American steel on the *West Coast* of the United States—not because the British were more efficient producers than the Americans, but because the British government decided to subsidize its steel companies in order to maintain employment in the British mills.[3] In response to such practices, the American industry has won legislation that introduces tariffs as soon as imports touch "trigger prices" that suggest "unfair" methods of competition. Meanwhile, however, the big American mills are being laid low by competition from *within* the United States, as new efficient "minimills" undersell the big plants of the older industry. Do trigger prices make sense under these circumstances?

protectionism vs. free trade   All this makes us think carefully about protectionism. No one disputes that a policy of high tariff walls and strict quotas would seriously harm the living standards of millions of Americans. But few deny that a policy

---

[3] For a still relevant discussion of the use of nationalized companies to promote national interests, see Joseph Monsen and Keith Walters, *Nationalized Companies: A Threat to American Business* (New York: McGraw-Hill, 1963), p. 106 and passim.

of completely free and open trade could severely damage the standards of living of hundreds of thousands of Americans caught in regions, industries, or occupations that are unable, for whatever reason, to meet international competition.

Hence the real political choice does not appear to be "free trade" or "protectionism," but a combination of both—a program that establishes a long-run trade policy designed to safeguard some sectors during a period of transition, to encourage and support exports where the market for them seems promising, and to bolster American productivity in general by addressing itself to fundamental problems, such as our educational system, as well as to specific research areas.

a managed trade policy Most European nations, and certainly Japan, have such policies of co-ordinated national effort—policies that usually entail the cooperative planning effort of management, finance, labor, and economic and technical specialists. As we have noted when speaking earlier of European policies, this certainly does not mean central planning. It refers, rather, to strategies aimed at securing an industry's place in the international economy—strategies that usually require the financing or negotiating powers of government, the drive and flexibility of management, and the cooperation of labor.

As a result, trade policies vary considerably from one nation to the next. In Japan, where trade policy has been very successful, it often takes the form of government financing of enterprise to allow it to make a very rapid jump into large-scale production. This is the way that Japan has seized the initiative in the microchip industry and robotization, and the way it is hoping to become the dominant force in the "fifth-generation" computer of the next decade. Swedish trade policy has been one of incentives for Swedish industry to change its course away from the ship construction, timber, and iron ore industries that are no longer promising vehicles for Swedish growth toward high-tech industries, combined with large-scale assistance to relocate labor from depressed industrial locations to expansive ones. In France, trade policy has been targeted on the mass-transit equipment industry in order to secure France's place in world manufacturing: The bid for New York City's subway cars was won a few years ago by a Canadian subsidiary of a French firm. In Germany, the industries that are being encouraged for world leadership are the emerging processes of powdered metal and ceramics.

the role of government The objection to the attempt to create a U.S. trade policy must be obvious. Why should government, with its bureaucratic tendencies and political vulnerabilities, do better than private management?

There are two answers to that objection. First, the present array of responses within America *is* a trade policy of sorts, but an incoherent one. Only the addition of government as a financing, negotiating, and pressuring agency can impose an overriding national interest on a congeries of conflicting private interests—at least so say the trade policy advocates.*

Second, the protagonists of managed trade assert it is a vain hope that the role of government can be reduced in the modern world. The enormous power of technology, the scale of modern industry, the complexity of modern business, and the political impatience of modern publics all point to a growing, not a dwindling, place for government in the conduct of the economic affairs of twenty-first century capitalism.

Whether we turn toward protectionism or toward trade policy depends, perhaps, mainly on whether American attitudes can be nudged toward cooperation and participation. Compared with foreign competitors, American business-government and management-labor attitudes have an antiquated air. Many businessmen still speak of government as if it were a foreign power occupying Washington, not a part of the capitalist system that seeks to coordinate the conflicts among regions, sectors, interests, and classes. Many managements still speak of labor as an unruly cost of production, not a resource of intelligence and morale. Many unions conduct their affairs as if the United States were still an insulated economic fortress. Such attitudes will have to change if we are to forge a trade policy that integrates the U.S. economy into the world system.[4]

KEY CONCEPTS AND KEY WORDS

Tight money

1. Controlling inflation in recent years has relied mainly on *tight money* policies that restrict the ability of banks to make loans, thereby forcing up interest rates. Tight money is very effective when applied without letup. But the cost of bringing down inflation by high interest rates is a high level of business failure and unemployment.

Institutional change

2. *Wringing inflation out of the system would require far-reaching institutional changes*: the end of indexing, restraining the ratchet power of big

---

* Perhaps a first step in this direction is the Trade and Competitiveness Act of 1988. In part, this is an outright protectionist measure, authorizing retaliatory practices against nations that use unfair trade practices against our exports—that is "unfair" by our standards, not theirs. Hence the bill has been greeted by sharp protests from abroad. But in the opinion of some, the bill may have another outcome. Because of its extension of governmental oversight, it may be the beginning of a coherent approach to our foreign trade—leading, some suggest, to the eventual appointment of a cabinet-level Secretary for Trade.

[4] For a sharp critique of U.S. policy, see Lester Thurow, *Head to Head: The Coming Economic Battle Among Japan, Europe, and America* (New York: William Morrow, 1992).

labor and big business, raising taxes automatically when inflation begins to accelerate. These are difficult political goals to achieve.

Incomes policies

3. *Incomes policies* mean that inflation is controlled by agreements to hold incomes—mainly wages and dividend payments—to levels that do not exceed increases in productivity. This is difficult to achieve on a voluntary basis because the temptations to cheat are very great.

Mandatory controls

4. *Mandatory controls work well in wartime, not so well in peacetime.* They may, however, provide a necessary breather during which incomes policies can be installed.

The politics of anti-inflationary policy

5. Controlling inflation is essentially a political matter. The trick is to discover policies that will gain the acceptance of the public. This may be harder to accomplish in a big, diversified country like the United States than in a small, cohesive one.

Human capital and infrastructure

6. It is uncertain that unemployment can be combated by supply-side policies alone. The challenge is to use government spending to generate jobs and create productivity for the private sector. One such approach is *building human capital* by aid to education and training, and rebuilding and *strengthening the public infrastructure* on whose efficiency much private productivity rests.

Structural unemployment

7. A second general approach to generating employment without inflation is to improve the workings of the labor market by matching available skills and jobs. *Remedying structural unemployment* is expensive and difficult, but it can greatly reduce the level of joblessness.

Trade policy

8. *Trade policies are attempts to concert the powers of government, enterprise, and labor* to establish a secure footing for a nation in the international economy. They are an effort to avoid the uncoordinated and often fruitless individual rescue operations that are the response of a country that has no policy.

Business-government and labor-management relations

9. Almost all foreign nations have trade policies. The institutional means and the specific market targets vary widely, but all seek to bring government and business into tandem, with labor actively cooperating. This represents an approach to business-government and management-labor relations that is quite different from that currently in favor in America.

QUESTIONS

1. Why are incomes policies so difficult to achieve? How would you personally feel about an incomes policy like that described in the footnote on page 215.

2. Do you think there is a realistic possibility that the United States will one day be "wrung dry" of its inflationary psychology, so that you would be willing to buy a thirty-year bond paying, say, 5 percent? Think hard about the reasons that make you answer this question yes or no.

3. How much inflation do you think is socially justifiable to gain "full" employment? Suppose that you had the following choices:

If the unemployment rate were:	inflation would be:
10 percent	2 percent
6 percent	6 percent
4 percent	15 percent
2 percent	25 percent

   Where do you personally think the nation would be best off? Where do you think labor would like to be? Business?

4. Do you think that infrastructure spending should be justifiable by the same criteria as private investment spending—namely, that it is profitable? If not, then what criteria would you suggest to decide whether, say, a road was worth the cost?

5. If American Airways should be forced to the wall by the competition of foreign nationalized airlines, what measures would you suggest to save it, or would you think it wise to allow it to go bankrupt?

6. The United Automobile Workers has proposed that we help employment in the auto industry by passing "local content" legislation, forcing all automakers, foreign or U.S., to produce higher and higher percentages of their cars within the United States as their share of the national market increases. Many economists dislike the policy as "protectionist." The UAW replies that nearly all other auto-manufacturing countries have local content laws. What are the pros and cons of the matter, as you see it?

7. Suppose that we had a government trade agency with representatives of industry, labor, and the public, and that the big steel producers turned to it for aid in modernizing their plants. Can you suggest some quid pro quos that such an agency could ask for in return for a massive loan? Suppose that some of these were a pledge not to abandon steel towns and a pledge to install the very best antipollution equipment, and that these pledges conflicted with the aim of lowering steel costs. This gives you an idea of the difficulty of creating a a workable trade policy. Can you suggest ways out of the dilemma?

13
SOCIALISM AND CAPITALISM

In our last chapter, we come back to the theme of the first—the trajectory of economic history. This time, however, we face to the future rather than to the past, and ask not where capitalism came from, but where it is going.

This is a question to which conventional economics does not generally address itself, and for good reason. For the question goes far beyond the competence of economists as such. As we have said before, in the end it will likely be considerations of political wisdom, of social morale, and of institutional adaptability that will determine the futures of the United States and Japan and the European nations that make up most of the capitalist world. The same is true for whatever is left of the former Soviet Union and the East European countries that comprise the once-socialistic world. And it is true once again for the Third World: the Brazils and Mexicos and Indias and Egypts that are struggling to find their places in the economic sun, some as capitalist economies, some as semi-socialist ones, and some—we instance Iran—as neither.

All the knowledge of the historian, the political scientist, and the philosopher would not allow us to foretell this immense story in detail. Nevertheless, economics may teach us a few lessons that bear on—even if they do not allow us to predict—the shape of things to come.

yesterday's outlook... Let us start by reviewing an extraordinary turnabout in the way we perceive economic history itself. Here we must look back to the late 1930s—a mere blink of the eye as historic chronologies usually unfold. The direction of world economic change seemed very clear in those days: World capitalism appeared to be on its way out, world socialism on its way in. Without a single exception, the Western capitalist nations had gone through, or were still embroiled in, the most devastating economic depression in history. Ahead lay a world war whose outcome, most observers quite correctly foresaw, would be the destruction of capitalist colonial empires abroad and the emplacement of "socialistic" welfare schemes at home. Who could entertain optimistic expectations for capitalism in the face of such events and prospects?

Meanwhile, the fortunes of socialism were rising as dramatically as those of capitalism seemed to be fading. The Russian Revolution had seized the imagination of much of the world. In the old colonial regions, socialist parties and leaders were already preparing to reorganize the lands of Asia and Africa under the banner of national planning, whose galvanizing force had been made evident by the Soviet example. The coming war seemed to the Third World a great turning point, signaling the end of the old order and the beginning of the new. With such expectations, who would not have painted the socialist future in bright colors?

. . . and today's

Need we say that things have not turned out that way? Capitalism is very much alive today, even though, as we know, it is not in perfect health. More striking, socialism is in the midst of a revolutionary transformation that is introducing into its midst many aspects of the capitalist system. And perhaps most surprising of all, South Korea and Mexico and other Third World countries generally have not left the fold of the capitalist system but have actually become more enmeshed in it. Some of that entanglement is the result of their financial indebtedness to their former political and military masters. But perhaps more significant, the entanglement also proceeds from the emergence of new centers of industrial production in many countries that were certainly not capitalist fifty years ago—Hong Kong, Singapore, Taiwan, South Korea—and the strong signs of further capitalist development elsewhere—Brazil, Mexico, India. In the face of these events, who can today declare that capitalism is dying or that socialism is the wave of the future?

why history changed course

Can we explain this astonishing change of historic course? Two generalizations will help us think about what has happened.

1. Capitalism has changed.

Capitalism is very much a vital economic force in modern history, but it is not the same capitalism as that to which the gloomy predictions of the past applied. The nature of that change has been spelled out in the pages of this book and does not need to be explained in detail. At its core is the introduction, into every advanced capitalist nation, of measures to cushion the social (and political) effects of economic malfunction. We can summarize the change by saying that macroeconomic policies to improve and maintain economic growth, however imperfect, have effectively prevented the disaster of another Great Depression.

As every reader of this book must know, that certainly does not mean that capitalism is today free of serious problems. Nonetheless, it helps explain the profound change that marks off capitalism's present self-assessment from that of the not-so-distant past. *The outlook for the future, at least in the main capitalist nations, no longer appears to be a choice between capitalism and socialism.* Rather, it concerns the *kind* of capitalism most likely to work well. The debates we have followed in our text—debates over Keynesian policies, welfare, government deficits, protectionism, industrial regulation—are taking place within a general consensus about the viability of capitalism very different from that of fifty years ago.

2. *Socialism has revealed unexpected economic difficulties.*

By and large, the early enthusiasts for socialism laid their bets on two aspects of a planned economic system. One was its capacity to move a backward, moribund economy off dead center. The other was the elimination of the inefficiencies and wastefulness of capitalism. One of those bets paid off, at least in part. The other did not.

The bet that paid off was the ability of central planning to bring backward nations into the modern world. This was most dramatically evidenced in the Soviet Union (into whose history we shall shortly look) and in China. No one can compare the old Tsarist empire or the hopelessly inefficient Chinese landlord system with the societies created by the Soviets or the Chinese communists and not recognize that an unprecedented transformation has taken place, however horrendous the cost.

Getting a society off dead center is one thing, keeping it going is another. Here is the bet that socialism lost. Without exception, the impressive socialist "takeoffs" were followed by increasingly disappointing, and finally disastrous, economic performance. Moreover, the reason for the failure was the same in every case—the vitality of the early stage of mobilization was followed by the inertia and then the downright disorganization of bureaucratization. The unexpected lesson of socialism was that planning was an easy word to spell, but a hard one to spell out. Planning was intended to be the remedy for the ills of capitalism. It became a remedy in many cases worse than the disease.

THE SOVIET SYSTEM

Let us begin by looking into the history of the Soviet system. We must start by realizing that the Russian system did not evolve gradually over time, as did capitalism. It was created, forcibly, after the Revolution of

1917. A semifeudal society dotted with a few large capitalist enterprises was taken over by revolutionaries who had read deeply in Marx but who knew nothing about how to organize a "socialist" economy.

Alas, Marx was of small use for the revolutionists because *Capital*, his great opus, was entirely about capitalism, not socialism. In those few essays in which Marx looked to the future, his gaze rarely traveled beyond the watershed of the revolutionary act itself. With the achievement of the revolution, Marx thought, a temporary regime known as "the dictatorship of the proletariat" would take over the transition from capitalism to socialism, and thereafter, a "planned socialist economy" would emerge as the first step toward a still less specified "communism."* In the latter state—the final terminus of economic revolution, according to Marx—there were hints that the necessary but humdrum tasks of production and distribution would take place by the voluntary cooperation of all citizens and that society would turn its serious attention to matters of cultural and humanistic importance.

Can occur in capitalist system

the early USSR In reality, the revolution presented Lenin, Trotsky, and the other leaders of the new Soviet Union with problems far more complex than this utopian long-term design. Shortly after the initial success of the revolution, Lenin nationalized the banks, the major factories, the railways, and the canals. In the meantime, the peasants themselves had taken over the large landed estates on which they had been tenants and had carved them up into individual holdings. The central authorities then attempted for several years to run the economy by requisitioning food from the farms and allocating it to factory workers, while controlling the flow of output from the factories themselves by a system of direct controls from above.

This initial attempt to run the economy was a disastrous failure. Under inept management, industrial output declined precipitously; by 1920, it had fallen to *14 percent* of prewar levels. As goods available to the peasants became scarcer, the peasants themselves were less and less willing to acquiesce in giving up food to the cities. The result was a wild

---

* What is the difference between *socialism* and *communism*? In the West, *socialism* has always cherished democratic political mechanisms, whereas *communism* has not. But within the socialist bloc, the distinction has traditionally been made differently. Socialism represented a stage of development in which it was still necessary to use "bourgeois" incentives in order to make the economy function; that is, people must be paid in proportion to the "economic value" of their work. Under communism, a new form of human society will presumably be achieved in which these selfish incentives would no longer be needed. Karl Marx's famous description of communism read: "From each according to his ability; to each according to his need." This utopian description of socialism and communism is very likely to be reexamined and may well be discarded, in light of the collapse of centrally planned socialism.

inflation, followed by a degeneration into an economy of semibarter. For a while, toward the end of 1920, the system threatened to break down completely. To forestall the impending collapse, in 1921 Lenin instituted a New Economic Policy, the so-called NEP. This was a return toward a market system and a partial reconstitution of actual capitalism. Retail trade, for instance, was opened again to private ownership and operation. Small-scale industry also reverted to private direction. Most important, the farms were no longer requisitioned but operated as profit-making units. Only the "commanding heights" of industry and finance were retained in government hands.

There ensued for several years a bitter debate about what course of action to follow next. While the basic aim of the Soviet government was still to industrialize and to socialize (that is, to replace the private ownership of the means of production by state ownership), the question was how fast to move ahead—and, indeed, *how* to move ahead. The pace of industrialization hinged critically on one highly uncertain factor: the willingness of the large, private peasant sector to deliver food with which the city workers could be sustained in their tasks. To what extent, therefore, should the need for additional capital goods be sacrificed in order to turn out the consumption goods that could be used as an inducement for peasant cooperation?

the drive *to total* *planning*   The student of Russian history—or, for that matter, of economic history—will find the record of that debate an engrossing subject.[1] But the argument was never truly resolved. In 1927, Stalin moved into command, and the difficult question of how much to appease the unwilling peasant disappeared. Stalin simply made the ruthless decision to appease him not at all, but to *coerce* him by collectivizing his holdings.

The collectivization process solved in one swoop the problem of securing the essential transfer of food from the farm to the city, but it did so at a frightful social (and economic) cost. Many peasants slaughtered their livestock rather than hand it over to the new collective farms; others waged outright war or practiced sabotage. In reprisal, the authorities acted with brutal force. An estimated 5 million "kulaks" (rich peasants) were executed or put in labor camps, while in the cities an equally relentless policy showed itself vis-à-vis labor. Workers were summarily ordered to the tasks required by the central authorities. The right to strike was forbidden, and the trade unions were reduced to impotence. Speedups were widely applied, and living conditions were allowed to deteriorate to very low levels.

---

[1] See Alexander Erlich, *The Soviet Industrialization Debate: 1924–1928* (Cambridge, Mass.: Harvard University Press, 1960).

The history of this period of forced industrialization is ugly and repellent, and it has left abiding scars on Russian society. It is well for us, nonetheless, to attempt to view it with some objectivity. If the extremes to which the Stalinist authorities went were extraordinary, often unpardonable, and perhaps self-defeating, we must bear in mind that industrialization on the grand scale has always been wrenching, always accompanied by economic sacrifice, and always carried out by the more or less authoritarian use of power. We have already seen what happened in the West at the time of the Industrial Revolution, with its heavy-handed exploitation of labor; and without "excusing" these acts, we have seen their function in paving the way for capital accumulation.

Without seeking to justify the Russian effort, it is worth pondering whether rapid industrialization, with its inescapable price of low consumption, could ever be a "popular" policy. Will poor people willingly vote for an economic transformation which will not "pay out" for twenty or forty years? We might note in passing that universal male suffrage was not gained in England until the late 1860s and 1870s. Aneurin Bevan has written, "It is highly doubtful whether the achievements of the Industrial Revolution would have been permitted if the franchise had been universal. It is very doubtful because a great deal of the capital aggregations that we are at present enjoying are the results of the wages that our fathers went without."[2]

plan vs. market   A massive industrialization drive requires a determined effort to hold consumption to a minimum and to transfer resources to capital building, an effort greatly facilitated, as we have seen, by the totalitarian political apparatus. But there is still another question to be considered: How are the freed resources to find their proper destination in an integrated and workable industrial sector?

Let us remind ourselves again of how this is done under a market economy. There, the signal of profitability serves as the lure for the allocation of resources and labor. Entrepreneurs, anticipating or following demand, risk private funds in the construction of the facilities that they hope the future will require. Meanwhile, as these industrial salients grow, smaller satellite industries grow along with them to cater to their needs.

The flow of materials is thus regulated in every sector by the forces of private demand, making themselves known by the signal of rising or falling prices. At every moment there emanates from the growing industries a magnetic pull of demand on secondary industries, while, in turn, the growth salients themselves are guided, spurred, or slowed down

---

[2] In Gunnar Myrdal, *Rich Lands and Poor* (New York: Harper, 1957), p. 46.

by the pressure of demand from the ultimate buying public. And all the while, counterposed to these pulls of demand, are the obduracies of supply—the cost schedules of the producers themselves. In the crossfire of demand and supply exists a marvelously sensitive social instrument for the integration of the overall economic effort of expansion.

And in the absence of a market? Clearly, the mechanism must be supplied by the direct orders of a central controlling and planning agency. The planning agency must provide a substitute for the forward-looking operations of the corporate management structure in a market economy. In the place of an IBM and a General Motors building their plants in anticipation of, or in response to, an insistent demand for their products, the planning body must itself set overall goals and objectives for economic growth. Not the consumer but the planners' own judgments and desires determine the force of "demand."

Establishing the overall objectives is, however, only the first and perhaps the easiest part of the planning mechanism. It is not enough to set broad goals and then assume that they will be fulfilled by themselves. We must remember that planning in a totalitarian economy is not superimposed on a market structure in which individuals take care of the "details" of production according to the incentives of price and profit. In a totally planned economy, each and every item that goes into the final plan must also be planned. Schedules of production are needed for steel, coal, coke, lumber, on down to nails and paper clips, for there is no "automatic" device by which these items will be forthcoming without a planning directive. Supplies of labor must also be planned; or if labor is free to move where it wishes, wage rates must be planned in order to draw labor where it is wanted.

Thus, supplementing and completing the master objective of the overall plan must be a whole hierarchy of subplans, the aggregate of which must bring about the necessary final result. And here is a genuine difficulty. For an error in planning, small in itself, if it affects a strategic link in the chain of production, can seriously distort—or even render impossible—the fulfillment of the total plan.

the postwar period   With all its difficulties, central planning worked in the years following World War II, when the ravaged Russian economy was rebuilt in a storm of energy resembling that of the early 1930s. Thereafter, however, the problems of socialism began to change. For once the essential work of rebuilding had been accomplished, the main task of planning shifted from construction to coordination. The challenge facing the planners was no longer to bring into being the basic framework of a modern industrial state but to make such a framework function effectively.

That proved to be much more difficult than the earlier effort. Under Stalin's successors, especially Nikita Khrushchev and Leonid Brezhnev, the system began to show alarming signs of failure. According to U.S. government estimates, real Soviet gross national product grew at an average annual rate of about 6.5 percent from 1965 to 1980, but by only 1.8 percent per year from 1980 to 1985. In a few parts of the economy, where no expense was spared and where the bureaucracy was subordinated to the highly demanding requirement of special "consumers," the system had its triumphs—the Soviets launched the first space shot, built impressive military planes and tanks, and created whole new cities in strategic regions.

But in other areas, where the special interests were not in a position to dominate the bureaucracy, very different results followed. Consumer goods were produced in quantity, but of such poor quality that warehouses bulged with unusable shoes and shoddy cloth. Although the USSR produced twice as much steel per capita as the United States, there was a chronic steel shortage because the material was used so wastefully. Lumber was in short supply because only some 30 percent of the Soviet timber harvest was utilized, compared with 95 percent in the United States and Canada.

Why was Russian planning an increasingly evident failure? Let us answer the question by learning how planning actually worked—at least how it worked until the era of *perestroika* (restructuring), to which we will shortly turn.

the "old" Soviet planning system   Until recently, Soviet planning was carried out in successive stages. It began at the center, where the Gosplan, the official state planning agency, laid out the basic guidelines for a five-year effort. This Five-Year Plan dictated such crucial decisions as the rates at which consumption and investment would grow, the foreign trade balance with the Soviet Union's satellite states, and the priorities for basic research.*

The overall plan was then broken down into shorter one-year plans. These one-year plans, specifying the output of major sectors of industry, were then transmitted to various government ministries concerned with, for example, steel production, rail transportation, or lumbering. In turn,

---

*The first Five-Year Plan, from 1928 to 1932, had as its basic objective the intensification of industrialization in heavy industry, with special emphasis on electrification; the second took as its main goal the development of transportation and the beginning of agricultural planning; the third plan (1938–1942) was essentially occupied with producing the needs for a war economy; the fourth, from 1946 to 1950, was mainly a plan of reconstruction from wartime damage, with continuing emphasis on heavy industry; a fifth plan, 1951 to 1955, emphasized a steep increase in output, with some stress being given (for the first time) to consumer goods. A sixth plan was scrapped in midcourse; a seventh (1959–1965) aimed to increase industrial output by 80 percent and agricultural output by 70 percent, and to bring significant increases in housing (a sector long neglected in the interests of industrialization) and in consumer goods generally.

the ministries referred the one-year plans further down the line to the heads of large industrial plants, to experts and advisers, and so forth. Thus, the overall design was unraveled into its constituent parts, until finally the threads were traced back as far as possible along the productive process—right to the officials in charge of factory operations.

In this way, the factory manager of a plant—say, a coking operation—would be given a set of instructions to make his operations dovetail with those of the industries to which his output would flow and from which his inputs would arrive. The manager would then confer with his staff of production engineers and plant supervisors and would transmit up the line his requirements for meeting his "targets"—perhaps an authorization to hire more workers or to order additional machines. In this way, "demand" requirements flowed down the chain of command and constraints of "supply" flowed back up, all coming together in a giant production blueprint (actually a vast series of computer printouts) in the Gosplan offices.

success
indicators

As we can imagine, the coordination and integration of these plans was a fantastically complicated task. Even with the most sophisticated planning techniques, the process was slow, cumbersome, and mistake-prone. To get around the constant shortages that cropped up and brought things to a grinding halt, factory managers were given strong financial incentives to *surpass* their planned output.

But this only introduced yet another problem. For the "success indicators" by which plan achievement was measured invariably produced their own bottlenecks and distortions. If the target for a textile mill was specified in yards of cloth, there was obviously a strong temptation to weave the cloth as loosely as possible to maximize the yardage from a given input of thread. If the success indicator was a measure of weight, the temptation was to skimp on quality or design. A cartoon in the satiric magazine *Krokodil* showed a nail factory proudly displaying its "record output"—one gigantic nail suspended by an immense gantry crane. The economic system was, in fact, soon heavily dependent on so-called *tolkachi*—wheelers and dealers who arranged for shipments to be rerouted, shortages to be filled, and excess inventories to be disposed of, either behind the authorities' backs or with their tacit permission.

collapse

It was to remove these suffocating inefficiencies that Mikail Gorbachev began to speak in 1985 of *glasnost*—openness—and of *perestroika*—the fundamental restructuring of the economic system.

What is perestroika? We must ask what perestroika was intended to be, because Gorbachev's plan was overtaken by a rush of events that rapidly brought the Soviet Union to the brink of economic and political chaos, the consequence of the increasing disorganization of the economy. The collapse itself was an astonishing phenomenon that took everyone by surprise and is still not clearly understood. In all likelihood, sclerosis simply mounted to crisis proportions. It became increasingly difficult to assure shipments from one factory or region to another, so that production began to fall precipitously. We speak of a "serious recession" in the United States when GNP drops by a percent or two; in the Soviet Union during the first years of the 1990s, production may well have dropped by 25 percent, perhaps even more. As food shortages began to appear in the major cities, *tolkachi* "fixers" gave way to hucksters. The black market was probably the only growth sector in the Russian economy. From there it was a short step to political disorganization as the Union itself began to come apart at the seams, and the prospect of political disruption raised the further economic spectre of a return to contending statelets.

perestroika   There we leave the story, whose next developments the reader will know more about than can this writer looking into the future. Let us turn, instead, to the fascinating question of what perestroika was intended to be. We can outline Gorbachev's proposal in terms of four fundamental changes:

1. Five-year plans would have continued to set the general objectives for the system, but they would have resembled European rather than Soviet old-style planning. Growth rates for GNP, levels of taxation, and regional encouragements would have been their target. A few military items would have remained strictly under the control of the bureaucracy (not so different from our own defense arrangements), but no consumer output would have been under Gosplan control.

2. Ministries of production would have been gradually converted into autonomous enterprises expected to live in a competitive market system. The only "success indicator" was to be the profits. It was not certain whether these enterprises would have been private businesses. Probably they were intended to be competitive state-owned undertakings.

3. Managers of these factories would have bought and sold what and where they pleased, at whatever prices they could get, exactly like private enterprise. The job security that protected Soviet workers (vastly lowering productivity) would give way to the normal relations of business employees and their bosses.

4. Many kinds of small undertakings were to be encouraged as purely private businesses—restaurants, beauty salons, automobile repair shops, and the like. More important, agricultural production was to be increasingly (but not totally) provided by household plots, not by collective farms.

could it   Probably not. Gorbachev's perestroika envisaged a kind of half-way
have   house between centralized planning and market incentives. One of the
worked?   reasons for the increasing dissatisfaction within the Soviet Union over

Gorbachev's leadership was precisely the impatience of its "liberal" market-oriented wing with measures of change that stopped short of a full-scale market system, and the unease of the "conservative" Party core over the threat to bureaucracy implicit in its proposals.

Behind these political struggles lie broad political and economic questions that affect not only the Soviets, but also the Eastern European socialist countries struggling to find some more effective mode of economic organization than central planning. Here are some of these problems:

1. It is one thing to wish to introduce "the market," and another to accept the changes it brings. Moving from a planned to a market society means making a *political*, not just an economic shift, in which power is transferred from government officials to a new class of capitalist entrepreneurs. That has occurred only once before in history, in the commercial revolution whose bloody and difficult course we witnessed in Chapter 3. That transformation took several centuries. Today's reformers want to accomplish it in a decade or two.

2. The promoters of capitalist rejuvenation stress the improvements that a market society will bring. They do not mention the unemployment, inflation, and intense domestic and foreign competition it will also bring. These unavoidable side effects of a transition to capitalism are likely to make their unwelcome presence felt long before economic growth and well-being arrive. Thus political pressures on a huge scale are virtually certain to plague the ex-communist countries for a very long time, not only delaying the advent of economic growth, but perhaps setting the stage for a retreat from the democracy that is an even more important goal than their economic progress.

3. Finally, there is a grab bag of knotty institutional and legal problems. How will the institutions and social classes of capitalism be introduced? Who will write the laws that establish and define private property? How will the property of the state—above all, its potentially profitable enterprises—be transferred into private hands? And whose hands will they be? And just as small stumbling blocks: How will a workable economy be established when there are no private banks, no commercial lawyers or accountants, virtually no checking accounts (all payments made in cash or in book entries between ministries and their factories), no Yellow Pages in the phone books, and very few phone books?

is socialism dead? This raises a question of central importance for ourselves, who are less interested in the analysis of the Soviet downfall than in the repercussions of this epochal event on the major theme of our book. That theme has been the trajectory of capitalism as the principal form of economic society in Western civilization. For a time it seemed as if centrally planned socialism would be a powerful contestant with capitalism, and very possibly its successor. In the aftermath of the debacle of central planning, is there anything left of "socialism" at all?

One part of that question can be disposed of with some degree of certainty. Socialism as a society built around a core of strong central planning is a form of economic society whose prospects appear very dim, at least for the advanced industrial nations. It is possible, however, that in underdeveloped countries, seeking to change backward peasant societies into modern industrial ones, centrally planned socialism may prove to be as successful as it was, for a time, in the Soviet Union. Thus some kind of "military socialism" may well continue for a time as the framework of China or of impoverished societies elsewhere that seek to make the painful ascent into industrial sufficiency.

But if the experience of the West is any lesson, this kind of socialism will not yield its hoped-for results, once the initial industrial undertakings have been completed. Again judging by this same experience, the creation of smooth-functioning complex economies geared to the fulfillment of consumers' needs will prove to be very difficult, perhaps impossible, under central planning. The inertia of bureaucracy and the stultifying atmosphere of political uniformity are deadly obstacles to economic dynamism. Dictatorial societies are not good breeding grounds for the entrepreneurial spirit. A successful centrally planned socialism does not seem a possibility over the foreseeable future.

the uncertain boundary of socialism

There is, however, another way of thinking about the future of socialism. Let us imagine a country that comprised the most desirable features of existing capitalist nations. It might (for example) combine the culture enjoyed by France, the school system of Sweden, the public health achievement of Canada, the income distribution patterns of Norway, the labor-management accords of Germany, the civil liberties of the Netherlands—or whatever other combination of national institutions pleases the reader. The question of socialism could then be posed as follows: What changes would be required to make this imaginary but unmistakably capitalist country into a "socialist" one—that is, into a political, social, and economic entity both unmistakably different from, and superior to, capitalism?

The question helps put the problem of socialism into its present historic context. For it poses as a matter of institutional realities, not ideological visions. Take, for example, the question of whether socialism in the future might not be "market socialism," using markets instead of central planning, while retaining some of the other institutions of socialism. The questions we now ask are: How do we decide which institutions to keep? Some kinds of planning? What kinds, and in what areas? A more egalitarian income distribution? How equal, and how attained? Worker participation? In what decisions, and how structured?

These are difficult questions to answer, precisely because they do not allow us to evade hard institutional realities by resort to rhetoric.

They force us to confront the discomfiting fact that the institutional boundary between advanced capitalism and democratic socialism is not easy to draw. They ask us to consider how far we wish to press for "socialist" ideals within the general institutional forms of capitalism, and whether and where we want to breach those boundaries.

Is there a final judgment? Perhaps it is to say that the adaptive capabilities of capitalism appear quite large within the near-term future, so that something resembling socialism might well be achieved in some nations, within a framework of private property and market relations. Over the longer term there are likely to be limits to that adaptive capability. For example, it is uncertain whether capitalism would be able to retain its vitality if the ecological vise really closed in, or if the relationship between the capitalist and precapitalist worlds would continue along its present antagonistic course. If these challenges arrive, they will usher in historic changes whose general nature we can only dimly perceive.

PROSPECTS FOR CAPITALISM

Will capitalism then continue to be the uncontested form of socioeconomic organization within the Western world—at least until these still distant problems become threatening realities? That likelihood poses a fitting question for our final consideration. What are the trends that appear imminent within modern capitalism? If socialism as a distinct form of economic society no longer seems on the immediate agenda, what movements, what strains and stresses, what problems and possibilities can we foresee for our own lives and for those of our children?

capitalism's problems   Our exploration of the course of economic history may help us think about this all-important question. It suggests that we approach the issue by asking if there is one central difficulty that threatens capitalism in the same manner that the bureaucratic disease threatens socialism. The question once put, the answer must surely come to mind. As we have seen throughout these chapters, the persisting problem of capitalism is to achieve objectives other than those that emerge spontaneously from the marketplace itself. Perhaps we can generalize that the great problem of capitalism is to realize political aims that do not spring from its economic workings, just as the great problem of socialism is to realize economic aims that do not spring from its political workings.

It is certainly easy to remind ourselves of the character of these capitalist problems. One of them is the tendency of market systems to tolerate unnecessary poverty, because the market does not generate mechanisms of distribution geared to the needs of the poor. Another problem is the failure of capitalisms to pay sufficient attention to the quality of life, turning a blind eye to the deficiencies and excesses that emerge from the guidance of the market—urban blight side by side with conspicuous consumption. Yet a third problem is the malfunctions generated by the workings of the system itself—its succession of booms and busts, its persisting inability to provide employment for all who seek it, its tendency to create huge enterprises that defy the very power of the nation-state itself.

the rise of capitalist "planning"

These difficulties are as deeply rooted in the workings of the market system of capitalism as the difficulties of socialism are rooted in the workings of its system of central allocation. Moreover, just as the problems of socialism could be ignored during its early stages, when the full force of the planning operation could work its mobilizing miracles, so the drawbacks of the market mechanism could be ignored in the middle phases of capitalism, while the system availed itself of its tremendous capacity to generate and satisfy demand.

But as a market society becomes more advanced, its requirements change, just as do those of a socialist society. These latter, as we have seen, increasingly require the flexibility and adaptability that central planning cannot give. And capitalisms begin to need the public guidance that the market cannot provide. *The result is that just as we see socialisms turning toward the market, we see capitalisms turning toward "planning."*

It is not central planning. The planning mechanisms of capitalism constitute that wide range of measures that we have followed in this book—measures by which the polity intervenes in, seeks to change the course of, and tries to overcome the problems that arise from the unhindered market. Planning in capitalism therefore embraces its fiscal and monetary policies, its programs of public investment, its measures of income support and redistribution, its regulation of big business—in short, the gamut of public activities whose various forms and modes of application we have followed in the pages past. Now, however, we no longer view these policies piecemeal, but see them as a response of the system to its problems, similar in mirror fashion to the quite opposite response of socialism to its chief functional difficulty.

politics vs. economics

Will these measures assure the longevity of capitalism? That question cannot be answered with certainty. We know from past experience that the malfunctions of capitalism can be very grave. We have also seen that many of these problems can be considerably redressed, even if not removed. Here, too, we have no alternative but to await the verdict of history. Perhaps we should say *verdicts*. We have spoken in this chapter about socialism and capitalism, but it would have been wiser to have spoken of socialisms and capitalisms. For it is likely that there will be successful capitalisms and unsuccessful ones, just as it is possible that some socialisms will flourish and some will not. In the end, it will likely be considerations of political wisdom, social morale, and institutional adaptability that will determine the futures of the nations that make up the capitalist as well as the socialist world.

A LAST WORD

One final word before we are done. Despite communism's collapse, we tend to speak of capitalism and socialism as systems in opposition, embodying contrary principles of political and economic life. Yet from the historian's viewpoint, it might be wise to conclude by emphasizing certain problems common to all modern industrial societies. In our time, three such problems seem of very great long-range significance.

1. *Control over technology.*

One of the most important attributes of modern history is lodged in a striking difference between two kinds of knowledge: the knowledge we acquire in physics, chemistry, engineering, and other sciences, and that which we gain in the sphere of social or political or moral activity. The difference is that knowledge in some sciences is cumulative and builds on itself, whereas knowledge in the social sphere does not. The merest beginner in biology soon knows more than the greatest biologist of a century ago. By way of contrast, the veteran student (or practitioner) of government, of social relations, of moral philosophy, is aware of his modest stature in comparison with the great social and moral philosophers of the past.

The result is that all modern societies tend to find that their technological capabilities are constantly increasing, while the social, political, and moral institutions by which those capabilities are controlled cannot match the challenges with which they are faced. Television, for example, is an immense force for cultural homogenization; medical technology changes the composition of society by altering its age groups and life expectancy; rapid transportation vastly increases mobility and social horizons; and the obliterative power of nuclear arms casts a pervasive anxiety over all of life. All these technologically rooted developments fundamentally alter the conditions and problems of life, but we do not know what social, political, and moral responses are appropriate to them. As a result, all modern societies experience the feeling of being at the mercy of a technological and scientific impetus that shapes the lives of their citizens in ways that cannot be accurately foreseen nor adequately controlled.

2. *The problem of participation.*

The second problem derives from the first. Because advanced societies are characterized by high levels of technology, they are necessarily marked by a high degree of organization. The technology of our era depends on the cooperation of vast masses of people, some at the levels of production, some at the levels of administration. The common undergirding of all advanced industrial societies lies not alone in their gigantic instrumentalities of production, but also in their equally essential and vast instrumentalities of administration, whether these be called corporations, production ministries, or government agencies.

The problem, then, is how the citizen is to find a place for his or her individuality in the midst of so much organization; how to express his or her voice in the direction of affairs, when so much bureaucratic management is inescapable; how to participate in a world whose technological structure calls for ever more order and coordination. This is a matter which, like the sweeping imperative of technology, affects both capitalisms and socialisms. In both kinds of societies, individuals feel overwhelmed by the impersonality of the work process, impotent before the power of huge enterprises—above all, the state itself—and frustrated at an inability to participate in decisions that seem more and more beyond any possibility of personal influence.

No doubt much can be done to increase the feeling of individual participation in the making of the future, especially in those nations that still deny elementary political freedoms. But there remains a recalcitrant problem of how the quest for increased individual decision making and participation can be reconciled with the organizational demands imposed by the technology on which all advanced societies depend. This is a problem that is likely to trouble societies—capitalist or not—as long as technology itself rests on integrated processes of production and requires centralized organs of administration and control.

3. *The problem of the environment.*

All industrial nations face an era in which exponential growth is beginning to absorb resources at rates faster than we may be able to provide them with new technologies; and all industrialized societies—indeed, the whole world—may soon be entering an era in which environmental limitations will impose a scaling down of expectations of growth.

In this period of long-run economic stringency, industrial nations of all kinds again seem likely to share common problems—not only in bringing about a controlled slowdown in output, but also in achieving social harmony under conditions that no longer allow their citizens to look forward to ever-higher standards of material consumption. Here, too, similar social and political problems may override differences in economic institutions and ideologies.

envoi In a larger sense, then, we go beyond economics to the common human adventure in which economic systems are only alternate routes conducting humanity toward a common destination. Perhaps it is well that we end our book with the recognition that the long history of the market system does not project us onto a final stage in social history. Rather we arrive at a state in which some kinds of problems—the pitifully simple problems of producing and distributing goods—find resolution only to reveal vastly larger problems springing from the very technology and organization that supplied the earlier answers.

KEY CONCEPTS AND KEY WORDS

Market vs. command

1. A striking change has occurred in our time. Socialism, the longtime challenger of capitalism, has suffered a tremendous setback. Socialist systems everywhere in the world are moving toward the market mechanism—the central mechanism of capitalism. In this chapter we trace the causes of, and prospects for, that change.

The command system

2. The Soviet economy was created by fiat, rather than evolving, as did our own. Following the Russian Revolution, the partly peasant and partly capitalist framework of Tsarist Russia was first organized into a halfhearted command system, then ruthlessly forced into a totalitarian structure by Stalin.

Industrialization and command

3. The early command system worked because it was able to mobilize resources for the relatively simple task of "forcing" industrialization atop a preindustrial base. In restrospect, we can see that some degree of political command seems always to accompany the wrenching transformation of industrialization, although Stalin's use of power was hideously excessive.

Planning: old style

4. After World War II's reconstruction was completed, the command system began to display serious difficulties. Command economies are good for mobilizing, but not for flexibility and adaptation. The old planning system no longer worked because its "success indicators" failed to generate the responses that the system needed to avoid shortages and mismatches.

Perestroika

5. In 1985, Mikhail Gorbachev announced a basic restructuring (*perestroika*) for the Soviet system—a restructuring that would have gone a long way, but not all the way, to introducing the fundamental institutions of capitalism. That plan was never actually instituted, as the increasing disorganization of economic life brought the economy to a near standstill. Severe political turmoil followed, and the final outcome remains unforeseeable.

The socialist debacle

6. Similar kinds of economic disorganization and political upheaval took place in virtually all the centrally planned socialisms of Europe. One by one, they have rejected communist political rule and sought to introduce a capitalist economy. The difficulties of such transformations are very great, and their success is uncertain.

Prospects for capitalism

7. Is capitalism thereby assured of its future? It is not likely to be challenged by any centrally planned economy. But it will certainly be characterized by the dynamic tendencies that have marked its history—above all, the strains and stresses of an expansive drive working within the encouragements and discouragements of a competitive market. In all likelihood this will drive capitalism in the direction of planning—not central planning, but the use of various means to lessen its instabilities and correct its market-driven inequities.

Long-run problems

8. The prospect for capitalism then becomes one of assessing the creative and adaptive capacities of different capitalisms, just as the future for socialism depends on the same capacities for the countries emerging from central planning. In the near term, these adaptive capabilities are potentially large. In the longer run, all modern nations may find their ultimate challenge in dangerous and runaway technologies and the tightening margin of ecological safety.

QUESTIONS

All the previous chapters have offered questions for review. Not this one. This is not a chapter to be "learned" so much as thought about. This time you must pose the questions.

NAME INDEX

A

Alberti, Leon Battista, 69
Allen, Frederick Lewis, 136–37
Amici, Jean, 53
Aquinas, Thomas, 35
Aristotle, 24–26, 36
Arkwright, Richard, 72, 74–77, 81, 104
Armour, Philip Danforth, 104

B

Beard, Miriam, 18
Berle, Adolf, 115–16, 119
Bernstein, Peter, 217n
Bevan, Aneurin, 230
Boccaccio, 27
Boswell, James, 77
Boulton, Matthew, 74, 76–77
Brezhnev, Leonid, 231

C

Cabral, Pedro, 48
Caesar, 45
Calvin, John, 49–50
Carlyle, Thomas, 75
Carnegie, Andrew, 104
Chandler, Alfred, 169n
Charlemagne, 27, 28
Cicero, 24
Cochran, Thomas, 110

Coeur, Jacques, 53
Colton, David, 106
Columbus, Christopher, 48
Cornwall, John, 175n

D

da Gama, Vasco, 48
da Vinci, Leonardo, 70
Dandolo, 46
Defoe, Daniel, 78
Demosthenes, 69, 70
Denison, Edward, 182
Dodd, Samuel, 112
Duryea, Charles E., 95

E

Edwards, 197
Eisenhower, Dwight D., 202
Eliot, Charles William, 113
Engels, Friedrich, 81, 89

F

Fisk, James, 106
Ford, Henry, 95
Frick, Henry Clay, 104
Friedman, Milton, 125, 139n

SUBJECT INDEX